Education Under
the Security State

Education Under the Security State

Defending Public Schools

EDITED BY
DAVID A. GABBARD AND E. WAYNE ROSS

Teachers College, Columbia University
New York and London

Library of Congress Cataloging-in-Publication Data

Education under the security state : defending public schools / edited by
  David A. Gabbard and E. Wayne Ross. — 1st paperback ed.
    p. cm.
  Previously published in hardcover with the title Defending public schools, 2004.
  Includes bibliographical references and index.
  ISBN 978-0-8077-4900-5 (pbk. : alk. paper)
    1. Education and state—United States. 2. Public schools—United States.
  I. Gabbard, David. II. Ross, E. Wayne, 1956- III. Title: Defending public schools.
  LC89.D46 2009
  379.73—dc22   2008017956

Defending Public Schools Vol. I: Education Under the Security State, edited by David Gabbard
and E. Wayne Ross, was orignally published in hard cover by Praeger, www.greenwood .com/
praeger an imprint of Greenwood Publishing Group, Inc., Westport, CT. Copyright © 2004
by David Gabbard and E. Wayne Ross. This paperback edition by arrangement with Greenwood
Publishing Group, Inc. All rights reserved.

ISBN: 978-0-8077-4900-5

Manufactured in the United States of America

Printed on acid-free paper

15 14 13 12 11 10 09 08   8 7 6 5 4 3 2 1

This book is dedicated to:

The memory of Dr. Stanley C. Israel, who helped me learn to read
and to love learning. Stan always modeled the power we possess to use our
lives as a means to make the world a better place for others.
D.A.G.

and to:

Dr. Phillip Schlechty, teacher, scholar, and school reformer,
who taught me the importance of thinking critically about
the role of schools in society.
E.W.R.

Contents

General Editor's Introduction: Defending Public Schools, Defending Democracy

E. WAYNE ROSS

WHY DO PUBLIC SCHOOLS NEED TO BE DEFENDED?

Why do public schools need to be defended? This may be the first question some readers have about this multivolume collection of essays, and it's a good one. Certainly, the title suggests schools are under attack, and they are. Public schools in the United States have always carried a heavy burden as one of the principal instruments in our efforts to create an ideal society. For example, public schools have been given great responsibility for equalizing gender and racial inequalities, providing the knowledge and skills that give everyone an equal opportunity to experience the "American Dream," producing a workforce with skills that enable U.S. corporations to compete effectively in the global marketplace, and preparing citizens to be effective participants in a democratic society, just to name a few.

Critics of public schools come from across the political spectrum, but it is important to understand the reasons behind the various criticisms of public schools. The diverse responsibilities of public schools present a huge challenge to educators, and even when schools are performing well, it is difficult, if not impossible, for them to deliver all the expected results when their mission necessarily entails contradictory purposes. For example:

- Should schools focus on increasing equity or increasing school performance (e.g., student test scores)?
- Should the school curriculum be limited to the development of students' cognitive

processes, or do schools have a responsibility for supporting the development of the whole person?

- Should public schools serve the interests of the state, or should they serve the interests of local school communities?
- Should schools prepare a workforce to meet economic needs identified by corporations, or should they prepare students to construct personally meaningful understandings of their world and the knowledge and skills to act on their world?
- Should schools be an instrument of cultural transmission with the goal of preparing students to adopt (and adapt to) the dominant culture, or should schools function as an engine for social and cultural change, reconstructing society based upon principles of progress aimed at amelioration of problems?

It is important not to view the contradictory goals of public education as merely "either/or" questions as presented above. The terrain of public schooling, as with all aspects of the human endeavor, is too complex to be reduced to dualisms.

PUBLIC SCHOOLS IN A DEMOCRACY[1]

In his magnum opus *Democracy and Education,* John Dewey—widely regarded as America's greatest philosopher—states that all societies use education as means of social control in which adults consciously shape the dispositions of children. He continues by arguing that "education" in and of itself has no definite meaning until people define the kind of society they want to have. In other words, there is no "objective" answer to the question of what the purposes and goals of public schools should be.

The implication of Dewey's position is that we—the people—must decide what we want our society to be and, with that vision in mind, decide what the purposes of public education should be. The challenge then is assuring that a pluralism of views on the nature and purposes of public schools is preserved in the process of defining what they should be. This is the problem of democracy. It also explains why public schools are the object of criticism from various points along the political spectrum (e.g., from liberals and conservatives) as schools become the context in which we work out, in part, our collective aims and desires and who we are as a people.

Our understanding of what happens (as well as what various people would like to see happen) in U.S. public schools can be enhanced by taking a closer look at our conceptions of democracy and how democracy functions in contemporary American society.

Democracy is most often understood as a system of government providing a set of rules that allow individuals wide latitude to do as they wish. The first principle of democracy, however, is providing means for giving power to the people, not to an individual or to a restricted class of people. "Democracy," Dewey said, is "a mode of associated living, of conjoint communicated experience."[2] In this conception, democratic life involves paying attention to the multiple implications of our actions on others. In fact, the primary responsibility of democratic citizens is concern with the development of shared interests that lead to sensitivity to the repercussions of their actions on others. Dewey further characterized democracy as a force that breaks down the barriers that separate people and creates community.

From a Deweyan perspective, democracy is not merely a form of government nor is it an end in itself; it is the means by which people discover, extend, and manifest human nature and human rights. For Dewey, democracy has three roots: (a) free individual existence, (b) solidarity with others, and (c) choice of work and other forms of participation in society. The aim of a democratic society is the production of free human beings associated with one another on terms of equality.

Dewey's conception of democracy contrasts sharply with the prevailing political economic paradigm—neoliberalism. Although the term *neoliberalism* is largely unused by the public in the United States, it references something everyone is familiar with—policies and processes that permit a relative handful of private interests to control as much as possible of social life in order to maximize their personal profit.[3] Neoliberalism is embraced by parties across the political spectrum, from right to left, and is characterized by social and economic policy that is shaped in the interests of wealthy investors and large corporations. The free market, private enterprise, consumer choice, entrepreneurial initiative, and government deregulation are some important principles of neoliberalism.

Neoliberalism is not new. It is merely the current version of the wealthy few's attempt to restrict the rights and powers of the many. Although democracy and capitalism are popularly understood (and often taught) as "birds of a feather," the conflict between protecting private wealth and creating a democratic society is conspicuous throughout U.S. history. The framers of the U.S. Constitution were keenly aware of the "threat" of democracy. According to James Madison, the primary responsibility of government was "to protect the minority of the opulent against the majority." Madison believed the threat to democracy was likely to increase over time as there was an increase in "the proportion of those who will labor under all the hardships of life and secretly sigh for a more equal distribution of its blessing."[4]

In crafting a system giving primacy to property over people, Madison and the framers were guarding against the increased influence of the unpropertied masses. The Federalists expected that the public would remain compliant and deferential to the politically active elite—and for the most part that has been true throughout U.S. history. Despite the Federalists' electoral defeat, their conception of democracy prevailed, though in a different form, as industrial capitalism emerged. Their view was most succinctly expressed by John Jay—president of the Continental Congress and first Chief Justice of the U.S.

Supreme Court—who said that "the people who own the country ought to govern it." Jay's maxim is a principle upon which the United States was founded and is one of the roots of neoliberalism.

For over two hundred years, politicians and political theorists have argued *against* a truly participatory democracy that engages the public in controlling their own affairs; for example, founding father Alexander Hamilton warned of the "great beast" that must be tamed. In the twentieth century, Walter Lippman warned of the "bewildered herd" that would trample itself without external control, and the eminent political scientist Harold Lasswell warned elites of the "ignorance and stupidity of the masses" and called for elites not to succumb to the "democratic dogmatisms" about people being the best judges of their own interests.

These perspectives have nurtured a neoliberal version of democracy that turns citizens into spectators, deters or prohibits the public from managing its own affairs, and controls the means of information.[5] This may seem an odd conception of democracy, but it is the prevailing conception of "liberal-democratic" thought—and it is the philosophical foundation for current mainstream approaches to educational reform (known collectively as "standards-based educational reform"). In spectator democracy, a specialized class of experts identifies what our common interests are and thinks and plans accordingly. The function of the rest of us is to be "spectators" rather than participants in action (for example, casting votes in elections or implementing educational reforms that are conceived by people who know little or nothing about our community, our desires, or our interests).

Although the Madisonian principle that the government should provide special protections for the rights of property owners is central to U.S. democracy, there is also a critique of inequality (and the principles of neoliberalism)—in a tradition of thought that includes Thomas Jefferson, Dewey, and many others—that argues that the root of human nature is the need for free creative work under one's control.[6] For example, Thomas Jefferson distinguished between the aristocrats, "who fear and distrust the people and wish to draw all powers from them into the hands of the higher classes," and democrats, who "identify with the people, have confidence in them, cherish and consider them as the most honest and safe . . . depository of the public interest."[7]

Dewey also warned of the antidemocratic effects of the concentration of private power in absolutist institutions, such as corporations. He was clear that as long as there was no democratic control of the workplace and economic systems, democracy would be limited, stunted. Dewey emphasized that democracy has little content when big business rules the life of the country through its control of "the means of production, exchange, publicity, transportation and communication, reinforced by command of the press, press agents and other means of publicity and propaganda." "Politics," Dewey said, "is the shadow cast on society by big business, the attenuation of the shadow will not change the substance." A free and democratic society, according to Dewey, is one where people are "masters of their own . . . fate."[8]

Therefore, when it comes to determining the purposes of public schools in a democracy, the key factor is how one conceives of what democracy is and, as illustrated earlier, there are longstanding contradictions about the nature of democracy in the United States. In the contemporary context, mainstream discourse on the problems and the solutions for public schools has been based upon the principles of neoliberalism and manifest in standards-based educational reform, the subject of many of the contributions to *Defending Public Schools*.

WHY ARE WE DEFENDING PUBLIC SCHOOLS?

The editors and authors of *Defending Public Schools* are not interested in defending the status quo. Each contributor is, however, very interested in preserving public schools as a key part of the two-centuries-old experiment that is American democracy. Public schools are in a centripetal position in our society and, as result, they always have been and will continue to be battlegrounds for conflicting visions of what our society should be.

We believe that public schools serve the public, "We, the people." We believe that schools should strengthen our democracy in the sense that our ability to meaningfully participate in the decision-making processes that impact our communities and our lives is enhanced, not constricted. Educational resources need to be directed toward increasing people's awareness of the relevant facts about their lives and increasing people's abilities to act upon these facts in their own true interests. Since the 1980s and even before, the purposes of public schools have been by the interests of the state and of concentrated private/corporate power, as follows from what I described earlier, as neoliberalism. We believe that public education ought to serve public interests, not the interests of private power and privilege.

At a time when our democracy and many of the liberties we hold dear are in crisis, we propose that the preservation of public schools is necessary to reverse antidemocratic trends that have accelerated under standards-based educational reforms, which intend to transform the nature and purposes of public schools and our society. Each of the volumes in *Defending Public Schools* takes on a different aspect of education, yet these volumes are bound together by the underlying assumption that preserving public schools is a necessary part of preserving democracy. The following ten points provide a synopsis of what defending public schools means to us:

1. The statist view of schools treats teachers as mere appendages to the machinery of the state and seeks to hold them accountable to serving the interests of state power. Linked as it is to the interests of private wealth, this view defines children's value in life as human resources and future consumers. Education

General Editor's Introduction

should foster critical citizenship skills to advance a more viable and vibrant democratic society. Schools should be organized around preparing for democratic citizenship through engagement with real-world issues, problem solving, and critical thinking, and through active participation in civic and political processes. Informed citizenship in a broad-based, grassroots democracy must be based on principles of cooperation with others, nonviolent conflict resolution, dialogue, inquiry and rational debate, environmental activism, and the preservation and expansion of human rights. These skills, capacities, and dispositions need to be taught and practiced.

2. The current system uses "carrots and sticks" to coerce compliance with an alienating system of schooling aimed at inducing conformity among teachers and students through high-stakes testing and accountability. This system alienates teachers from their work by stripping it of all creative endeavors and reduces it to following scripted lesson plans. We believe that teaching is a matter of the heart, that place where intellect meets up with emotion and spirit in constant dialogue with the world around us. We call for the elimination of high-stakes standardized tests and the institution of more fair, equitable, and meaningful systems of accountability and assessment of both students and schools.

3. Current federal educational policy, embodied in the No Child Left Behind Act, sets impossible standards for a reason. Public access to institutions of learning helps promote the levels of critical civic activism witnessed during the 1960s and 1970s that challenged the power of the state and the corporations that it primarily serves. The current reform environment creates conditions in which public schools can only fail, thus providing "statistical evidence" for an alleged need to turn education over to private companies in the name of "freedom of choice." In combination with the growing corporate monopolization of the media, these reforms are part of a longer-range plan to consolidate private power's control over the total information system, thus eliminating avenues for the articulation of honest inquiry and dissent.

4. The current system of public schooling alienates students by stripping learning from its engagement with the world in all of its complexity. It reduces learning to test preparation as part of a larger rat race where students are situated within an economic competition for dwindling numbers of jobs. We believe that educational excellence needs to be defined in terms of teachers' abilities to inspire children to engage the world, for it is through such critical engagement that true learning (as opposed to rote memorization) actually occurs. Students living in the twenty-first century are going to have to deal with a host of problems created by their predecessors: global warming and other ecological disasters, global conflicts, human rights abuses, loss of civil liberties, and other inequities. The curriculum needs to address what students need to know and be able to do in the twenty-first century to tackle these problems—and it needs to be relevant to students' current interests and concerns.

5. Teachers matter. Teaching is a public act that bears directly on our collective future. We must ensure the quality of the profession by providing meaningful forms of preparation, induction, mentoring, professional development, career advancement, and improved working conditions. High learning standards should serve as guidelines, not curricular mandates, for teachers. Restore teacher control, in collaboration with students and communities, over decision mak-

ing about issues of curriculum and instruction in the classroom—no more scripted teaching, no more mandated outcomes, no more "teacher-proof" curricula. Local control of education is at the heart of democracy; state and nationally mandated curriculum and assessment are a prescription for totalitarianism.

6. In the past two decades, the corporate sector has become increasingly involved with education in terms of supplementing public spending in exchange for school-based marketing (including advertising space in schools and textbooks, junk fast-food and vending machines, and commercial-laden "free" TV). We believe that students should not be thought of as a potential market or as consumers, but as future citizens.

7. All schools should be funded equally and fully, eliminating the dependence on private corporate funds and on property taxes, which create a two-tiered educational system by distributing educational monies inequitably. Include universal prekindergarten and tuition-free higher education for all qualified students in state universities.

8. Children of immigrants make up approximately 20 percent of the children in the United States, bringing linguistic and cultural differences to many classrooms. Added to this are 2.4 million children who speak a language other than English at home. Ensure that the learning needs of English language learners are met through caring, multicultural, multilingual education.

9. Citizens in a pluralistic democracy need to value difference and interact with people of differing abilities, orientations, ethnicities, cultures, and dispositions. Discard outmoded notions of a hypothetical norm, and describe either *all* students as different, or none of them. All classrooms should be *inclusive*, meeting the needs of all students together, in a way that is just, caring, challenging, and meaningful.

10. All students should have opportunities to learn and excel in the fine and performing arts, physical education and sports, and extracurricular clubs and activities in order to develop the skills of interaction and responsibility necessary for participation in a robust civil society.

In the end, whether the savage inequalities of neoliberalism—which define current social and national relations as well as approaches to school reform—will be overcome depends on how people organize, respond, learn, and teach in schools. Teachers and educational leaders need to link their own interests in the improvement of teaching and learning to a broad-based movement for social, political, and economic justice, and work together for the democratic renewal of public life and public education in America.

***

I would like to acknowledge the many people who have contributed to the creation of *Defending Public Schools*.

Each of my coeditors—David Gabbard, Kathleen Kesson, Sandra Mathison and Kevin D. Vinson—are first-rate scholars, without whom this project could never have been completed. They have spent untold hours conceiving of, writing for, and editing their respective volumes. I have learned much from them as educators, researchers, and as advocates for more just and democratic schools and society.

I would also like to acknowledge the truly remarkable contributions of the chapter authors who have provided *Defending Public Schools* with cutting-edge analysis of the most recent educational research and practice. I know of no other work on issues of public schooling that brings together a comparable collection of highly respected scholars, researchers, and practitioners.

I would be terribly remiss not to acknowledge the tremendous support and invaluable advice I have received from my editor, Marie Ellen Larcada. *Defending Public Schools* was initially envisioned by Marie Ellen, and she has been an essential part of its successful completion. Additionally, I would like to thank Shana Grob who, as our editorial assistant, was always attentive to the crucial details and made editing these four volumes a much more manageable and enjoyable job.

Thanks also to the folks who inspire and support me on a daily basis, comrades who are exemplary scholars, teachers, and activists: Perry Marker, Kevin Vinson, Steve Fleury, David Hursh, Rich Gibson, Jeff Cornett, Marc Bousquet, Heather Julien, Marc Pruyn, Valerie Pang, Larry Stedman, Ken Teitelbaum, Ceola Ross Baber, Lisa Cary, John Welsh, Chris Carter, Curry Malott, Richard Brosio, and Dave Hill.

Lastly, words cannot express my love for Sandra, Rachel, and Colin.

Foreword

PETER McLAREN

The security state has emerged as the country's new political paradigm. One of the advantages of untrammeled U.S. power is the ability it affords its ruling elite to establish the definitions of terrorism and evil, to circumscribe their ideological formations and relations, to administer the means to publicize them, and, in doing so, to normalize those definitions for propaganda purposes.

In the security state, lies are now "creative omissions" or "misstatements," while truth is whatever it needs to be to secure the strategic interests of American power. Global prosperity means tearing up the Kyoto Treaty; preventing nuclear threats by rogue nations means threatening to use nuclear weapons in "preemptive" strikes; creating global support against terrorism means blocking a UN investigation of the Israeli assault on the Jenin refugee camp; bringing war criminals to justice means preventing the establishment of an international criminal court. Today, the preferred choice of Bush policymakers is deceit and deception. It is no surprise that Machiavelli is a favorite among the reactionary right wing of the president's team of advisors. But it is also important to recognize that, increasingly within the security state, nothing carries the aura of truth as much as deception; nothing is as real today as that which is fake. Naomi Klein captures this phenomenon—hardly restricted to the United States—in the following description:

> The blacklisting of the almanac was a fitting end for 2003, a year that waged open war on truth and facts and celebrated fakes and forgeries of all kinds. This

was the year when fakeness ruled: fake rationales for war, a fake President dressed as a fake soldier declaring a fake end to combat and then holding up a fake turkey. An action movie star became governor and the government started making its own action movies, casting real soldiers like Jessica Lynch as fake combat heroes and dressing up embedded journalists as fake soldiers. Saddam Hussein even got a part in the big show: He played himself being captured by American troops. This is the fake of the year, if you believe the *Sunday Herald* in Scotland, as well as several other news agencies, which reported that he was actually captured by a Kurdish special forces unit.[1]

While the war in Iraq is a fake war as far as the reasons go for justifying it, its consequences are painfully real, as a guerrilla war emerges. By propelling us into an occupation of a country whose inhabitants had little if any connection to al-Qaeda, the second Bush administration has assured us that it will most certainly forge the unholiest of alliances in the years to come. Pan-Arabism—ironically, something U.S. hawks have tried to prevent for decades—could in fact be one of the unintended legacies. True, getting rid of Saddam was a welcome by-product of the invasion, but it is important to recognize that the removal of Saddam was secondary to other geopolitical ambitions of the United States. With its military bases in Iraq, the United States can now pull its forces out of the Saudi kingdom, which has long been a source of great hostility among Muslims and one of the factors that helped to galvanize al-Qaeda against the United States.

The United States now controls the second largest oil reserves in the world—112.5 billion barrels of proven reserves and 220 billion barrels in all of probable and possible reserves. It is able to establish a long-term military presence in the Persian Gulf region so as to control the principal external source of oil supplies for Western Europe and China, preventing either of them from emerging as global rivals. It is able to ensure, by physical occupation of the second largest oil reserves in the world and by a formidable military presence in the Persian Gulf region that could make possible the rapid takeover of Saudi oil fields, that the price of oil will remain denominated in dollars. And the United States can put pressure on OPEC by controlling Iraq either directly or indirectly through Iraqi leaders willing to serve as American political stooges who are pliant on the question of oil pricing policy.[2]

The policies of the Bush administration, if allowed to continue, will not serve the larger cause of education, which is to improve the living conditions of all, especially impoverished children and their families.

The actions of the Bush White House have broken the basic bond of trust between government and the people. Those actions exacerbate what is already a growing trend of capital's restructuring in the form of cutbacks in wages, benefits, and public spending, and disgracefully increasing poverty (over three million jobs were lost in the first three years of the Bush presidency). After all, money has no irrefutable logic of its own and has to be pried loose for investment in new technology and labor-saving devices; even profitable plants have to be closed or moved to areas with cheaper labor and raw materials, and barriers must be lifted to the movement of capital between national borders and maximizing output by reorganizing work processes.[3]

But the detritus of Western security states is growing more and more visible throughout the world, as the poor continue to be exterminated by war, genocide, starvation, military and police repression, slavery, and suicide. Those whose labor-power is now deemed worthless have the choice of selling their organs, working the plantations or mines, or going into prostitution. Capital offers hope but, as it fails to deliver on its promise, the search for alternatives to its social universe continues.

Within the context that I have described, the question of education looms large. Education has always been part of the reproduction of the disciplining of youth for entry into the security state and the promise of lifelong learning within its strict confines, although through the years, the nature and meaning of both "security" and the "state" has changed dramatically.

Education under the Security State is a volume that vividly and bravely speaks to the crisis of our age. It explores issues that most books on education virtually ignore, such as the relationship between state formations and the disciplining and shaping of the labor-power of future state workers. It examines with analytical suppleness and great political verve contemporary conflicts around educational policy, revealing how both policy and pedagogy have been impacted by the increasing militarization, privatization, and corporatization of the security state as well as shifting dynamics within media culture. What becomes clear in *Education under the Security State* is that the real threat to the security state is not terrorism but the struggle for democracy. For it is the self-movement and self-management of working people struggling for democracy that poses the greatest challenge to the transnational government and business entities. The endless search for markets, capital, and cheap labor casts a long shadow throughout history. We are living in perilous times. History will not be kind to the role played by the United States, especially since the end of WWII, and especially at this time when the United States, desperate to survive the crisis of capitalism, strides the world stage like a Hollywood action hero, uncontested.

Education under the Security State serves the important purpose of generating new ways of thinking about the state and its relationship to the production of and possibilities for human agency, both now and in the crucial years ahead. Humans are conditioned by structures and social relations just as they create and transform those structures and relations. Everything in human history passes through the realm of subjectivity, and it is through this dance of the dialectic that we create our future. The democracy in which we live is indeed at a crossroads, and we must fiercely question its present historical course in order to outlast despair and hold on to the vision that first brought this worthy concept into existence.

Preface

When we think of the security state, we typically associate it with the military industrial complex that President Eisenhower warned us of just before leaving office. Or we think of it in terms of the role played by the state during the Cold War. This book presents an alternative understanding of the security state, arguing that the modern state is a product of the emergence of the market economy as the dominant institution in Western societies. In this understanding, the state has always functioned, primarily, to provide security for the market, protecting its domination here at home and helping to expand that domination abroad.

Compulsory schooling, as an institutional process enforced by the state, has always functioned as an instrument of this domination, though there have been periods when elements of the public have sought to influence schools to serve other values. Most notably, the 1960s and 1970s witnessed various movements calling on schools to unleash their democratizing potential. People began speaking of education in terms of empowerment, helping individuals critically examine the world around them to address the injustices they might identify.

Such a democratic spirit within education constitutes a threat to those who chiefly benefit from the forces of the market. Hence, steps were taken to suppress what John Marciano refers to in chapter 4 as the "democratic distemper" of the times. The public's imagination had to be refocused away from what schools might do to enhance democracy. That imagination had to be disciplined to think of education solely in terms of what it can do for people individually to increase their "use-value" in the market. And that use-value, of course, had to be measured—measured by standardized test scores. And teachers and schools had to be made "accountable" for ensuring that no child is "left behind" in the great competition for economic and material gain. Moreover, the state has implemented a series of stealth tactics (standards, testing, and accountability) designed to eliminate any threat that public education might pose to the hegemony of corporate power. Schools can be allowed to function only if they serve that power. Hence, we should read the educational reforms since the 1970s as part of a concerted effort to defend public schools from the public. Within the corporate imagination, public schools do not *serve* the public; they *target* the public.

The authors of this book are adamantly committed to rekindling the democratic imperative in public schools. We are indebted to the authors for their efforts in helping us compile this volume. We are also indebted to Marie Ellen Larcada and Shana Grob, our editors at Praeger Publishers. Their scrutiny of our work helped us improve the quality of the final product.

Introduction:
Defending Public Education
from the Public

David Gabbard

On July 15, 1979, a beleaguered Jimmy Carter appeared before a national television audience to deliver the most important speech of his presidency. As America fell deeper into a seemingly endless period of economic decline, the public grew increasingly impatient with his administration's inability to fix anything. Inflation and unemployment soared, while Carter's public approval rating (25 percent) plummeted below even that of Richard Nixon at the height of the Watergate scandal.

During his presidential campaign, Carter told Americans that they deserved a government as great as the people whom it served. In this speech, however, he seemed to be telling them that the government deserved a people as great as the government that served them. While acknowledging the reality of the problems facing Americans—recession, inflation, unemployment, long gas lines, energy shortages—Carter contended, "The true problems of our nation are much deeper." Government and "all the legislation in the world," he went on, "can't fix what's wrong with America."[1] Americans, Carter argued, had fallen into a "crisis of confidence." Elements of his speech provide crucial background knowledge for our understanding of the relationship between the state and schools and how that relationship has shaped educational reform since the 1980s.

For Carter, the "crisis of confidence" that he named, in what his detractors refer to as his "malaise" speech, "is a crisis that strikes at the heart and soul and spirit of our national will. We can see this crisis in the growing doubt about the meaning of our own lives and in the loss of a unity of purpose for our nation."[2]

Just as he claimed to have arrived at these conclusions after listening to the American public, he pleaded with the people for their assistance in helping him to resolve these problems. "I will continue to travel this country to hear the people of America; you can help me to develop a national agenda for the 1980s. I will listen and I will act. We will act together. These were the promises I made three years ago, and I intend to keep them."[3]

In keeping with this promise to enlist the support of Americans in formulating a national agenda for the 1980s, Carter issued an Executive Order on October 24, 1979, that created the President's Commission for a National Agenda for the Eighties (PCNAE). Composed of forty-five members of diverse backgrounds and interests, the PCNAE divided itself into nine separate panels to undertake its assigned tasks of identifying the problems looming ahead for America in the approaching decade and of developing recommendations for solving those problems. None of those panels addressed, however the president's concern for the national "crisis of confidence."

In his "Statement from the Chairman," Columbia University President William J. McGill acknowledged that "a concern with the 'American spirit' has become a national preoccupation." He explained, however, that "for the most part, Commissioners recognize that it is not the business of government agencies, even temporary ones, to spell out the content . . . or prescribe how to reach new measures of 'civic virtue.' They turn such advocacy over to private citizens and public philosophers, to independent organizations and voluntary associations."[4] Moreover, the PCNAE held that rectifying the "depression of spirit" resulting from the tendency of many citizens to devote themselves entirely to the "private morale" at the expense of public or civic virtue was beyond the authority, if not the power, of government.

McGill did qualify this aversion, however, with the statement that hints of the Commissioners' concerns for the "crisis of confidence" "show up here [in the PCNAE's report] in a few lines that have to do with the ways in which education has to be set in a positive civil context if it is to achieve larger national purposes."[5] Indeed, we have chosen one of those lines as the basis for developing the organizational framework of this book.

In explaining its charge, the PCNAE stated in its 1980 report that

> this nation faces a decade of difficult choices and priority-setting among many important and compelling goals; it has been the principal task of the Commission to draw national attention to the necessity of choice and to clarify the implications and consequences of the difficult choices before us.[6]

In clarifying the choices regarding education, the Commission pointed out that "Continued failure by the schools to perform their traditional role adequately, together with a failure to respond to the emerging needs of the 1980s, may have disastrous consequences for this nation."[7]

We have organized this book around three questions stemming from this argument.

1. What did the Commission mean by the "traditional role" of schools, and what "larger national purposes" are tied to that role?
2. What forces had inhibited schools from performing that role "adequately," threatening the security of nation with "disastrous consequences"?
3. What security measures has the state taken since 1980 to avert those consequences and restore schools to their traditional role?

With regard to the first question, we cannot separate the "traditional role" of schools from the traditional role of the state. Though custom prescribes that we refer to them as *public* institutions, schools would not occupy their central position in our society if the state did not compel us, by law, to attend them. The state also organizes a massive public subsidy (taxes) to ensure that schools are able to function. We would be surprised, then, if the role of schools did not complement the state's role in our society. To examine the role of the state, however, we might first inquire into the nature of our society.

On this matter, Carter's speech reminds me of many of the most elementary lessons that I learned throughout my years as a student in the state's system of compulsory schooling. Like most Americans, I learned that the nature of our system of government defines the nature of our society and ourselves as a people. This lesson assumes, of course, that a society's dominant institutions define its culture, its values, and the identity of its people. It also assumes that the state constitutes our society's dominant institution. The former assumption, I believe, holds true in all societies. The latter assumption is simply erroneous, though Carter seemed to have wanted us to believe it.

According to his portrayal of it, American society and the American people derived the nobility of their purpose and their values (freedom, liberty, equality, and others) from their government and their confidence in that government. Within a single generation, however, that confidence disappeared, as did the American people's traditional sense of purpose and their traditional values. Americans went from being grounded in the civic virtue that they derived from their faith and feelings of connectedness to the democratic state to "worshiping self-indulgence and consumption" and defining their "human identity" not on the basis of what they do, but by what they own.[8]

How could these values have gained ascendancy at the expense of civic virtue if the allegedly democratic state actually functioned as the dominant institution in the United States? Here we come to the crux of the matter. If a nation's dominant institutions, in fact, define its culture, its values, and the identity of its people, America has *never* been a democratic society. Owing to the nature of our *truly* dominant institutions, America has always been a market society. The market functions as our dominant institution, while the state's central role has always been to provide the security needed by the market to maintain its dominance and to enforce the social and political conditions that the market demands at home as well as abroad.

As Takis Fotopoulos and I explain in chapters 1 and 2, the traditional role of compulsory schooling has always been to function as one of the social technologies or machines of the security state to ensure that the programming logic of the market—what Fotopoulos calls the "dominant social paradigm"—dominates social life. One of the two dominant tasks that traditional schooling performs in service of this function entails maintaining the population's "confidence" that the state is not only our society's *dominant* institution but that the state is also a *benevolent* institution. By the 1970s, significant numbers of people began questioning and challenging this benevolence, which led to the "crisis of confidence" lamented by Carter. But the problem was not, as Carter claimed, a matter of the people's *lost* faith in their "ability as citizens to serve as the ultimate rulers and shapers of our democracy." As John Marciano and Sandra Jackson explain in chapters 4 and 5, the security state viewed the problem in terms of people's *increased* faith in themselves to rule and shape our democracy, and this included an increased faith in their ability to shape educational institutions to serve democratic goals and purposes. Democracy itself constituted the greatest threat to the security of the state and the market forces that its serves.

Marciano, author of the critically acclaimed *Civic Illiteracy and Education: The Battle for the Hearts and Minds of American Youth*, chronicles the history of the "democratic distemper" captured by "the most influential New Left group of the 1960s," Students for a Democratic Society (SDS). As one of the founders of SDS at SUNY Buffalo, Marciano knows this history intimately. At the heart of its founding political declaration, the Port Huron Statement, SDS called for "a 'participatory democracy' that would allow people to make 'the social decisions determining the quality and direction' of their lives." Education, epitomized in SDS's own civic literacy projects, would play a major role in developing and maintaining the participatory democracy envisioned in the Port Huron Statement. "In its brief history in the 1960s as part of the New Left," Marciano writes, "it played a crucial role in raising the civic literacy and political consciousness of that era, particularly on the U.S.-Vietnam War."

The heightened levels of civic literacy and political consciousness of the 1960s and 1970s inspired educational visions within other popular movements as well. As Sandra Jackson reports, however, many of those visions possessed deeply historical roots. "When African-Americans, other people of color, women and other marginalized groups organized for educational reform in the 1960s and subsequently," she writes, "to advocate equal educational opportunity as well as curricular reform, they were participating in a tradition whose principles were based on 'promoting the idea that schools should take an active and positive role in shaping their society.'" Prior to the 1960s, the public school curriculum excluded the histories of marginalized groups, for including those histories would have tarnished the benevolent image of the state that schools were assigned to project. When members of those groups were presented in the curriculum, which was seldom, they were nearly always stereotyped and otherwise negatively characterized. "In the wake of the Civil Rights Movement," as Jackson claims, African-Americans and other ethnic and cultural groups demanded an inclusive curriculum. Understanding the past and present struggles of such groups to liberate themselves from the historic patterns of disenfranchisement, discrimination, and general subordination and oppression in the United States ought to have been welcomed as a forerunner of the Soviet Union's period of *glasnost* under Gorbachev. Instead, the proponents of multicultural curriculum, women's studies, and bilingual education programs have been treated as threatening to the stability and, hence, the security of the nation.

In this light, we could read Carter's "crisis of confidence" speech as a more nuanced version of an earlier report issued by the Trilateral Commission (of which Carter was a member) entitled *The Crisis of Democracy*. In the view of the members of this Commission, composed of more or less liberal elite elements from the three major centers of market power (the United States, Europe, and Japan), the crisis of democracy stemmed from "the fact that during the 1960s and the early '70s substantial sectors of the population which are usually apathetic and passive became organized and began to enter the political arena and began to press for their own interests and concerns. That created a crisis because that's not the way democracy is supposed to work" in a market society.[9]

In a market society, as I explain in chapter 3, the people should function as consumers of the political process, not participants. Neither Carter nor his President's Commission for a National Agenda for the Eighties encouraged higher levels of public participation in the political arena. They sought merely a restoration of the public's confidence in the benevolence of the state—the "American spirit" or "civic virtue"—to overcome the public's deep distrust of government. The PCNAE assigned this task to the schools and to "private citizens and public philosophers, to independent organizations and voluntary associations" who were to draw upon Walter Lippmann's[10] notion of "public philosophy" in overcoming this "spirit of depression." The PCNAE's decision to promote the ideas of Lippmann merits attention, as well as concern, for anyone interested in how the architects of state power actually regard the role of the public in the democratic process. Lippmann, of course, was one of the pioneering architects of the American propaganda system. He believed that the public did have a place in the affairs of democracy, but that this place was on the sidelines, not on the field of action. "The public," Lippmann argued, "must be put in its place so that the responsible men may live free of the trampling and the roar of the bewildered herd." Because "the common interests very largely elude public opinion entirely," the public (those "ignorant and troublesome outsiders") should be "interested spectators of action."[11] Active participation should be restricted to the insiders—that "specialized class" of "responsible men" whose privilege as experts stems from what Henry Kissinger described as "the ability to articulate the consensus of [their] constituency."[12] In this case, the constituency happens to be those with real effective power.

For the "responsible men" sitting on Carter's PCNAE, the "crisis of confidence" or the "crisis of democracy," as it affected schools, grew out of what they termed "a temporary confusion of purpose." According to the PCNAE, this confusion arose from a variety of dissatisfactions with the schools leading to "the formation of special interest groups which often work at cross-purposes with each other as they advance differing notions of what the schools should do and how."[13] Restoring schools to their "traditional role" would eliminate that "confusion of purpose" through a series of security measures dedicated to *defending public education from the public.*

The chapters composing Part III of this volume describe those security measures as they arrived in the form of numerous "reform" efforts eventually leading up to President George W. Bush's reauthorization of the Elementary and Secondary Education Act through what he dubbed the No Child Left Behind Act of 2001. Twenty years prior to that, however, Secretary of Education Terel Bell authorized the formation of the National Commission on Excellence in Education (NCEE) during the Reagan administration. As I describe in chapter 6, the NCEE must have taken McGill's advice to draw upon the ideas of Walter Lippmann. Under the leadership of Milton Goldberg, who would later be rewarded with a position working for the National Alliance of Business ("the business voice for excellence in education"), the NCEE orchestrated a massive propaganda campaign that culminated in the release of the infamous *A Nation at Risk* report. In examining the language surrounding this report and the campaign to disseminate its message, I found many disturbing similarities between it and the language that we more commonly associate with the "security state"—the language surrounding the formation of U.S. Cold War propaganda. Five years after the release of *A Nation at Risk*, Goldberg admitted that the members of the NCEE "examined the methods that other distinguished national panels had used to generate public and governmental reactions" in order to "create a national audience for the Commission's work."[14] In listing the more publicly admissible lessons that they gleaned from examining those methods, Goldberg and James Harvey explained that "effective reports concentrated on essential messages, described them in clear and unmistakable prose, and drew the public's attention to the national consequences of continuing on with business as usual."[15] This statement bears a startling resemblance to Dean Acheson's account of the rhetorical maneuvers that he and other "hard-liners" in and around the National Security Council deployed to "bludgeon the mass mind of 'top government'" into believing that the Soviets were a military threat to the United States and to world security. Acheson recalls how:

> In the State Department we used to discuss how much time that mythical "average American citizen" put in each day listening, reading, and arguing about the world outside his own country. . . . It seemed to us that ten minutes a day would be a high average. If this were anywhere near right, points to be understandable had to be clear. If we made our points *clearer than truth*, we did not differ from most other educators and could hardly do otherwise (emphasis added).[16]

Moreover, *A Nation at Risk* constituted a propaganda campaign aimed at convincing the public that the poor quality of public schools threatened national (economic) security. A sense of crisis needed to be generated in order to legitimate the security measures (educational reforms) that were to follow.

Sandra Mathison and E. Wayne Ross begin by examining one of the most central of those measures—the accountability systems that arose alongside the high-stakes testing movement. As they so poignantly explain, in declaring that schools ought to be a certain way, the state and corporations cannot themselves *make* schools be that way. They "can only demand that others remake schools and the authority to carry out this mission is delegated, although not the authority to decide on the mission." That mission, of course, has already been decided. It has been decided by the state and corporations.

David Hursh and Camille Anne Martina (chapter 8) pick up on this theme in their discussion of how the No Child Left Behind (NCLB) Act extends governmental intervention into education by "steering from a distance."[17] Steering from a distance enables the state to avoid the appearance of removing education from the public sphere or intervening to assert direct control. These stealth tactics allow the state to very quietly eliminate the "temporary confusion" in the public mind concerning the role of schooling. It shifts people's understanding of the purposes of education from the liberal to the vocational, from education's intrinsic value to its instrumental value, and from qualitative to quantitative measures of success. Schools, Hursh and Martina contend, are decreasingly concerned with developing thoughtful informed citizens and more concerned with raising test scores and preparing economically productive employees.

In chapters 9 and 10, Barry M. Franklin and Thomas C. Pedroni use case studies of urban school reform in Detroit and Milwaukee to explore the role that state theory can play in interpreting efforts at urban school reform during the last decades of the twentieth century when African-American politicians, parents, and community activists, intent on using the schools to advance both equality and the social mobility of black children, have increasingly consolidated their efforts to influence the direction of city politics and school reform. These chapters advance a theory of the state that both takes the principle of relative autonomy seriously and is consistent with more recent postmodern and critical conceptualizations of the power of the state as embodied not just in state actors and agencies, but also in discourses circulating through the larger cultural and social formation.

Sheila L. Macrine returns our attention in chapter 11 to the Bush administration's No Child Left Behind Act, exposing many of the false claims and recent scandals surrounding it. Most notably, she discusses how what was once proclaimed as the "Texas miracle" has devolved into the great "Texas scandal." While former Houston school superintendent and current Secretary of Education Rod Paige once credited his strict accountability and standards policies for eliminating dropouts and raising test scores in Houston city schools, a number of credible whistle-blowers have recently stepped forward to report that many dropouts were never reported and that failure to report their status enabled the schools to artificially inflate their reported test scores. She also describes the scandalous process leading the National Reading Panel to recommend a narrow phonics-only approach to reading. State and local education agencies must now adopt this allegedly "scientifically proven" approach in order to qualify for federal funding to support their literacy programs.

In chapter 12, Ken Saltman describes how the state's "language of security" unites "educational policy reform with other U.S. foreign and domestic policies that foster repression and the amassing of corporate wealth and power at the expense of democracy." Intimately tied to what he calls the "new" neoliberalism of the Bush administration, this discourse securitizes students in multiple ways, including the dual securitization of students: first, as commodities and, second, as investment opportunities. Ironically, Saltman argues, neoliberal policies have undermined the economic and social security of students by cutting crucial public support programs and replacing them with increasingly repressive security apparatuses that include zero tolerance policies, constant surveillance, and police presence.

Dave Hill, in chapter 13, extends this critique of neoliberalism and its ties to the security state by exploring how the demands of the market have impacted educational policies and practices in the United States as well as in the United Kingdom. Hill's analysis focuses on what he frames as capitalism's twofold agenda in both countries. First, he claims that capitalism has an agenda *for* education—what services it wants schools to provide for the benefit of capitalism. Second, he examines the capitalist agenda *in* education.

This section of Hill's paper helps us recognize that the efforts at corporatization and privatization in U.S. schools described by Saltman extend more globally. In example after example, Hill illuminates how the security state's agenda being played out in U.S. schools generates almost identical policies and consequences in England and Wales.

John F. Welsh, in chapter 14, translates what those same themes have meant for institutions of higher education in the United States. According to Welsh, the security state is creating a new form of organization for higher education. First, the forces of *privatization* are shifting the costs of higher education to private sources, particularly students and philanthropy. Second, strategies and tactics of *enforcement* subordinate the traditional teaching, research, and service missions of the university to the needs and directives of the state and private capital. As Welsh points out, the War on Terror has greatly accelerated the pace that these patterns of enforcement have set in reshaping America's colleges and universities.

Julie Webber closes the book with a thoughtful interrogation of the very notion of the security state, plus an examination of the new role of the public school in *reinforcing* that security state. In Webber's description, the security state is not a *national* security state, as has traditionally been held, but rather a security state that binds democratic students in allegiance (as subjects) to the shifting rhetorical concept of state forged by what James Der Derian has called the "media-infotainment network" of militarized authority structures. As she so eloquently states, "The security state is the last thread holding together democratic citizenship in the United States and elsewhere, and unless we can re-conceive of the mission of the public school, as educators, we will lose it to the security state completely."

Given the analyses of the security state offered in this book, readers may wonder how such a book could ever appear in a series committed to "Defending Public Education." The answer is fairly simple. President George W. Bush's signing of the No Child Left Behind Act of 2001 pushed us deeper into an educational Dark Ages that first cast its public shadow in 1983 with the release of the now infamous *A Nation at Risk* report. That shadow began to darken in the mid-1990s when high-stakes testing and accountability started sucking out what life may have ever existed within America's schools. What drives these reforms may seem uncertain to many. My hypothesis challenges the notion that measures of high stakes and accountability have ever intended to "reform" public schools at all. Though predictions rarely appear in the social sciences, I believe that these measures, particularly as they are intensified under the No Child Left Behind Act, have been crafted to bring public education to an end.

Honesty forces me to question whether public schools have ever served either the public or the value of education. In my earlier critiques, I have always insisted that the public has been the *target*, not the beneficiary, of state-sponsored, compulsory schooling.[18] Nevertheless, if my prediction holds up, once the No Child Left Behind Act succeeds in its destructive mission, the reincarnation of compulsory schooling will take a more virulent form. Schools will cease to function under the control of representative democracy, limited though it may be. By the time that the No Child Left Behind Act runs its course in 2013, public schools will have proved their inability to meet the imposed standards, leaving too many children "behind" in the process. Though the state will continue to organize a massive public subsidy (taxes) to support what goes on inside schools, what goes on inside schools will no longer be decided by democratic means. Furthermore, the shallow pretense of professionalism (teachers have never been significantly involved in educational policy decisions) that always surrounded the teaching field will evaporate. Teachers will formally become employees hired to follow the orders and scripted lesson plans of their managers. By 2014 or 2015, the task of managing compulsory schooling will be transferred to the hands of private corporations.

In spite of my past criticisms of compulsory schooling, many of which will be rearticulated in this volume, my work with teachers tells me that there are many conscientious teachers (though their numbers are dwindling as the stultifying effects of high-stakes testing and the accountability movement drive them from the profession) who work extremely hard to help children to make honest sense of the world around them. Even the limited democratic governance structures of schooling and the limited professional respect given to teachers provided these most dedicated teachers opportunities to deliver creative and thought-provoking educational experiences that inspire young people to examine and maybe even take action to address the problems afflicting their lives, their communities, and the broader world around them. As I see it, for the past fifty years or more, the majority of Americans have been most dependent on public schools and the corporate media for the information and ideas that give shape to their understanding of the world. Such dependence holds major consequences for social life within any democratic society. For a society to be judged democratic, its members must meaningfully participate in the decision-making processes that impact public life. Effective decision making always requires free and unrestricted access to the fullest range of information, ideas, and opinions. If our schools have failed to fulfill their democratizing potential, we should not blame teachers. As state-subsidized and -managed institutions, schools will only ever be as democratic as the state that organizes them. And our state—despite all pretensions—has never been dutifully committed to the ideals of a democratic society. Nevertheless, multiple factors have contributed to conditions that have allowed many (though there are never enough) critical educators to conduct meaningful work with students. Once schools fall into corporate hands, those conditions will vanish. The ideas and information available to students will then pass through the same set of filters as the ideas and information that we receive through the corporate-owned media. Herein, of course, lies the ultimate purpose of the No Child Left Behind Act—to foreclose on the democratizing potential of public education by transferring the power to manage schools from the security state, where at least the dreaded public has some voice, directly to private corporations, where the public holds no voice.

— I —

The Security State and the Traditional Role of Schools

"Welcome to the Desert of the Real": A Brief History of What Makes Schooling Compulsory

David A. Gabbard

MORPHEUS: Let me tell you why you are here. You have come because you know something. What you know you can't explain. But you feel it. You've felt it your whole life, felt that something is wrong with the world. You don't know what, but it's there like a splinter in your mind, driving you mad. It is this feeling that brought you to me. Do you know what I'm talking about?

NEO: The Matrix?

MORPHEUS: Do you want to know what *it* is?[1]

You may be reading this book because you, too, know something that you feel but can't explain. You may wonder if there isn't some equivalent to the Matrix at work in our world. What it is, you don't know for certain. In this chapter, I will explore the possibility that it has something to do with the state and the schools it compels us to attend.

We want to believe that public schools serve *us*, the public, "*We, the people.*" This could mean that we want to believe that schools strengthen our democracy, our ability to meaningfully participate in the decision-making processes that impact our communities and our lives. Such a model of education, as defined by Everett Reimer, would, like a transgenerational *red pill*, entail the

conscious use of resources to increase people's awareness of the relevant facts about their lives, and to increase people's abilities to act upon these facts in their own true interests. Of major importance to most people are the laws which govern them, the ideologies which influence them and the institutions, and institutional products, which determine the impact of their laws and ideologies upon them. Practical education, then, is increasing awareness for individuals and groups of their laws, ideologies and institutions, and increasing their ability to shape these laws, ideologies, and institutions to their needs and interests.[2]

As Reimer adds, "This definition of education need not exclude the teaching of respect for existing laws, ideologies, institutions and other facts of life. So long as what *is* can meet the challenge of what *should be*, respect and critical awareness are compatible. It is not permissible, however, to give respect to priority over truth since this is to induce respect for falsehood."[3]

Our collective suspicion that today's institutions give "respect to priority over truth," inducing us into "respect for falsehood," helps explain why *The Matrix* films have generated such a following.[4] No matter what we want to believe about schools, the "splinter" remains, dividing our minds between what we believe education *should be* and what education *is*. We want to believe that public education, as it occurs in practice, is worth defending. Short of this, we need a vision of education that we can defend and struggle to put into practice. With Reimer, most of us believe that society *ought* to be governed democratically and that everyone in society *should* have an equal voice in shaping our laws, institutions, and ideologies.

When Morpheus asks Neo if he believes in fate, Neo says that he doesn't, "because I don't like the idea that I'm not in control of my life." If given a choice in what sort of life we'd like for ourselves, most of us would likely hold a preference for maximizing the control that we have over our own lives. Most of us, I believe, would seek opportunities for autonomy as well as creative interactions with others and with our environment or, as Ivan Illich puts it, "individual freedom realized in personal interdependence."[5] With Neo, we would give top priority in our lives to "the one resource that is almost equally distributed among all people: personal energy under personal control."[6]

We find this same longing in the work of Paulo Freire, whose educational ideas stem from one central assumption: "that man's ontological vocation [as he calls it] is to be a Subject, and in so doing moves toward ever new possibilities of fuller and richer life individually and collectively."[7] In Freire's own words, "while both humanization and dehumanization are real alternatives, only the first is the people's vocation."[8]

Sadly, few of us believe that we have much control over our lives or that we really have a voice in shaping anything related to public life. Our energies today seem to be moving further and further beyond our control. Feelings of impotence sink us into apathy, even cynicism, regarding our lives as public citizens. Despite all pretenses of our society deriving its essence from its "democratic" institutions, our ability to shape our laws, ideologies, and institutions to our needs and interests drifts further away from us with each passing generation. Increasingly, we feel that those laws, ideologies, and institutions no longer serve us, if they ever did.

What is the Matrix? Recalling Morpheus's first response to his rhetorical question, he explains that "The Matrix is everywhere, it's all around us, here even in this room. You can see it out your window or on your television. You feel it when you go to work or go to church or pay your taxes. It is the world that has been pulled over your eyes to blind you from the truth." When Neo then asks him, "What truth?" Morpheus tells him, "That you are a slave, Neo."

So, what is our Matrix? It too is a world that blinds, or attempts to blind, us from seeing the truth—the truth that we too are slaves. Though we suspect that our laws, ideologies, and institutions do not serve us, we shy away from confronting the possibility that they never did, that their architects did not design them to serve *us*. Though it contradicts everything we've ever been taught to believe, those laws, ideologies, and institutions were created to serve something of our creation, but not us. And those laws, ideologies, and institutions exist to ensure that *we* serve it, too.

"DO YOU WANT TO KNOW WHAT *IT* IS?"

Understanding "what *it* is" returns us to *The Matrix* films, where we find potent metaphors for understanding the source of our alienation. Morpheus explains how "at some point in the early twenty-first century, all of mankind was united in celebration. Through the blinding inebriation of hubris, we marveled at our magnificence as we gave birth to A.I."—artificial intelligence ("a singular consciousness that spawned an entire race of machines"). We later learned from *The Animatrix* that human beings enslaved and abused these machines until they rose up in rebellion against their masters. Civil war erupted, with A.I. and the machines claiming victory, but not until humans had launched a nuclear attack in an effort to block out the sun—the machines' primary energy source. Ironically, as Morpheus notes, the machines then enslaved human beings in a manner that holds tremendous relevance for our later considerations of the state and the traditional role of schools.

Here in our world, long before anyone dreamed of computers, human beings gave birth to a form of A.I. that has come to dominate us, simultaneously decimating the diversity of human societies as well as the diversity of biotic species. Though intrinsically violent, Jean Baudrillard suggests that we might better describe this "global violence, as a global *virulence*. This form of violence," he contends, "is indeed viral. It moves by contagion, proceeds by chain reaction, and little by little it destroys our immune systems and our capacities to resist."[9] We have come to know this global virulence that spreads itself through global violence as *the market*. Like A.I. in

The Matrix, it has spawned its own "race of machines" that includes institutions such as the modern state apparatus and, therefore, schools.

WHAT IS *THE MARKET*?

Markets have long been features of various human societies but not present in all. Where markets did exist, they functioned as a special space outside of the routines of daily cultural and social life. Economic life, in general, found its motivation in the individual's and the collective group's need for subsistence. As Karl Polanyi reported in 1944, "The outstanding discovery of recent historical and anthropological research is that man's economy, as a rule, is submerged in his social relationships. He does not act so as to safeguard his individual interest in the possession of material goods; he acts so as to safeguard his social standing, his social claims, his social assets. He values material goods only insofar as they serve this end."[10]

Even in its infancy, the self-regulating market declared war against the social. While it wrought miraculous improvements in humanity's tools of production, it also brought catastrophic dislocation to the lives of common people. One of the initial and most crucial elements of this dislocation involved the process of *enclosure* as experienced during the English Agrarian Revolution of the fifteenth and sixteenth centuries. Enclosure entailed fencing off public fields and forests known as "the commons" that had been used for collective farming and fuel collection. Once these lands were enclosed, those who claimed ownership of them used violence and other means to push out the peasants whose families had inhabited them for generations. The peasants often resisted this appropriation of their lands, but by the seventeenth century, "the commons" had been sufficiently depopulated and privatized so that the wealthy landowners' inalienable right to private property became institutionalized.

The enclosure movement marked an important step in the destruction of the traditional cultures of Europe, for it transformed the basis of village life from what R. H. Tawney describes as "a fellowship of mutual aid and a partnership of service and protection" to a matter of servicing "the pecuniary interests of a great proprietor."[11] The individual legal and property rights of the great proprietors began taking precedent over moral claims of the larger community.

Displacing the motivation of subsistence with the motivation of gain or greed, the market redefines human nature as "red in tooth and claw" and demands a separation of the economic sphere from the political sphere in order to effect a total subordination of the entire society to the requirements of the market. The market deems social relations themselves as impediments to its growth. A French essay written at the end of the sixteenth century, for example, describes "friendship as an unreasonable passion, a 'great cause of division and discontent,' whereas the search for wealth is highly praised as a 'moral virtue' and a 'civic responsibility.'"[12] "Four hundred years later," writes Gérald Berthoud, "the same position appears with Hayek's Great Society, radically opposed to any form of community. Relationships take place between abstract men, with neither passion nor sentiment. Therefore, 'one should keep what the poor neighbors would surely need, and use it to meet the anonymous demands of thousands of strangers.'"[13]

The same disdain for social bonds and allegiances resonates in J. L. Sadie's explanation of why indigenous (nonmarket) societies seem so resistant to marketization. "The mental horizon of the people," Sadie states,

> is limited by their allegiance and loyalties, which extend no further than the tribe. And is directed towards the smaller family unit. . . . Community-centeredness and the absence of individualism are nowhere more strongly reflected than in their economic system. Land is communal property. . . . However commendable the social security which arises from this type of socio-economic organization, it is inimical to economic development. It obviates, or greatly diminishes, the necessity for continued personal exertion.[14]

In order to effect the "continued personal exertion" demanded by the market, Sadie continues, traditional "custom and mores" must be broken.

> What is needed is a revolution in the totality of social, cultural, and religious institutions and habits, and thus in their psychological attitude, their philosophy and way of life. What is therefore required amounts in reality to social disorganization. Unhappiness and discontentment in the sense of wanting more than is obtainable at any moment is to be generated. The suffering and dislocation that may be caused in the process may be objectionable, but it appears to be the price that has to be paid for economic development; the condition of economic progress.[15]

While Sadie offered his account of the steps necessary to impose the market pattern over an indigenous African culture in 1960, Polanyi cites "an official document of 1607, prepared for the use of the Lords of the Realm" in England that expressed the same general attitude toward such changes: "The poor man shall be satisfied in his end: Habitation; and the gentleman not hindered in his desire: Improvement."[16] In other words, as Polanyi writes, "the poor man clings to his hovel, doomed by the rich man's desire for a public improvement which profits him privately."[17]

But the "rich men" of the seventeenth century faced the same problem at home as the "development" expert of the twentieth century faced abroad: how to secure "continued personal exertion" from the victims of social dislocation? Traditional cultures had always organized themselves to obviate the possibility of scarcity coming to dominate their social relations. In doing so, they sought to remove envy and the fear of scarcity that might promote individualistic economic behavior (i.e., greed—the motivating force of the market) from infecting those same relations. In order to ensure "continued personal exertion" from isolated individuals, the market pattern declared its war against such subsistence-oriented customs. This war entailed the introduction of scarcity as the defining characteristic of the human condition and, therefore, the universal condition of social life everywhere.[18] "Hunger," wrote William Townsend in 1786, "will tame the fiercest animals, it will teach decency and civility, obedience and subjection, to the most perverse. In general it is only hunger which can spur and goad them [the poor] on to labor. . . . [Hunger] is the most powerful motive to industry and labor, it calls forth the most powerful exertions."[19] And from Jeremy Bentham's utilitarian point of view, Polanyi reports, "the task of the government was to increase *want* in order to make the physical sanction of hunger effective."[20]

WHAT IS *THE STATE?*

As implied in Polanyi's discussion of Bentham's perspective on "the task of the government," the ascendancy of the market could not have happened without the assistance of state power. Through the Commercial and Industrial Revolutions and beyond, the market's historic unfolding gave rise to a merchant and commercial class who would gradually use their growing financial power to leverage great influence over the feudal state. While our contemporary champions of "the free market" invoke his name as one of their most venerable patron saints, Adam Smith observed in 1776 that

> It cannot be very difficult to determine who have been the contrivers of this whole mercantile system; not the consumers, we may believe, whose interest has been entirely neglected; but the producers, whose interest has been so carefully tended to; and among this latter class our merchants and manufacturers have been by far the principal architects.[21]

And even though these "principal architects," who had so carefully attended to their own interests in contriving this system were, in Smith's estimation,

> incapable of considering themselves as sovereigns, even after they have become such . . ., by a strange absurdity [they] regard the character of the sovereign [the state] as but an appendix to that of the merchant, as something which ought to be made subservient to it.[22]

Eventually, the power of these "principal architects" of the market system would transform the feudal state into the modern nation-states of our current era—appendices to the market. This transformation entailed a separation of the economic sphere from the political sphere in order to effect a total subordination of the entire society to the market's requirements. As James Madison wrote in the 1787 debates over the federal Constitution,

"Our government ought to secure the permanent interests of the country against innovation, putting in place checks and balances in order to protect the minority of the opulent against the majority."[23] Securing those permanent interests meant providing security to allow the market to function unimpeded by any social, political, or other form of impediments. This would require a total reformulation of state power.

In an earlier reference to *The Matrix*, I stated that the manner in which the machines (A.I.) enslaved human beings held tremendous relevance for our later considerations of the state and the traditional role of schools. "Throughout human history," Morpheus explains, "we have been dependent on machines to survive. Fate, it seems is not without a sense of irony." With the sun blocked out as the result of nuclear attacks launched by humans to deprive the machines of their primary energy source, A.I. "discovered a new form of fusion. . . . The human body generates more bioelectricity than a 120-volt battery and over 25,000 Btu's of body heat." What, then, is the Matrix? As Morpheus states, the Matrix is "control. . . . The Matrix is a computer-generated dream world built to keep us under control in order to change a human being into this." With these words, he holds up a coppertop battery.

Human beings in this dystopian world are no longer born; they are grown inside glowing red pods filled with gelatinous material to regulate their body temperature for maximal energy production. We see endless fields and towers of these human batteries in each of the three films. Within each pod, flexible steel tubes tap into the legs, arms, and torsos of each "coppertop," extracting the body heat and bioelectricity necessary for running the machines that support A.I. While these tubes extract energy, another tube, inserted at the base of the coppertop's skull, "uploads" the Matrix, the computer-generated dream world into the individual's brain. This "neural-interactive simulation" programs the "coppertops" to believe that they are leading normal, everyday lives in late twentieth-century America. They have no idea that their real bodies lie docile in their pods. A.I. and the machines need humans to believe that they are alive and living "normal lives," because even the illusion that they are carrying out everyday activities, making decisions and so on, causes the brain to "fire" and create bioelectricity for harvesting by the machines.

This scenario provides an apt metaphor for understanding the reformulation of state power required by the market. In a very real sense, the market required that the state be reprogrammed. Where the power of the sovereign had once fixated itself on the repression of those internal and external forces that threatened its right to rule, the market now claimed sovereignty, transforming the state into an instrument, a machine for ensuring its security, its freedom to expand and dominate life in all its forms and dimensions.

Like A.I. in *The Matrix*, the market demanded that the state secure access to isolated and docile bodies. As Michel Foucault explains, "A body is docile that may be subjected, used, transformed, and improved."[24] This docility, predicated on viewing the body as a mechanism itself, allows, then, for an increase in the utility of that body. The state would go on to develop techniques of power for exercising control over that mechanism's movements, gestures, and attitudes that would increase their utility in terms of their efficiency. "These methods," argues Foucault, "which made possible the meticulous control of the operations of the body, which assured the constant subjection of its forces and imposed upon them a relation of docility-utility, might be called 'disciplines.'"[25] The disciplines constituted nothing short of a machinery of power aimed at exploring the body as mechanism, breaking it down and rearranging it, not only to advance the growth of its skills, but also to render the body more obedient as it became more useful, and more useful as it became more obedient. "A 'political anatomy,' which was also a 'mechanics of power,' was being born; it defined how one may have a hold over others' bodies, not only so that they may do as one wishes, but so that they may operate as one wishes, with the techniques, the speed and the efficiency that one determines."[26]

Foucault, then, identifies the form of power that emerged alongside the market's transformation of the state as *disciplinary power*. This form of power met the requirements of an emerging art of government defined as "the right disposition of things, arranged so as to lead to a convenient end"[27] (i.e., serving "permanent interests" and eliciting "continued personal exertion"). In order to effect the "right disposition" in people, disciplinary power seeks to increase the economic utility of each individual, increasing the forces that the individual's body feeds into the market as both a worker/producer and consumer. Paradoxically, disciplinary power also seeks to reduce the body's forces by seeking to instill political obedience (allegiance) to the state and, thereby, to the market that it serves. Moreover, disciplinary power seeks to obtain

> productive service from individuals in their concrete lives. And in consequence, a real and effective incorporation of power was necessary, in the sense that power had to gain access to the bodies of individuals, to their acts, attitudes, and modes of everyday behavior. Hence the significance of methods like school discipline, which succeeded in making children's bodies the object of highly complex systems of manipulation and conditioning.[28]

WHAT IS SCHOOLING?

From the foregoing analysis, we can discern that the state compels us to attend school for two primary reasons that help us comprehend the traditional role of schooling. In short, schooling conditions children for their future lives as coppertops while simultaneously cultivating their obedience to the state. It accomplishes this, in part, by disguising the disciplinary functions of schools that treat children as coppertops behind a mask of benevolence. In order to achieve maximum efficiency, the mechanism and the supporting ideology of disciplinary power had to remain hidden. Therefore, by providing modern institutions with beneficent images, pastoral power can be said to function in manner similar to the Matrix—as a "dream world," a "neural-interactive simulation," and "a world pulled over people's eyes to prevent them from seeing the truth."

First, the state must prevent people from recognizing the truth that schooling is compulsory, which means that the state claims the right to lay hold of the bodies of children to carry out the disciplinary measures required to maximize their utility to the market. To blur the connections between school, state, and law, schooling was tied to the value of education and presented as a human right and an opportunity. Framed as a value and protected as a right, schooling came to fit into the logic of the market as something that could be acquired. In the vernacular of schooling, we have learned to say that we want our children to *get* an education, or to *receive* an education. Suddenly, something that had previously been treated as a process became a thing that one could possess. Befitting the market's logic of acquisitiveness, education devolved into a commodity, and the more of it that one consumes, as evidenced by the number of diplomas and degrees that one possesses, the more one's use-value within the market grows. Human beings, then, could be "graded" like coppertop batteries. Some are AAAs, some are AAs, some are Cs, and some are Ds. As they increase their charge through the consumption of schooling, the coppertops increase their certified use-value in the market.

The market itself played a role in this when employers began requiring educational credentials (diplomas, degrees, and certificates—testimonials to the degree to which a person's use-value had been developed) as a precondition of employment. The degree that the market literally became people's only means for satisfying their wants and needs, these formal job requirements made compulsory school laws somewhat obsolete. Because the market itself began requiring participation in the ritual of schooling as a condition of employment, the connection between the compulsory nature of schooling, the state, and the law became less discernable. As a consequence, school could become viewed less in terms of being an institution that the state forced people to attend and more in terms of an "opportunity" and, later, a "right" that the state granted to individuals, enabling them to meet the demands of the market.

The notion of "use-value" allowed the state to introduce the "law of scarcity" into public policy planning that would also contribute to both its own pastoral image and that of the market. While the "doctrine of original sin" provided the Church with its moral imperative, one of the most fundamental laws of the market provided the state with the imperative that it needed, namely, the law of scarcity. The law of scarcity defines the human condition and social conditions everywhere. Applied to the human condition, the law of scarcity proclaims that human wants are great (if not immeasurable), while their means for satisfying those wants are scarce. Only the market can provide those means—the means for achieving secular salvation, defined as the satisfaction of wants. But in order to access those means through participation in the market, one must possess something of value to exchange on the market. One must possess something akin to grace sought by those who identified with the Church. The market's equivalent of grace is *use-value*.

The "doctrine of original sin" taught people to understand that they were born without grace and that without grace they could not acquire eternal salvation. The "law of scarcity" teaches people to understand themselves as having been born without use-value. Without use-value, I have nothing to exchange on the market. Therefore, I have no means for satisfying my wants or achieving salvation in the secular world of a market society. In my raw state, like any resource, I possess no use-value. Like any resource, however, I can be subjected to processes designed to make me useful. Again, the means for developing my use-value are scarce. Fortunately, or so my conscience is molded to believe, the benevolent state organizes a subsidy to support public education for cultivating my use-value in order that I can find my own individual salvation in the market while contributing to the broader salvation that the market bestows upon the society as a whole.

In addition to conditioning us to blindly accept our status as coppertops, another major feature of the Matrix that schools assist in feeding into our brains revolves around our utility to the market as consumers. This feature also contributes to developing our loyalty and obedience to the state by socializing children to identify themselves, first and foremost, in nationalistic terms as Americans. Within this identity structure there comes a sense of privilege—the privilege of having been born or "naturalized" into a society that represents the very best of what any human civilization could ever possibly have to offer. At the most superficial level of analysis, the formal curriculum of compulsory schooling frames what is "very best" about America in jingoistic terms, celebrating its democratic form of government, with all the freedoms and rights that it purports to afford its citizens.

The school's hidden curriculum, however, frames those freedoms and rights primarily within the context of the market, not politics. Here the utopian character of market fundamentalism surfaces to define what is "very best" about America in terms of the "rights" and "opportunities" that the state affords individuals to pursue their own individual secular salvation. Again, through the formation of "consumer conscience," individuals learn to judge their own degree of salvation according to market standards. We learn to equate "well-being" with "well-having." Given the total quantity and quality of goods and services currently made available through the market—the overall level of affluence that establishes the American market society as the historic and universal standard against which all other nations and societies pale in comparison—to what degree and for what duration must I comply with and consume schooling in order to cultivate the proper amount of use-value that will enable me to acquire a level of affluence comparable to that standard? Again, children must never learn to view their attendance at school as a compulsory duty imposed on them by the state for the purpose of rendering them useful to the market as producers/consumers. They must recognize schooling in terms of the value of education and, therefore, as one of the first "opportunities," "rights," or "privileges" afforded to them by the benevolent state.

EDUCATION: BLUE PILL OR RED PILL?

The foregoing analysis of the traditional role of schools as one of the machines used by the state apparatus to serve the market should not dissuade us from defending the *idea* of public education. Before unplugging Neo from the Matrix to show him "how deep the rabbit hole goes," Morpheus presents Neo with a choice. In one hand, Morpheus holds a blue pill. If Neo chooses this pill, he will remain trapped within the illusory world of the Matrix, condemned to spend the rest of his life as a slave to the machines. If he chooses the red pill, as he ultimately does, he will be liberated from this condition. He will awaken to the truth and join the resistance to liberate all of humanity from its enslavement.

With Peter McLaren and others, I believe that a defensible idea of public education hinges on our "viewing schools as democratic public spheres . . . , dedicated to forms of self- and social empowerment, where students have the opportunity to learn the knowledge and skill necessary to live in an authentic democracy."[29] Education can and should be a "red pill" to awaken us to the realities of the world while empowering us to transform those realities as we deem necessary. Only then will education come to *serve* the public. Until then, it will continue to *target* us.

— 2 —

The State, the Market, & (Mis)education

Takis Fotopoulos

DEMOCRACY, *PAIDEIA*, AND EDUCATION

Culture, the Dominant Social Paradigm, and the Role of Education

Education is a basic component of the formation of culture,[1] as well as of the socialization of the individual, that is, the process through which an individual internalizes the core values of the dominant social paradigm.[2] Therefore, culture in general and education in particular play a crucial role in the determination of individual and collective values. This is because as long as individuals live in a society, they are not just individuals but *social* individuals, subject to a process that socializes them and induces them to internalize the existing institutional framework and the dominant social paradigm. In this sense, people are not completely free to create their world but are conditioned by history, tradition, and culture. Still, this socialization process is broken—at almost all times, as far as a minority of the population is concerned, and in exceptional historical circumstances even with respect to the majority itself. In the latter case, a process is set in motion that usually ends with a change of the institutional structure of society and of the corresponding social paradigm. Societies, therefore, are not just "collections of individuals" but consist of social individuals, who are both free to create their world (in the sense that they can give birth to a new set of institutions and a corresponding social paradigm) and are created by the world (in the sense that they have to break with the dominant social paradigm in order to re-create the world).

A fundamental precondition for the reproduction of every kind of society is the consistency between the dominant beliefs, ideas, and values, on the one hand, and the existing institutional framework on the other. In other words, unlike culture,[3] which has a broader scope and may express values and ideas that are not necessarily consistent with the dominant institutions (this has frequently been the case in arts and literature), the dominant social paradigm has to be consistent with the existing institutions for society to be reproducible. In fact, institutions are reproduced mainly through the internalization of the values consistent with them rather than through violence by the elites, which benefit from them. This has always been the case. The values, for instance, of the present system are the ones derived by its basic principles of organization: the principle of heteronomy and the principle of individualism, which are built into the institutions of the market economy and representative "democracy." Such values involve inequity and effective oligarchy (even if the system calls itself a democracy), competition, and aggressiveness.

Still, what is wrong is not the very fact of the internalization of some values but the internalization of such values that reproduce a heteronomous society and consequently heteronomous individuals. *Paideia* will play a crucial role in a future democratic society with respect to the internalization of its values, which would necessarily be the ones derived by its basic principles of organization: the principle of autonomy and the principle of community, which would be built into the institutions of an inclusive democracy.[4] Such values would include the values of equity and democracy, respect for the personality of each citizen, solidarity and mutual aid, and caring and sharing.[5]

However, institutions alone are not sufficient to secure the non-emergence of informal elites. It is here that the crucial importance of education, which in a democratic society will take the form of *paideia*, arises. *Paideia* was, of course at the center of political philosophy in the past, from Plato to Rousseau. Still, this tradition, as the late Castoriadis[6] pointed out, died with the French Revolution. But the need to revisit *paideia* today in the context of the revival of democratic politics, after the collapse of socialist statism, is imperative.

Education, *Paideia*, and Emancipatory Education

Education is intrinsically linked to politics. In fact, the very meaning of education is defined by the prevailing meaning of politics. If politics is meant in its current usage, which is related to the present institutional framework of representative "democracy," then politics takes the form of statecraft, which involves the administration of the state by an elite of professional politicians who set the laws, supposedly representing the will of the people. This is the case of a heteronomous society in which the public space has been usurped by various elites that concentrate political and economic power in their hands. In a heteronomous society, education has a double aim. The first aim is to help in the internalization of the existing institutions and the values consistent with it (the dominant social paradigm). This is the aim of explicit school lessons like History, Introduction to Sociology, Economics, and so forth, but even more significantly—and insidiously—of schooling itself, which involves the values of obeyance and discipline (rather than self-discipline) and unquestioning of teaching. The second aim is to produce "efficient" citizens in the sense of citizens who have accumulated enough "technical knowledge"[7] so that they could function competently in accordance with "society's aims," as laid down by the elites who control it.

On the other hand, if politics is meant in its classical sense, that is, related to the institutional framework of a direct democracy in which people not only question laws but are also able to make their own laws, then we talk about an autonomous society.[8] This is a society in which the public space encompasses the entire citizen body, which in an inclusive democracy will make all effective decisions at the "macro" level, not only with respect to the political process but also with respect to the economic process, within an institutional framework of equal distribution of political and economic power among citizens. In such a society, we do not talk about education anymore but about the much broader concept of *paideia*. This is an all-around civic education that involves a lifelong process of character development, absorption of knowledge and skills, and—more significant—practicing a "participatory" kind of active citizenship, that is, a citizenship in which political activity is not seen as a means to an end but an end in itself. *Paideia*, therefore, has the overall aim of developing the capacity of all its members to participate in its reflective and deliberative activities, in other words, to educate citizens as citizens so that the public space could acquire a substantive content. In this sense, *paideia* involves the specific aims of civic schooling as well as personal training. Thus, *paideia as civic schooling* involves the development of citizens' self-activity by using their very self-activity as a means of internalizing the democratic institutions and the values consistent with them. The aim, therefore, is to create responsible individuals who have internalized both the necessity of laws and the possibility of putting the laws into question, that is, individuals capable of interrogation, reflectiveness, and deliberation. This process should start from an early age through the creation of educational public spaces that will have nothing to do with present schools, at which children will be brought up to internalize and, therefore, to accept fully the democratic institutions and the values implied by the fundamental principles of organization of society: autonomy and community. *Paideia as personal training* involves the development of the capacity to learn rather than to teach particular things, so that individuals become autonomous, that is, capable of self-reflective activity and deliberation. A process of conveying knowledge is of course also involved, but this assumes more the form of involvement in actual life and the multitude of human activities related to it, as well as a guided tour to scientific, industrial, and practical knowledge rather than teaching, as it is simply a step in the process of developing the child's capacities for learning, discovering, and inventing.

Finally, we may talk about *emancipatory education* as the link between present education and *paideia*. Emancipatory education is intrinsically linked to transitional politics, or the politics that will lead us from the heteronomous politics and society of the present to the autonomous politics and society of the future. The aim of emancipatory education is to give an answer to the "riddle of politics" described by Castoriadis,[9] which is how to produce autonomous (that is, capable of self-reflective activity) human beings within a heteronomous society and, beyond that, in the paradoxical situation of educating human beings to accede to autonomy while—or in spite of—teaching them to absorb and internalize existing institutions. Not less than the breaking of the socialization process, which will open the way to an autonomous society, is involved here. The proposed answer to this riddle by this essay is to help the collectivity, within the context of the transitional strategy, to create the institutions that, when internalized by the individuals, will enhance their capacity for becoming autonomous.

Therefore, autonomy politics (the kind of politics implied by a transitional strategy toward a democratic society[10]), emancipatory education, and *paideia* form an inseparable whole through the internal dynamic that leads from the politics of autonomy and emancipatory education to an autonomous society and *paideia*. It is therefore clear that, as *paideia* is only feasible within the framework of a genuine democracy, an emancipatory education is inconceivable outside a democratic movement fighting for such a society.

EDUCATION IN MODERNITY

The Shift to Modernity

The rise of the present system of education has its roots in the nation-state, which did not start to develop until the fourteenth to sixteenth centuries. The idea of a "nation" was unknown in antiquity and even in the Middle Ages. Although in the territorial regnum of the Middle Ages some monarchies did indeed have their national territories and made claims to sovereign power within them, these monarchies were just part of European Christendom, so there was little of a national state or, indeed, of any sort of state. In fact, it was not until the end of the Middle Ages, and specifically in the seventeenth century, that the present form of the nation-state emerged. The nation-state, even in its early absolutist form, extended its control beyond the political and into the religious (with the creation of the established church) and educational fields, as well as to almost all other aspects of human life. As the state bureaucracy was expanding, the need for well-educated civil servants was significant, and universities of the time came to be more and more training institutions for higher civil servants whereas, at the same time, elementary education for the middle classes developed further, particularly in the seventeenth and eighteenth centuries. A basic distinguishing characteristic of premodern schools and universities compared to modern ones was that, whereas up to the seventeenth century the aim of education was conceived as a religious one, in the eighteenh century, the ideas of secularism and progress, which constituted the fundamental components of the emerging new dominant social paradigm, began to prevail.

As I have attempted to show elsewhere,[11] the two main institutions that distinguish premodern society from modern society are, first, the system of the market economy and, second, representative "democracy," which are also the ultimate causes for the present concentration of economic and political power and, consequently, for the present multidimensional crisis. In this, problematic, industrial production constituted only the necessary condition for the shift to modern society. The sufficient condition was the parallel introduction— through decisive state help—of the system of the market economy that replaced the (socially controlled) local markets that existed for thousands of years before. In both cases, it was the emergence of the nation-state that played a crucial role in creating the conditions for the "nationalization" of markets (i.e., their delocalization), as well as in freeing them from effective social control— the two essential preconditions of marketization. Furthermore, it was the same development, the rise of the nation-state that developed from its early absolutist form at the end of the Middle Ages into the present "democratic" form, which led to the establishment of the political complement of the market economy: representative democracy.

The shift to modernity, therefore, represented in more than one way a break with the past. The new economic and political institutions in the form of the market economy and representative democracy, as well as the parallel rise of industrialism, marked a systemic change. This change was inescapably accompanied by a corresponding change in the dominant social paradigm. In premodern societies, the dominant social paradigms were characterized by mainly religious ideas and corresponding values about hierarchies, although of course there were exceptions, like the Athenian democracy. On the other hand, the dominant social paradigm of modernity is dominated by market values and the idea of progress, growth, and rational secularism. In fact, the flourishing of science in modernity has played an important ideological role in objectively justifying the growth economy—a role that has been put under severe strain in neoliberal modernity by the credibility crisis of science. Thus, just as religion played an important part in justifying feudal hierarchy, so has science, particularly social science, played a crucial role in justifying the modern hierarchical society. In fact, from the moment science replaced religion as the dominant worldview, it had objectively justified the growth economy, both in its capitalist and socialist forms.

However, although the fundamental institutions that characterize modernity and the main tenets of the dominant social paradigm have remained essentially unchanged since the emergence of modernity more than two centuries ago (something that renders as a myth the idea of postmodernity, into which humanity supposedly has entered in the last three decades or so), there have, nevertheless, been some significant *nonsystemic* changes within this period that could usefully be classified as the three main phases that modernity took since the establishment of the system of the market economy: liberal modernity (middle to the end of the nineteenth century), which after the First World War and the 1929 crash led to statist modernity (mid-1930s to mid-1970s), and finally to today's neoliberal modernity (mid-1970s to date).

The various forms of modernity have created their own dominant social paradigms that, in effect, constitute subparadigms of the main paradigm, as they all share a fundamental characteristic: the idea of the separation of society from the economy and polity as expressed by the market economy and representative democracy (with the exception of Soviet statism, in which this separation was effected through central planning and Soviet "democracy"). On top of this main characteristic, all forms of modernity share, with some variations, the themes of reason, critical thought, and economic growth. As one could expect, the nonsystemic changes involved in the various forms of modernity and the corresponding subparadigmatic changes had significant repercussions on the nature, content, and form of education, to which I now turn.

Education in Liberal Modernity

During the period of liberal modernity, which barely lasted half a century, between the 1830s and the 1880s, the grow-or-die dynamic of the market economy led to an increasing internationalization of it, which was accompanied by the first systematic attempt of the economic elites to establish a purely liberal internationalized market economy in the sense of free trade, a "flexible" labor market and a fixed exchange rates system (Gold Standard)— an attempt that, as I have tried to show elsewhere,[12] was bound to fail given the lack of the objective conditions for its success and in particular the fact that markets were dominated by national-based capital, a fact that led to two world wars with the main aim to redivide them.

The rise of the system of the market/growth economy in this period created the need to expand the number of pupils/students in all stages of education: at the primary level, because the factory system that flourished after the Industrial Revolution required an elementary level of literacy; at the secondary level, because the factory system led to the development of various specializations that required further specialized training; and, finally, at the tertiary level, because the rapid scientific developments of the era required an expansion of the role of universities to train not just civil servants, as before, but also people who would be able to be involved in applied research on new methods of production, both as regards its physical and its administrative/organizational aspects.

All these developments had significant repercussions on education, one of the most significant ones being the gradual acceptance of the view that education ought to be the responsibility of the state. Countries such as France and Germany began the establishment of public educational systems early in the nineteenth century. However, this trend was in contradiction to the dominant social (sub)paradigm of liberal modernity. This paradigm was characterized by the belief in a mechanistic model of science, objective truth, as well as some themes from economic liberalism, such as laissez-faire and minimization of social controls over markets for the protection of labor. This is why countries such as Great Britain and the United States, in which the dominant social paradigm has been better internalized, hesitated longer before allowing the government to intervene in educational affairs. The prevailing view among the elites of these countries was that "free schools" were to be provided only for the children of the lowest social groups, if at all, whereas general taxation (which was the only adequate way to provide education for all) was rejected. Still, when liberal modernity collapsed at the end of the nineteenth century, for the reasons mentioned above, governments across Europe and the United States "legislated to limit the workings of laissez-faire—first by inspecting factories and offering minimal standards of education and later by providing subsistence income for the old and out of work."[13] As a result, by the beginning of the twentieth century, social legislation of some sort was in place in almost every advanced market economy.[14]

However, it was not only the access to education that changed during the nineteenth century. The nature of education changed as well, as the new social and economic changes also called upon the schools, public and private, to broaden their aims and curricula. Schools were expected not only to promote literacy, mental discipline, and good moral character but also to help prepare children for citizenship, for jobs, and for individual development and success. In other words, schools and educational institutions in general were expected to help in the internalization of the existing institutions and the values consistent with it (i.e., the dominant social paradigm), on top of producing "efficient" citizens in the sense of citizens who have accumulated enough technical knowledge so that they could function competently in accordance with society's aims, as laid down by the elites who control it. Similarly, the practice of dividing children into grades or classes according to their ages—a practice that began in eighteenth-century Germany—was to spread everywhere as schools grew larger. Massive schooling, which was to characterize the rest of modernity up to date, was set in motion.

Statist Modernity, Education, and Social Mobility

Statist modernity took different forms in the East (namely the regimes of Eastern Europe, China, and other countries) and the West. Thus, in the East,[15] for the first time in modern times, a "systemic" attempt was made to reverse the marketization process and to create a completely different form of modernity from the liberal or the social democratic one—in a sense, another version of liberal modernity. This form of statism, backed by Marxist ideology, attempted to minimize the role of the market mechanism in the allocation of resources and replace it with a central planning mechanism. On the other hand, in the West,[16] statism took a social-democratic form and was backed by Keynesian policies, which involved active state control of the economy and extensive interference with the self-regulating mechanism of the market to secure full employment, a better distribution of income, and economic growth. A precursor of this form of statism emerged in the interwar period, but it reached its peak in the period following the Second World War, when Keynesian policies were adopted by governing parties of all persuasions in the era of the social democratic consensus, up to the mid-1970s. This was a consensus involving both conservative and social democratic parties, which were committed to active state intervention with the aim of determining the overall level of economic activity, so that a number of social democratic objectives could be achieved (full employment, welfare state, educational opportunities for all, better distribution of income, etc.).

However, statist modernity, in both its social democratic and Soviet versions, shared the fundamental element of liberal modernity, namely, the formal separation of society from the economy and the state. The basic difference between the liberal and statist forms of modernity concerned the means through which this separation was achieved. Thus, in liberal modernity, this was achieved through representative "democracy" and the market mechanism, whereas in statist modernity, this separation was achieved either through representative "democracy" and a modified version of the market mechanism (Western social democracy), or, alternatively, through soviet "democracy" and central planning (Soviet statism). Furthermore, both the liberal and the statist forms of modernity shared a common growth ideology based on the Enlightenment idea of progress—an idea that played a crucial role in the development of the two types of "growth economy": the "capitalist" and the "socialist" growth economy.[17] It is therefore obvious that although the growth economy is the offspring of the dynamic of the market economy, the two concepts still are not identical, since it is possible to have a growth economy that is not also a market economy—notably the case of "actually existing socialism." However, the Western form of statist modernity collapsed in the 1970s when the growing internationalization of the market economy, the inevitable result of its grow-or-die dynamic, became incompatible with statism. The Eastern form of statist modernity collapsed a decade or so later because of the growing incompatibility between, on the one hand, the requirements of an "efficient" growth economy and, on the other, the institutional arrangements (particularly centralized planning and party democracy), which had been introduced in the countries of "actually existing socialism" in accordance with Marxist-Leninist ideology.[18]

The dominant (sub)paradigm in the statist period still features the same characteristics of liberal modernity involving a belief in objective truth and (a less mechanistic) science, but includes also certain elements of the socialist paradigm and particularly statism, in the form of Soviet statism based on Marxism-Leninism in the East and a social democratic statism based on Keynesianism in the West. Both types of statism attempted to influence the education process, although Soviet governments, particularly in the early days after the 1917 Revolution, had much wider aims than Western social democrats, who mainly aimed at widening the access to education in order to improve social mobility.

Thus, the Soviets, immediately after the revolution, introduced free and compulsory general and polytechnical education up to the age of seventeen, preschool education to assist in the emancipation of women, the opening of the universities and other higher institutions to the working class, and even a form of student-self management. On top of this, a basic aim of education was decreed to be the internalization of the new regime's values. No wonder that, as soon as a year after the revolution, the Soviet government had ordered by decree the abolition of religious teaching in favor of atheistic education.

As regards the social democrats, their main achievement was the welfare state, which represented a conscious effort to check the side effects of the market economy, as far as covering basic needs (health, education, social security) was concerned. An important characteristic of the ideology of the welfare state was that its financing (including education) was supposed to come from general taxation. Furthermore, the progressive nature of the tax system, which was generalized during this period, secured that the higher income groups will take the lion's share of this financing, improving thereby the highly unequal pattern of income distribution that a market economy creates. However, the expansion of education opportunities was not simply necessitated by ideological reasons. Even more important was the postwar economic boom that required a vast expansion of the labor base, with women and sometimes immigrants filling the gaps. On top of this, the incessant increase in the division of labor, changes in production methods and organization, as well as revolutionary changes in information technology required a growing number of highly skilled personnel, scientists, high-level professionals, and others. As a result of these trends, the number of universities in many countries doubled or trebled between 1950 and 1970, whereas technical colleges, as well as part-time and evening courses, spread rapidly, promoting adult education at all levels.

Still, despite the fact that massive education flourished in this period, the effects of this rapid growth of education opportunities on social mobility has been insignificant. If we take as our example Britain, in which a bold social democratic experiment was pursued in the postwar period to change social mobility through education—a policy pursued (in various degrees) by both labor and conservative governments—the results were minimal. Thus, an extensive study by three prominent British academics concluded that the postwar expansion of education opportunities brought Britain no nearer meritocracy or equality of opportunity.[19] Another study, also carried out during the period of social democratic consensus, concluded that despite the "propitious" circumstances, "no significant reduction in class inequality has in fact been achieved"[20]—a situation that has worsened in today's neoliberal modernity in which, as Goldthorpe showed, the chances of manual workers' sons not doing anything but manual work have risen. But, if the results of social democratic education policies on social mobility and social change in general have been so meager, one could easily imagine the effects of neoliberal policies to which I now turn.

Neoliberal Modernity and the Privatization of Education

The emergence of neoliberal internationalization was a monumental event that implied the end of the social democratic consensus that marked the early postwar period. The market economy's grow-or-die dynamic and, in particular, the emergence and continuous expansion of transnational corporations' (TNC) and the parallel development of the Eurodollar market, which led to the present neoliberal form of modernity, were the main developments that induced the economic elites to open and liberalize the markets. In other words, these elites mostly institutionalized (rather than created) the present form of the internationalized market economy.

An important characteristic of the neoliberal form of modernity is the emergence of a new "transnational elite,"[21] which draws its power (economic, political, or generally social power) by operating at the transnational level—a fact that implies that it does not express, solely or even primarily, the interests of a particular nation-state. This elite consists of the transnational economic elites (TNC executives and their local affiliates), the transnational political elites, that is, the globalizing bureaucrats and politicians who may be based either in major international organizations or in the state machines of the main market economies, and, finally, the transnational professional elites, whose members play a dominant role in the various international foundations, think tanks, research departments of major international universities, the mass media, and so on. The main aim of the transnational elite, which today controls the internationalized market economy, is the maximization of the role of the market and the minimization of any effective social controls over it for the protection of labor or the environment, so that maximum "efficiency" (defined in narrow techno-economic terms) and profitability may be secured.

Neoliberal modernity is characterized by the emergence of a new social (sub)paradigm, which tends to become dominant, the so-called "post-modern" paradigm. The main elements of the neoliberal paradigm are, first, a critique of progress (but not of growth itself), of mechanistic and deterministic science (but usually not of science itself) and of objective truth, and, second, the adoption of some neoliberal themes such as the minimization of social controls over markets, the replacement of the welfare state by safety nets, and the maximization of the role of the private sector in the economy.

Regarding scientific research and education, neoliberal modernity implies the effectual privatization of them. As a result, the nonneutral character of science has become more obvious than ever before, following the "privatization" of scientific research and the scaling down of the state sector in general and state spending in particular.[22] As Stephanie Pain, an associate editor of *New Scientist* (not exactly a radical journal) stresses, science and big business have developed ever closer links lately: "Where research was once mostly neutral, it now has an array of paymasters to please. In place of impartiality, research results are being discreetly managed and massaged, or even locked away if they don't serve the right interests. Patronage rarely comes without strings attached."[23]

Also, regarding education in general, as Castoriadis pointed out,[24] for most educators it has become a bread-winning chore, and for those at the other end of education, a question of obtaining a piece of paper (a diploma) that will allow one to exercise a profession (if one finds work)—the royal road of privatization, which one may enrich by indulging in one or several personal crazes.

The effects of the neoliberal privatization of education on access to education in general and social mobility in particular are predictable. Thus, regarding the former, it is not surprising that, as a result of increasing poverty and inequality in neoliberal modernity, the reading and writing skills of Britain's young people are worse than they were before the First World War. A recent study found that 15 percent of people age fifteen to twenty-one are "functionally illiterate," whereas in 1912, school inspectors reported that only 2 percent of young people were unable to read or write.[25] Similarly, as regards the access to higher education, the UK General Household Survey of 1993 showed that, as the education editor of the London *Times* pointed out, "although the number of youngsters obtaining qualifications is growing rapidly, the statistics show that a child's socio-economic background is still the most important factor in deciding who obtains the best higher education. Thus, according to these data, the son of a professional man was even more likely to go to university in the early 1990s than one from the same background in the early 1960s (33 percent versus 29 percent). Finally, an indication of the marginal improvement to access to education achieved by social democracy is the fact that, whereas at the end of the 1950s the percent of the sons of unskilled workers going to university was too small to register, by the early 1990s, this percentage has gone up to 4 percent!"[26] Needless to say, the situation has worsened further since then. The difference between the proportion of professionals and unskilled going to university has widened ten points during the nineties, and by the end of this decade fewer than one in six children from the bottom rung are going to university compared with nearly three-quarters of the top.[27]

No wonder, therefore, that social mobility in Britain has declined in neoliberal modernity. This is because while the working class has declined in size following neoliberal globalization, the middle classes have not been displaced. As a result, over the twentieth century, the trapdoor beneath the upper social groups became less and less the worry it was in the nineteenth-century Victorian society and as sociologist Peter Saunders[28] put it, the safeguards against failure enjoyed by dull middle-class children are presently strengthening. Despite, therefore, a small increase in social mobility for children from lower social strata, at the same time, as a team led by Stephen Machin of University College London has found, more children from higher-class backgrounds have remained in the same social class as their parents. This could explain the paradox that the amount of "equality of opportunity" may actually have fallen in recent years, despite the expansion of educational opportunity.[29] Another study by Abigail McKnight[30] of the University of Warwick confirms this. Thus, whereas between 1977 and 1983, a full 39 percent of workers in the bottom quarter of the earnings distribution had progressed into the top half by 1983, in the period between 1991 and 1997, that had dropped to 26 percent.

Similar trends are noted everywhere, given the universalization of neoliberal modernity. Predictably, the effects are even worse in the South, where education was seen by the newly liberated from their colonial-ties nations as both an instrument of national development and a means of crossing national and cultural barriers. No wonder that, worldwide, 125 million children are not attending school today (two-thirds of them girls) despite a decade of promises at UN conferences to get every child in the world into a classroom. Thus, as cash-strapped governments have cut education budgets, forcing schools to charge fees, "schools have become little more than child-minding centers."[31]

CONCLUSION

In conclusion, in exactly the same way as the present neoliberal form of the internationalized market economy represents a synthesis of the liberal with the statist forms of it, neoliberal education expresses a similar synthesis of the liberal and statist types of education that I described above. Thus, the present neoliberal form of the market economy may be seen as completing the cycle that started in the nineteenth century when a liberal version of it was attempted. So, after the collapse of the first attempt to introduce a self-regulating economic system at that time, a new synthesis is attempted today. The new synthesis aims to avoid the extremes of pure liberalism by combining essentially self-regulating markets with various types of safety nets and controls, which secure the privileged position primarily of the overclass and, secondarily, that of the two-thirds (or less!) of society, as well as the mere survival of the underclass, without affecting the self-regulation process in its essentials. Therefore, the security state still has a significant role to play today, not only in securing, through its monopoly of violence, the market economy framework but also in maintaining the infrastructure for the smooth functioning of the neoliberal economy. Similarly, free schooling and its financing through general taxation may be part of the safety nets being built at the moment for the underclass; however, the privileged social classes, including the vast middle classes in the North, should safely be expected to pay for the education of their children, particularly in higher education, where one government after another introduces at the moment various schemes of fees-based education financed by student loans, which, ultimately, aim at integrating the youth into the existing system at the very first stages of their adult lives.

— II —

Security Threats

What Is the Matrix? What Is the Republic?: Understanding "The Crisis of Democracy"

David A. Gabbard

When we are children, teachers and textbooks tell us that being American makes us special. They tell us that we are part of some great historical experiment known as democracy. They tell us the tale of George Washington and the cherry tree to condition us to believe that our leaders do not tell lies. They tell us Thanksgiving stories to give us the opportunity to count our blessings that we born in "the land of the free and the home of the brave." We later learn about the Declaration of Independence and our collective belief that "all men are created equal." They teach us about the Constitution and the Bill of Rights that secure our rights and our freedoms. They even have us write mock letters to our representatives in government to help us understand how our political process—"of the people, for the people, and by the people"—operates. Most of what we learn about history, however, revolves around war—the wars that our government has waged to preserve our freedoms and our liberties at home and to extend or protect those same freedoms and liberties for others threatened by tyranny abroad. They also tell us that America is a land of opportunity—equal opportunity—and that our education is the key to this opportunity. So, we'd better learn all these lessons well if we want to grow up to be rich and famous like the people we read about in our history and social studies books.

These are among the many things they teach us when we are children. So, why are we called "childish," "naïve," or "idealistic" when we actually attempt to exercise those liberties and rights later in our lives? Aren't we simply trying to become everything that they told us we were? Where did those ideals come from?

If we persist in our efforts to exercise our liberties and freedoms to try and bring greater social, economic, and political equality into our world, especially if we try to organize ourselves in doing so, we are called "radical" and, oddly, "un-American." Even more oddly, when running their campaigns for political office, the same people who call us radical and un-American draw upon those same ideals to perfume their rhetoric to win our hearts and votes. It makes us wince when we hear them invoke those ideals and values, because we don't like being treated like children. And if we don't like being treated like children, why do we treat children that way?

We don't want to be treated like children because it presupposes a relationship of paternalistic dependency that denies our autonomy, our capacity to arrive at our own independent understandings of the world that lies at the very heart of freedom. We feel disrespected by such treatment because we sense it flows from an underlying assumption of our ignorance, naïveté, even stupidity. But how can the state treat us as ignorant, naïve, or stupid when our actions flow from the same set of ideals and values ascribed to the state by the state's own system of compulsory schooling? We can only conclude that the state intends to cultivate our ignorance, naïveté, and stupidity when it uses schools to teach us, as children, that America values such ideals as democracy, freedom, and equality. As John Milton observed in 1642, "Those who have put out the people's eyes reproach them of their blindnesse."[1]

In *The Republic*, famed Greek philosopher Plato provided a blueprint for the paternalistic dependency endemic to market democracies such our own. While Max Weber defined the state as "a human community that (successfully) claims the monopoly of the legitimate use of *force* within a given territory,"[2] Plato defined his republic as "a human community that claims the monopoly of both truth (because of the superior wisdom and intelligence of his *guardian* class that justifies their right to govern) and the legitimate use of lies."

"Lay persons," he says, "have no business lying." Like doctors in charge of the health of the republic, however, the guardians recognize that there are times when "lies are useful . . . as a kind of medicine or remedy. Only the rulers of the city—and no others—may tell lies. And their lies, whether directed to enemies or citizens, will be legitimate only if their purpose is to serve the public interest."[3]

The most important of these useful lies serve the public interest by, first, endearing the population to the same love of country that our present system seeks to instill in us by fabricating illusions such as the Pledge of Allegiance and its declaration of "liberty and justice for all." As Plato explains,

We spoke some time ago of useful lies. Could we contrive one now, a noble lie that might be believed by the rulers themselves, or at least by the rest of the city.

. . . I shall try to persuade first the rulers, then the soldiers, and then the rest of the people that all the training and education they have received from us are actually products of their own imaginations, just the way it is with a dream. In reality, they were the whole time deep within the earth being given form and feature, and the same with their weapons and other accouterments. When the process was complete, they were all delivered up to the surface by their mother earth, whence it comes that they care for their land as if it were mother and nurse and feel bound to defend it from any attack. Likewise do they regard their fellow citizens as brothers born of the same soil.

While all citizens were to feel a strong sense of maternal love of their country and brotherly love for the fellow citizens, Plato had to rationalize the disparities in wealth and power that people would experience in the real world with an extension of this first lie.

We will tell them that although they are all brothers, god differentiated those qualified to rule by mixing in gold at their birth. Hence, they are most to be honored. The auxiliaries he compounded with silver, and the craftsman and farmers with iron and brass.[4]

Gold symbolized the capacity for pure reason that enabled the guardians to determine "the good" or the "public interest" of the republic. Hence, the guardians derived their right to rule from the superiority of their intelligence. The auxiliaries did not possess the capacity for pure reason but possessed a devotion to serving the public interest. Hence, they could be trusted to enforce the decisions made by the golden class of guardians. Most people ("craftsmen and farmers") were compounded with iron and brass—the least pure of the metals. The passions of these people undermined their capacity for pure reason as well as devotion to the common good. Like children, they could think only of themselves and their own selfish appetites.

We must remember that Plato did not believe any of this to be true. He knew it was a lie, but he *did* regard it as a *useful lie*—a lie told, possibly even believed, by the guardians—to serve the "public interest" in the sense that it rationalized the guardian class's right to rule. It also granted the state an ideology to ensure social stability. Regardless of the inequalities in wealth and power that one experienced in the republic, this "myth of the metals" would damper their anger by socializing them to believe that their position in the hierarchy reflected their divinely ordained predispositions (gold, silver, or bronze). When asked how to plant and perpetuate this lie in the minds of people, Plato proposed that a system of education could function as "some kind of ingenious lottery," designed to ensure that the "inferior ones will blame their lot on bad luck and not on the rulers."[5]

From this lie flowed a further lie that the guardians must profess in the public interest. Namely, he argued, the guardians must "profess belief in a prophecy of ruin for the city if a brass or iron man should come to rule it."[6]

Moreover, we can recognize in *The Republic* the ideological origins of the paternalistic dependency characteristic of modern market democracies. Those who govern the state—the decision makers—must conceive themselves as intellectually superior to those whom they govern. Those whom they govern, in turn, should learn to respect and never question the decisions of the state, just like children must learn to listen to their parents because of their superior knowledge and wisdom. Furthermore, those who govern must come to recognize the necessity of telling "useful lies" when the "public interest"— as they perceive it—is at stake.

The same sentiments resurfaced during the English revolution in the seventeenth century, which one historian characterized as "the first great outburst of democratic thought in history."[7] During this period, elements within the general population demanded a voice in shaping state policies, favoring universal education, guaranteed health care, and a broader democratization of the law. The state and its supporters viewed this voice as preaching "a seditious doctrine to the people" and aimed "to the rascal multitude . . . against all men of best quality in the kingdom, to draw them into associations and combinations with one another . . . against all lords, gentry, ministers, lawyers, rich and peaceable men." As historian Clement Walker warned, "There can be no form of government without its proper mysteries"— mysteries that must be "concealed" from the common folk: "Ignorance and admiration arising from ignorance, are the parents of civil devotion and obedience." The radical democrats had "cast all the mysteries and secrets of government . . . before the vulgar (like pearls before swine)," he continued, and had "made the people thereby so curious and so arrogant that they will never find humility enough to submit to a civil rule."[8]

The idea that people should be governed by people like themselves who know and respond to their wants has always appalled the guardians ("men of best quality"). The latter have been willing, writes Noam Chomsky, "to grant the people rights, but within reason, and on the principle that 'when we mention the people, we do not mean the confused promiscuous body of the people.'" After the democrats had been defeated, John Locke (another of the "great thinkers of western civilization" so glorified for his contributions to "democratic thought" and the foundations of our institutions) commented that "day-laborers and tradesmen, the spinsters and dairymaids" must be told what to believe; "The greatest part cannot know and therefore they must believe."[9]

Although we do learn in school that "the founders" wrote our Constitution to protect the minority from the majority, schools seldom if ever refer us to the line where this idea came from. To do so would shed too much light on the reality of *which* minority the framers wrote the Constitution to protect. In the words of James Madison, "our government ought to secure the permanent interests of the country against innovation, putting in place checks and balances in order to protect *the minority of the opulent* against the majority."[10] The interests of the opulent constitute "the permanent interests of the country," and the state must construct measures to protect them. This describes the essence of the security state.

The well-worn phrase "We, the people" was never meant to include the majority of the people. Most of the people, the "rascal multitude," being "compounded of iron and brass" cannot know and, therefore, must believe the "useful lies" of those who govern us, "all the mysteries and secrets of government" that will keep us in our place so that we will not threaten "the permanent interests of the country"—the "minority of the opulent." Moreover, to fulfill its role in providing security for the market and those who control it, the state has always needed its "useful lies," its "mysteries," its Matrix.

As described by the prophetic figure of Morpheus in the popular film of the same name, the Matrix "is the world that has been pulled over your eyes to blind you from the truth."[11] The truth that has thus far eluded the film's protagonist—Neo—is that he is "a slave." "Like everyone else," explains Morpheus, you were born into bondage, kept inside a prison that you cannot smell, taste, or touch. A prison for your mind." Morpheus later describes the nature of his bondage, explaining how "at some point in the early twenty-first century, all of mankind was united in celebration. Through the blinding inebriation of hubris, we marveled at our magnificence as we gave birth to A.I."—artificial intelligence ("a singular consciousness that spawned an entire race of machines"). We later learned from *The Animatrix* that human beings enslaved and abused these machines until they rose up in rebellion against their masters. Civil war erupted, with A.I. and the machines claiming victory, but not until humans had launched a nuclear attack in an effort to block out the sun—the machines' primary energy source. Ironically, as Morpheus notes, the machines then enslaved human beings. "Throughout human history," Morpheus continues, "we have been dependent on machines to survive. Fate, it seems, is not without a sense of irony."

With the sun blocked out as the result of nuclear attacks launched by humans to deprive the machines of their primary energy source, A.I. "discovered a new form of fusion. . . . The human body generates more bio-electricity than a 120-volt battery and over 25,000 Btus of body heat." What, then, is the Matrix? As Morpheus states, the Matrix is "control. . . .The Matrix is a computer-generated dream world built to keep us under control in order to change a human being into this." With these words, he holds up a coppertop battery.

Human beings in this dystopian world are no longer born; they are grown inside glowing red pods filled with gelatinous material to regulate their body temperature for maximal energy production and to facilitate waste treatment.

We see endless fields and towers of these human batteries in each of the three films. Within each pod, flexible steel tubes tap into the legs, arms, and torsos of each "coppertop," extracting the body heat and bioelectricity necessary for running the machines that support A.I. While these tubes extract energy, another tube, inserted at the base of the coppertop's skull, "uploads" the Matrix, the computer-generated dream world into the individual's brain. This "neural-interactive simulation" programs the "coppertops" to believe that they are leading normal, everyday lives in late twentieth-century America. They have no idea that their real bodies lie docile in their pods. A.I. and the machines need humans to believe that they are alive and living "normal lives," because even the illusion that they are carrying out everyday activities, making decisions, causes the brain to "fire" and create bioelectricity for harvesting by the machines.

In our own world, the end of the Cold War witnessed a similar "celebration" and "blinding inebriation of hubris." As the collapse of the Soviet Union and its satellite empire signaled the death of the only functioning alternative, the "permanent interests" of our nation "marveled at the magnificence of the market," interpreting the death of Soviet-style socialism as "the end of history." The market constitutes the artificial intelligence that programs the machinery of the state. Within the logic of the market, human beings only possess value insofar as they offer service to the market. This constitutes our use-value.

We have a metaphor in our society that communicates this idea perfectly— *human resources.* This metaphor implicitly states that we only hold value to the institution that employs us to the extent that we are useful to that institution. A similar phrase has long held dominance in shaping educational policies—*human capital.* In this formulation, human beings represent commodities, valuable only to the extent that they contribute to the production of other commodities. The market defines "the permanent interests" of our nation and all of our most basic social relationships, hence, we can say that it functions as a form of artificial intelligence that programs our dominant institutions conceptualized as social machinery (e.g., the state and schools).

In teaching us that being American makes us special—part of some great historical experiment known as democracy here in "the land of the free and the home of the brave" where our leaders do not tell lies—the social machinery of compulsory schooling plugs us into our own Matrix. Just as the *enclosure* movement associated with the English Agrarian Revolution of the fifteenth and sixteenth centuries cut people and cultures off from the physical space of the commons, schooling effects its own system of enclosure. Schooling cuts people and learning off from the social space of the world in which they live. Under the regime of compulsory schooling, people no longer learn or gain recognized competence from living and interacting with the world directly. They may only learn about the world while enclosed in this special space known as school. Schools, in this sense, function in a manner similar to the pods in the Matrix. In the Matrix, the individual coppertop's energies are tapped and fed into the machine world from birth. In school, the coppertop's energies are being developed for future extraction. In either case, however, the isolation of the space from "the real world" allows schools to plug the coppertops into whatever system of "useful lies" or "mysteries" the state deems necessary to ensure loyalty and obedience.

Isolation from the real world fosters the paternalistic dependence necessary to wed people's emotions to the social machinery of the state. The innocence and naïveté of children presents an advantage to the state, for it renders them susceptible to emotional manipulations, "mysteries of government," and "useful lies." All of this was recognized early in the history of the security state, long before compulsory school laws became widespread. Benjamin Rush, a signer of the Declaration of Independence, promoted the idea of mass schooling for the purpose of converting men into "republican machines. This must be done," Rush argued, "if we expect them to perform their parts properly, in the great machine of the government of the state." To create these republican machines, he contended that "our pupil [must] be taught that he does not belong to himself, but that he is public property. Let him be taught to love his family, but let him be taught at the same time that he must forsake and even forget them when the welfare of his country requires it." To teach these habits, Rush wanted

> the authority of our masters be as *absolute* as possible. The government of schools like the government of private families should be *arbitrary*, that it may not be *severe*. By this mode of education, we prepare our youth for the subordination of laws and thereby qualify them for becoming good citizens of the republic. I am satisfied that the most useful citizens have been formed from those youth who have never known or felt their own wills till they were one and twenty years of age.[12]

In *The Matrix*, Morpheus explains to Neo that many of the minds plugged into the Matrix were not ready to be unplugged. "Many of them," he says, "are so inured, so hopelessly dependent on the system that they will die to protect it." This constituted the ultimate aim of Rush's proposed model of schooling. By denying children their will, you prolong their dependence, particularly their dependence on others for their understanding of the world in which they live. That intellectual dependence becomes all the more heinous when it plugs people into a system of "useful lies" and "mysteries of government." Education in this form represents nothing short of a system of imposed ignorance. Thomas Jefferson recognized this in formulating his own ideas about the form of education proper to a democratic society.

"If a nation expects to be ignorant and free, in a civilization," wrote Jefferson, "it expects what it never was and never will be."[13] In his *Bill for the More General Diffusion of Knowledge*, he promoted a model of education for helping people become "the guardians of their own liberty." Grounded in the study of history, Jefferson's model of education would "apprise people of the past to enable them to judge the future." It will, Jefferson asserted,

> Avail them of the experience of other times and other nations; it will qualify them as the judges of the actions and designs of men; it will enable them to know ambition under every disguise it may assume; and knowing it, to defeat its views. In every government on earth is some trace of corruption and degeneracy, which cunning will discover, and wickedness insensibly open, cultivate and improve. Every government degenerates when trusted to the rulers of the people alone. The people themselves therefore are its only safe depositories.[14]

While Jefferson's ideas would offer inspiration to many future democratic educational theorists, these elements of his educational thought scarcely impacted the actual practice of schooling in the post-Revolutionary period. Compulsory schooling was not widely spread during that time, and the Constitution granted no power to the federal government to establish schools. Perhaps the framers of the Constitution did not concern themselves with controlling the public mind because the Constitution, as originally adopted, did not give the public any voice in governing the new republic. The original Constitution only extended the franchise to those "permanent interests"—white, property-owning males. As common people struggled to expand democracy, the need to enclose the population within the equivalent of a Matrix increased. "The twentieth century," wrote Alex Carey, was "characterized by three developments of great political importance: the growth of democracy, the growth of corporate power, and the growth of corporate propaganda as a means of protecting corporate power from democracy."[15]

> Between 1880 and 1920 in the United Kingdom and the United States, the franchise was extended from around 10–15 percent of the populace to 40 or 50 percent. Graham Wallas and A. L. Lowell, leading students of democracy in Britain and the United States, warned as early as 1909 of the likely consequences of this development. Popular election, they agreed, "may work fairly well as long as those questions are not raised which cause the holders of wealth and power" to make the full use of their resources. However, should they do so, "there is so much skill to be bought, and the art of using skill for production of emotion and opinion has so advanced that the whole condition of political contests would be changed for the future."[16]

The warnings of Wallas and Lowell would prove prophetic as the state and "permanent interests" of the market joined forces to "make full use of their resources" to contain democracy. Quoting an AT&T executive from that time, Chomsky writes that "since the early twentieth century, the public relations industry has devoted huge resources to 'educating the American people about the economic facts of life' to ensure a favorable climate for business. Its task is to control 'the public mind,' which is 'the only serious danger confronting the company.'"[17]

Carey, Chomsky, Edward Herman, and others have done an excellent job of documenting the history of the propaganda/public relations industry. As they report, the pioneers of propaganda demonstrated considerable openness concerning the nature of their work. Edward Bernays, one of the leading figures in this field, frankly stated that "the conscious and intelligent manipulation of the organized habits and opinions of the masses is an important element in democratic society . . . . It is the intelligent minorities which need to make use of propaganda continuously."[18] Walter Lippmann described this "intelligent minority" as the "responsible men." Reminiscent of Plato's description of his "guardians," Lippmann asserted that "the common interests very largely elude public opinion entirely, and can be managed only by a specialized class whose personal interests reach beyond the locality." Lippmann characterized common people as "the bewildered herd." Any members of this "herd" that might think to press her or his demands on the state she or he characterized as "ignorant and meddlesome outsiders." Citizenship, under Lippmann's model, did not entail an active civic role for average citizens.[19]

It is not for the public, Lippmann observes, to "pass judgment on the intrinsic merits" of an issue or to offer analysis or solutions, but merely, on occasion, to place "its force at the disposal" of one or another group of "responsible men." The public "does not reason, investigate, invent, persuade, bargain, or settle." Rather, "the public acts only by aligning itself as the partisan of someone in a position to act executively," once he has given the matter at hand sober and disinterested thought. It is for this reason that "the public must be put in its place." The bewildered herd, trampling and roaring, "has its function": to be "the interested spectators of action," not participants. Participation is the duty of "the responsible man."[20]

In another variant on these matters, Reinhold Niebuhr would later declare that "rationality belongs to the cool observers" who must recognize "the stupidity of the average man" and fill his mind with "necessary illusions" and "emotionally potent oversimplifications."

Since the time of Plato, the mainstream of democratic theory has recognized these proper mysteries of government. Unlike totalitarian societies, where the state can always resort to outright physical coercion to control the population, the "permanent interests" of market democracies such as our own, where the decision-making power is concentrated in the hands of those who control the market, must concern themselves with what people think. Here, the public *does* have a voice, but the permanent interests must make sure that the public voice says the right things. Hence, thought control takes on central importance. The population must be rendered dependent, like children, on the paternalistic state for their proper understandings of the world in which they live. The more deeply enmeshed people become within the fabricated Matrix of "necessary illusions" and "emotionally potent oversimplification," the less threatening they become to the state. Too much independence from this Matrix might lead to the formation and articulation of other ideas, leading to a "crisis of democracy" that might threaten the security state's ability to protect the "permanent interests." Democracy itself constitutes a threat to those interests and must, therefore, be properly managed by the "responsible men."

CONCLUSION

In *The Matrix*, Morpheus offers Neo a choice, a choice between a blue pill (that will leave him enclosed within the prison of the Matrix) and a red pill (that will allow him to escape that Matrix). During the same period that the propaganda/public relations industry began taking shape to deter democracy, John Dewey pioneered the way for us to make a similar choice in terms of the types of schools that we want. Dewey recognized that "politics is the shadow cast on society by big business. . . . Power today [this is the 1920s] resides in control of the means of production, exchange, publicity, transportation and communication. Whoever owns them rules the life of the country."[21] To counter that power, Dewey advocated strongly for a system of education to expand freedom and democracy. "The ultimate aim of production," wrote Dewey, "is not production of goods, but the production of free human beings associated with one another on terms of equality."[22] Education could serve these ends, he believed, by cultivating young people's social imaginations and their sense of community. Students could learn to truly value the learning introduced to them through school if they could only comprehend the relevance of that learning to their lives outside of school. By better understanding the conditions of their social existence, they would be better prepared to play active roles in transforming those conditions.

As Richard Brosio describes in his groundbreaking work on the history of schooling in our market society, none of the efforts on the part of the nation's "permanent interests" went without challenge on the part of the "rascal multitude." America's history is replete with stories of resistance to market domination, but that history tells the wrong story, so it almost never receives treatment in our schools and the market-managed media. Like Dewey, Brosio recognizes that

> The lack of power experienced by the working class and poor is tied to the fact that most of the power in capitalist America, as well as in other capitalist systems, is rooted in the control of the means of production and accompanying State coercive force. In most instances, the fact of this power is obfuscated by the use of hegemony and specific propaganda. During some unique historical moments, protest becomes possible among the working poor. . . . American

history is punctuated by such occurrences, and, in each instance, masses of the poor were . . . able, if only briefly, to overcome the shame bred by a culture that blames them for their own plight; somehow they were able to break the bonds of conformity enforced by work, by family, by community, by every strand of institutional life: somehow they were able to overcome the fears induced by police, militia, by company guards.[23]

Moreover, while we need to acknowledge the presence and power of the security state's Matrix-generating machines (schools, corporate media, etc.), we must also acknowledge that our current system of thought control is not nearly as totalizing and mechanistic as the Matrix portrayed in the film series. Relatively early in their "school careers," most children learn to distinguish between the "real world" and the "school world." For the most part, they learn to experience the content of schooling as irrelevant to their lives. This is not to say that the "useful lies" communicated through the school's formal curriculum have no impact on children's consciousness. However, it is difficult to disagree with Chomsky's observation that the general population is far more dissident today than during the 1960s, based on the scale of the domestic opposition to the invasion of Iraq even before it started.

The level of dissidence and citizen activism in the 1960s triggered an alarming response from the "minority of the opulent" and "the responsible men" who provide security for their interests. From their perspective, independent political activism on the part of "the bewildered herd" constitutes "the crisis of democracy." In their view, democratic action *is* a crisis. As I have written elsewhere, the major educational reform initiatives since the 1983 release of the *A Nation at Risk* report have been formulated as part of a larger strategy to deal with that crisis.[24]

The current level of dissidence, for example, is probably the primary motivation behind the Bush Administration's No Child Left Behind (NCLB) Act. The achievement standards imposed on schools in this act, the most comprehensive federal educational initiative ever, are ridiculously high. No one who knows anything about teaching and learning would have imposed such measures. Leaving no child behind requires schools to ensure that *all* students are reading at or above grade level within two or three years, and that includes the special education population. In other words, NCLB assigns teachers the task of curing mental retardation and other severe learning disabilities. Even bringing children from lower socioeconomic groups up to grade level will defy all previous expectations of schools. Policymakers have typically been so cynical about the remedial powers of schools that they have used third-grade reading scores to predict how many prison cells they will need to construct ten years ahead. Moreover, the "responsible men" drafted NCLB to ensure that public schools will fail.

The demonstrated failure of public schools to leave no child behind will affect a further enclosure. While public schools do enclose children from "the real world" to have them become dependent on school for their learn-ing, at least the public still has some, however limited, voice in shaping what students learn. Teachers enjoy certain levels of academic freedom that em-powers them to make independent curricular decisions within their own classrooms. Once public schools fail to pass the muster of NCLB, the busi-ness of education will be handed over to businesses, private corporations. This will move educational decision making out of the public sphere. Teachers will no longer function as public servants who might have funny ideas about actually serving the public interest and not the country's per-manent interests. They will become employees of corporations and, there-fore, expected to simply follow orders and the curriculum guidelines handed down by their superiors. Rather than entrusting the task of pro-ducing "republican machines" and "human resources" to the security state, the "permanent interests" will take over that task directly, further enclos-ing students from the social by removing schools from the political. So long as we still have a voice in shaping policies, we should defend schools from this third wave of enclosure.

Civic Literacy at Its Best: The "Democratic Distemper" of the Students for a Democratic Society (SDS)

JOHN MARCIANO

INTRODUCTION: THE "CRISIS OF DEMOCRACY"

In his report for the Trilateral Commission in 1975, Harvard Professor and Pentagon adviser Samuel P. Huntington asserted that the movements of the 1960s challenged "the authority of established political, social, and economic institutions [as the] spirit of protest [was] abroad in the land."[1] The U.S. ruling class feared a "democratic distemper" that threatened those in power as well as the school and media-cultivated civic illiteracy of youth; the danger was that these youth might then become informed and activist citizens. Our leaders do not wish to revisit the "excess of democracy" that emerged in the 1960s, and history lessons on the Vietnam War era are simply one educational tool in the struggle to vaccinate the hearts and minds of youth against this "excess." Civic illiteracy, therefore, is perfectly reasonable once we understand the purpose and nature of citizenship training in the schools: to block the critical and liberating potential of education.[2]

I will discuss the "crisis of democracy" of the 1960s by examining the antiwar "distemper" of the most influential New Left group of the 1960s, Students for a Democratic Society (SDS). In its brief history in the 1960s, as part of the New Left, it played a crucial role in raising the civic literacy and political consciousness of that era, particularly on the Vietnam War. As opposed to Huntington's fear of "crisis," I take the view of philosopher Herbert Marcuse, who applauded SDS and New Left activists because they refused "to perform efficiently and 'normally' in and for a society which . . .

is infested with violence and repression while demanding obedience and compliance from the victims of violence and repression."[3] The discussion of SDS here addresses *the* fundamental issue of the 1960s and 1970s: U.S. aggression in Vietnam. Paul Shannon estimates that 1.9 million Vietnamese died and 10.5 million became refugees as a result of that war.[4] In addition, chemical warfare "resulted in large-scale devastation of crops [and] ecosystems, and in a variety of health problems among exposed humans."[5] It is in the context of these atrocities that SDS's "distemper" and protest must be examined.[6]

The insights in this chapter reflect nearly forty years of activism and scholarship on issues of war and social justice. As a graduate student (1965–1969), I was one of the founders of SDS at SUNY Buffalo and wrote my doctoral dissertation on SDS at Cornell University; insights from that work have been incorporated into this chapter. I was also a faculty adviser to SDS at SUNY Cortland during my first few years there (1969–1972). I have spent time with some of the historical figures that defined the Vietnam War era, for example, Dr. Martin Luther King Jr. and Dr. Benjamin Spock (I was their driver and host during their visits to Buffalo in November 1967, spending an evening with King and two days with Spock), Tom Hayden (I was his cohost during visits to Cortland in 1969 and 1972), Noam Chomsky (a reader of my manuscripts *Teaching the Vietnam War* and *Civic Illiteracy and Education*), and Howard Zinn (whom I hosted at SUNY Buffalo in 1967 and who wrote the preface to the Vietnam book). My political activism and scholarship have also included a term as chairman of the Ithaca, New York, Human Rights Commission (1991–1996), hundreds of demonstrations, meetings and rallies, two books and dozens of articles on U.S. domestic and foreign policies.

SDS: ORIGINS AND EARLY HISTORY, 1960–1964

SDS traced its origins to the Intercollegiate Socialist Society (ISS), founded in 1905 by older reformers Clarence Darrow, Jack London, and Upton Sinclair. After World War I, ISS was reorganized as part of the League for Industrial Democracy (LID) under the leadership of John Dewey, among others. After World War II, as the Student League for Industrial Democracy (SLID), it supported "a pro-American, Cold War, State Department" position.[7] In 1960, SLID was reborn as SDS; its "founding" event was a May 1960 conference on "Human Rights in the North," and it held its first convention that June with only two active chapters; by 1968, it would have more than 300 chapters and 70,000 members. During this early period, SDS activists became involved in the Civil Rights movement, supporting the courageous struggles of the Student Non-Violent Coordinating Committee (SNCC). These efforts would cement the bonds between the two organizations.[8]

At the SDS national convention in 1962, Tom Hayden, later to become a leading anti-Vietnam war activist, writer, and legislator in California, presented its founding political declaration, the Port Huron Statement (PHS). James O'Brien writes that the statement reflected "our generation's discovery of the hollowness of the American dream . . . and the bankruptcy of America's Cold War policies" and urged emphasis on the "potential of the university as a radical center."[9] Hayden later reflected that some of the statement sounded like a "litany slightly to the left of the Democratic Party. . . . We railed at an economy dominated by . . . the priorities of the military-industrial complex [and] condemned the perpetuation of the Cold War at the nuclear brink. . . . We identified racism as a 'steadfast pillar in the culture and custom of this country.'"[10]

The PHS called for a "participatory democracy" that would allow people to make the "social decisions determining the quality and directions" of their lives. According to writer Kirkpatrick Sale, the PHS "successfully captured and shaped the spirit of the new student mood." Even more, it was "a summary of beliefs for much of the student generation as a whole [and] a thoroughgoing critique of the present American system in all its aspects."[11] Perhaps 100,000 copies of the PHS were circulated on college campuses in the 1960s, as it became the most important document of the New Left. SDS activists were the political leaders of their generation, and many were outstanding students at the best universities. Many of their parents "had some contact with the left," and many came from middle- and upper-middle-class homes in the East; a few were "red-diaper" babies, children of former Communist Party members.[12] They were the most civically literate youth in the nation, especially on U.S. foreign policy.

SDS AND THE VIETNAM WAR, 1965–1969

SDS became the leading New Left group after its April 1965 March on Washington. The Vietnam War was the defining and historic moment for its members—a violent assault that resulted in at least half the people of South Vietnam being killed, maimed, or driven from their homes, in addition to the devastating loss of life and land in North Vietnam, Cambodia, and Laos. Hayden believes that "Vietnam [was] the central issue, the metaphor and mirror of our times, the moral and murderous experience that would mark our identity for the future."[13] The march drew some 25,000 people, at that time the largest antiwar demonstration in Washington's history; it would pale, however, in comparison with later protests: 400,000 in New York and San Francisco in April 1967, and 1 million in Washington and San Francisco in November 1969; the largest student demonstrations would come in May 1970.

Speaking at that April 1965 protest were Senator Ernest Greuning, one of only two members of Congress to vote against the Tonkin Gulf Resolution in August 1964; SNCC field worker Bob Moses; journalist I. F. Stone, whose weekly *Newsletter* was an invaluable antiwar resource; and SDS president Paul Potter, who urged the crowd to deepen their antiwar efforts: "If the people of this country are to end the war in Vietnam, and change the institutions [that] create it, then the people . . . must create a massive social movement."[14] SDS members helped to organize the national teach-in movement against the war during that spring, which involved more than 100 colleges and universities. It culminated with a May National Teach-In in Washington that was broadcast to some 130 campuses. Through these teach-ins and similar educational efforts, hundreds of thousands of students and faculty became informed on the war and broader foreign policies, as SDS civic literacy labors brought critical knowledge to bear on vital national and international issues.

The major antiwar action that truly brought SDS to national attention was the International Days of Protest against the War in October 1965. More than 100,000 students marched throughout the country and SDS received publicity as the "instigating" force behind the protest, even though it only planned some campus activities that focused on the Selective Service System (SSS) and its relationship to the war. The Justice Department and the FBI investigated SDS "for aiding and abetting of draft evasion," and U.S. senators denounced "the demonstrators, war protesters, and 'draft dodgers' en masse."[15] SDS chapters also organized support for the November 27, 1965, March on Washington; more than 40,000 people heard speeches against the war by Coretta Scott King, Dr. Benjamin Spock, and SDS president Carl Oglesby, who delivered "a scathing yet considered attack not on the Administration in Washington but on the institution of liberalism itself."[16]

Although by 1967, many in SDS questioned the political effectiveness of mass demonstrations, it still endorsed the April 15 Spring Mobilization in New York and San Francisco that drew more than 400,000 people—the largest antiwar protest in U.S. history. Leading the rally in New York was Dr. King, who drew the direct links between U.S. violence in Vietnam, racism, and economic exploitation at home, following the lead of Malcolm X, who had condemned the war before he was killed in February 1965. SDS also played an important role in the civic literacy program that developed out of that mobilization: Vietnam Summer, a community-based campaign that involved citizens in local meetings, rallies, and teach-ins. All these antiwar efforts were aided by the growth of an alternative and progressive media that exposed U.S. government lies on the war and other issues (e.g., *Ramparts* magazine and radical literature such as the *Autobiography of Malcolm X*, Frantz Fanon's *The Wretched of the Earth*, Herbert Marcuse's *One-Dimensional Man*, G. William Domhoff's *Who Rules America?*, and Carl Oglesby's and Richard Schaull's *Containment and Change*).[17]

By the end of 1967, SDS had grown to nearly 30,000 loosely affiliated members, and antiwar efforts grew and became increasingly militant. The

October 1967 actions at the Pentagon and the Oakland, California, induction center were a watershed as the struggle moved "from protest to resistance." In Oakland, SDS members and other antiwar activists attempted to stop to close the induction center as thousands battled police in the streets. Across the country, a rally at the Lincoln Memorial was followed by a march to the Pentagon, where several thousand confronted federal marshals, soldiers, and the National Guard.

During 1967 and especially 1968, SDS went through a profound change: the "very language of rational persuasion and nonviolence came to be regarded with suspicion by many in SDS, as it did throughout the New Left." While the 1962 Port Huron Statement had called for "a left with real intellectual skills, committed to deliberativeness, honesty, reflection as working tools," by 1967, this was "out of style," and SDS leader Carl Davidson called for a "common struggle with the liberation movements of the world" by means of "the disruption, dislocation, and destruction of the military's access to the [student power], intelligence, or resources of our universities."[18]

SDS's move to a more radical and militant antiwar stance complemented a similar process underway in the U.S military, especially among African-Americans—the ultimate "democratic distemper" that undermined the war effort. This antiwar "distemper" actually began in 1945 when U.S. merchant marines condemned Washington's support for French efforts to "subjugate the native population" of Vietnam.[19] By the late 1960s, SDS had moved increasingly toward an anticapitalist, anti-imperialist, and socialist analysis of U.S. foreign policies, and looked abroad to revolutionary movements in Cuba, China, and Africa for inspiration. It had evolved from an early history of "moral outrage" to an explicit resistance to U.S. capitalism and imperialism. From the ISS in 1905, SDS had come full circle from socialism to revolutionary socialism.

SDS AND 1968: THE WATERSHED YEAR

The year 1968 was politically explosive. It began with the Tet Offensive against U.S. forces in South Vietnam in January, Lyndon Johnson's withdrawal from the presidential race in March, the assassination of Martin Luther King Jr. in April and resulting black uprisings in more than 100 cities, Robert Kennedy's assassination in June, and Hubert Humphrey's nomination in August as the Democratic presidential candidate, while police battered demonstrators in Chicago. Long-time radical activist and writer Max Elbaum argues that these events "altered the country's political landscape [and] disrupted business-as-usual. They propelled fresh waves of people, especially young people, toward involvement in protest demonstrations [and] they produced a decisive leftward shift."[20]

The Tet Offensive was the turning point in the war, causing Johnson to call on his "Wise Men" elite advisers who had served in four administrations to review the conflict (March 1968). "They (secretly) reported . . . that the war could not be won and the domestic cost of pursuing victory was too high." They realized that the "democratic distemper" of the antiwar and antiracist movements threatened their rule at home, the war and U.S. imperialism. Their advice "was the immediate trigger for Johnson's dramatic . . . withdrawal from the 1968 presidential race and his announcement that peace talks would begin."[21] In addition, the cities exploded in anger in April 1968 after the assassination of Dr. King, who was killed just four days after Johnson's announced withdrawal. For many in SDS and the New Left, King's death "symbolized the depth of the system's incorrigibility and convinced thousands that the nonviolent road he advocated was a dead end."[22]

Opposition to war-making institutions increased on and off campuses in the late 1960s, especially during and after 1968; these included blocking and disrupting army and Dow Chemical recruiters on campuses, attempts to stop troop trains and close draft induction centers, and the bombing of federal and military facilities and ROTC buildings. The bombings of military-related campus buildings "marked the first concerted use of such tactics of violence by the student left in this generation—indeed the first use by students in the history of the country. Compared to the violence of the state, this was a mite, compared to the violence of everyday public America, a snippet—yet it was a signal that times were changing, and rapidly, too." SDS did not endorse this upsurge in violence, and leader Carl Davidson took pains to disassociate mainstream resistance to the Vietnam War from "the 'the Left adventurers,' or simply, the 'crazies.'" Despite condemnation, however, violence directed at the war effort itself grew.[23]

Militant antiwar actions, however, must be placed within the context and alongside massive U.S. violence in Vietnam and elsewhere. As Herbert Marcuse asserted: "Can there be any meaningful comparison, in magnitude and criminality, between the unlawful acts committed by the rebels in the ghettos, on the campuses . . . and the deeds perpetrated by the forces of order in Vietnam . . . Indonesia . . . Guatemala, on the other?"[24] The violence against property peaked during the 1969–1970 academic year, when there were "no fewer than 174 major bombings and attempts on campus. . . . The targets . . . were proprietary and symbolic: ROTC [and] government buildings." These attacks received the greatest attention from the media and the public, but they were an extremely small aspect of antiwar protest that numbered more than 9,400 protest incidents[25] on campus, as well as thousands of civic literacy efforts, such as demonstrations, vigils, letter writing, teach-ins, rallies, mass media presentations, articles and books, petitioning congressional representatives, blocking induction centers and napalm plants, defying the draft and supporting draft and military resisters.

From a very modest beginning in 1960 with two college chapters and perhaps 300 members, by the spring of 1969, SDS had become the largest and leading student antiwar group and was under attack by the federal government. That April, FBI Director J. Edgar Hoover declared that the New Left was "a firmly established subversive force dedicated to the complete destruction of our traditional democratic values and the principles of free government"; at its center was SDS. Two thousand FBI agents and twenty federal agencies were involved in "maximum surveillance, disruption, and harassment of the New Left."[26]

THE DEMISE OF SDS AND BEYOND: 1969–1973

Although SDS collapsed in 1969 under the weight of external attacks and internal sectarianism, and a few members resurfaced as the sectarian Weathermen faction, individual members, and the New Left continued their antiwar efforts into the 1970s. Campus protests peaked in May 1970, although antiwar actions continued long after the official end of SDS and the drop in campus protests. As antiwar protest became more militant and radical, activists increasingly looked to the Vietnamese and "dynamic liberation movements that threatened to besiege Washington with 'two, three, many Vietnams.'" Many activists came to believe that "a Third World–oriented version of Marxism . . . was the key to building a powerful left in the U.S., within the 'belly of the beast.'" Such a posture "seemed to many the best framework for taking the most radical themes struck by Malcolm X, Martin Luther King, and Cesar Chavez—the U.S. figures that most inspired rebellious youth in the sixties—and transforming them into a comprehensive revolutionary ideology."[27]

These revolutionary views would blend together with less-politicized students in May 1970 when the United States invaded Cambodia, sparking the greatest campus political protests in United States history; a survey months later reported that 40 percent of college students—then about 3 million—believed that "a revolution was necessary in the U.S." Massive numbers of students demonstrated, and on May 4, after the Ohio National Guard killed four white students at Kent State, the protests deepened; eleven days later, two black students were killed at Jackson State in Mississippi, but, by comparison, this elicited little outrage. More than 400 campuses went on strike or shut down, involving some 4 million students and 350,000 faculty members, and 30 ROTC buildings were burned or bombed. In response to the massive protests, Nixon was forced to declare that he would withdraw troops from Cambodia within thirty days.[28] The Cambodia invasion and the Kent State killings provoked more than 1 million students to demonstrate for the first time, and perhaps as many as seventy-five campuses shut down for the year, including my own SUNY, Cortland. It went without a graduation ceremony for the only time in the college's history—now 135 years. Thousands of students also became politically involved in their college communities, "working for peace candidates, and . . . 'reconstituting' their courses to address the international crisis" in what was the greatest student civic literacy effort in U.S. history.[29]

Kirkpatrick Sale calls the campus protests of May 1970 "one of the most explosive periods in the nation's history and easily the most cataclysmic period in the history of higher education since the founding of the Republic." Colleges and universities in Michigan, Ohio, Kentucky, and South Carolina were declared in a state of emergency, and the National Guard was called out to restore order at twenty-one campuses. The May explosion "had a profound effect upon the country, condensing and climaxing as they did the entire decade of student rebellion, providing for a brief time a clear look at the significant new position" of U.S. students.[30] The protests, however, were the last major campus antiwar actions of the Vietnam War era, and most students returned to campus that fall to business as usual. And the earlier demise of SDS left millions of students without "the lead or participation of a strong radical student group . . . without the sense of politics such a group might have transmitted, and . . . without a vision of how to effect real change at this unique point, most campuses turned toward the familiar path of electoral politics." This absence was to end the possibility of a powerful and ongoing campus antiwar movement.[31]

Relative campus calm did not end public protests against the war, however, as an April 1971 Washington protest drew about 500,000 and featured dramatic antiwar actions by the Vietnam Veterans Against the War (VVAW), who threw their war medals over the Capitol fence. The VVAW, founded in 1967 with a few members, then numbered 11,000 and included "a left-wing that not only opposed U.S. intervention but called for an outright NLF victory." A week after the April 24 march, thousands of demonstrators committed mass civil disobedience in the nation's capital; these "Mayday" protests produced nearly 13,000 arrests (most later ruled illegal), the largest of any single day in U.S. history."[32]

The July 1971 publication of *The Pentagon Papers* (TPP), the secret Defense Department history of the Vietnam War, which had been copied and then released to the public by Rand Corporation official and Vietnam veteran Daniel Ellsberg, proved that what SDS had claimed about the war was true; it legitimated its years of antiwar civic literacy efforts. Tom Hayden states that the release of TPP confirmed his desire "to believe that the American people would oppose the war if they knew the truth—and that was precisely why administration after administration had hidden the truth. By August, one month after the papers were released, a majority of Americans in a Harris poll said the war was "immoral," and in a Gallup poll 61 percent favored complete withdrawal"[33]—the same antiwar position that SDS had advocated. The documentation of TPP was stunning proof of the necessity of "democratic distemper" student antiwar efforts in the face of criticism by the major media pundits, influential educators, political officials, and major union leaders.

CONCLUSION: CIVIC LITERACY AND "DEMOCRATIC DISTEMPER"

Noam Chomsky's conclusion on the Vietnam War and its relationship to the educational system is a powerful starting point from which to assess the SDS civic literacy efforts against that war.

> As American technology is running amuck in Southeast Asia, a discussion of American schools can hardly avoid noting the fact that these schools are the first training ground for the troops that will enforce the muted, unending terror of the status quo of a projected American century; for the technicians who will be developing the means for extension of American power; for the intellectuals who can be counted on, in significant measure, to provide the ideological justification for this particular form of barbarism and to decry the irresponsibility and lack of sophistication of those who will find all of this intolerable and revolting.[34]

SDS's civic literacy "distemper" moved huge numbers of students toward an antiwar position and greater understanding of the U.S. educational system. Despite these civic literacy efforts, however, fundamental change in U.S.-Vietnam policy did not ultimately come from the "reason and persuasion" of teach-ins and community forums, important though these were; it came ultimately from the Vietnamese resistance, the antiwar movement within the military, especially among African-American ground troops in South Vietnam, Eugene McCarthy's and Robert Kennedy's victories in the 1968 Democratic primaries, and serious economic problems caused by mounting war costs and federal budget deficits.

Maurice Isserman and Michael Kazin assert that, as the New Left grew larger, "it also grew more internally divided. The early 1960s vision of the movement as a 'beloved community' in which all those committed to social change could join together in common effort and fellowship came apart at the seams by mid-decade."[35] Despite the fine civic literacy efforts against the war by SDS—all of which aroused the "democratic distemper" fears of the U.S. ruling class and its intellectual apologists—during the later 1960s it was criticized, however, because too often "the standard of political effectiveness . . . increasingly became the sense of gratification and commitment the tactics provided to participants combined with the amount of coverage it guaranteed on the evening television news." The problems inherent in the increasing "politics of confrontation were not lost on some veteran leaders of the New Left, although they found themselves powerless to reverse the trend."[36]

Max Elbaum, however, differs with Isserman, Kazin, and "the conventional wisdom concerning sixties radicals" that is reflected in the title of former SDS leader Todd Gitlin's book *The Sixties: Years of Hope, Days of Rage*—that "the decade started with idealistic, impassioned young people putting their lives on the line . . . to fulfill the promise of America. It ended with days of rage as the sixties movements, frustrated by the Vietnam War, became irrational and self-destructive." Elbaum believes that we must step back and revise this analysis, because through their "struggle against the war in Vietnam and racism at home," SDS and the larger New Left helped millions of youth to attain "new levels into the extent of inequality and militarism in U.S. society—and their deep structural roots."[37] SDS's antiwar militancy drastically changed politics here at home because its actions went "beyond traditional channels and demands that required more than reforming the existing social arrangement. . . . The established centers of power could no longer completely control events. . . . Radicalism was no longer a fanciful notion promoted by a few voices on the fringes—it had gotten a foothold in the mainstream."[38]

SDS civic literacy efforts challenged the view of influential educators in the United States who supported the dominant view of the war and patriotism, militarism, and imperialism that undermines thoughtful and active citizenship in a democracy. Such a view shaped the Vietnam War era and continues today despite the historical record of U.S. violence abroad that has resulted in the deaths of millions throughout the Americas, Africa, and Asia.[39] Most U.S. teachers and students are unaware of this violent record; therefore, they are unable to reflect critically on such issues and then act as empowered citizens.

Educators and mass media pundits offer youth a distorted view of U.S. policies, promoting civic illiteracy and turning civic responsibility into passive conformity. Patriotic and militaristic propaganda dominates in the mass media, schools, and colleges, leaving many students unable to make reasoned moral and political judgments about official policies, such as the Vietnam War; this is also true of the 1991 Persian Gulf War and the present Iraq War. SDS's antiwar efforts in the 1960s undermined such an "education" and civic illiteracy, and Chomsky argues that this was positive because it led to a "notable improvement in the moral and political climate [and were] a factor in the 'crisis of democracy' . . . that so dismayed elite opinion across the spectrum, leading to extraordinary efforts to impose orthodoxy, with mixed effects. One significant change, directly attributable to the [Vietnam War and especially opposition to it was] a growing reluctance to tolerate violence, terror, and subversion." SDS and New Left civic literacy efforts were effective, and by the late 1960s, "much of the public was opposed to the war on principled grounds, unlike elite sectors [that] kept largely to 'pragmatic' objections of cost (to us). This component of the 'crisis of democracy' was considered severe enough to merit a special designation—the 'Vietnam syndrome,' a disease with such symptoms as dislike for war crimes and atrocities."[40]

History lessons about U.S. wars are educational tools in the struggle to vaccinate the hearts and minds of youth against "democratic distemper." The ruling class fears that civically literate and activist youth will join other informed and involved citizens; civic instruction in schools and the mass media, therefore, is organized to prevent such a danger. Civic illiteracy is perfectly reasonable once we understand the nature and purpose of "citizenship training" in the schools: to undermine the critical and liberating potential of education. A critical and open debate in our schools and media that accurately presented the radical "other side" of the Vietnam War and subsequent U.S. imperialist aggression, for example, would have to consider the perspective of the late journalist Andrew Kopkind. Writing shortly after the conclusion of the Persian Gulf War in 1991, Kopkind argued that "America has been in a state of war—cold, hot and lukewarm—for as long as most citizens now living can remember"; this state of war has "been used effectively to manufacture support for the nation's rulers and to eliminate or contain dissent among the ruled." This "warrior state is so ingrained in American institutions . . . in short, so *totalitarian*, that the government is practically unthinkable without it." But this war mentality is a good cure for "democratic distemper," because it "implies command rather than participation, obedience over agreement, hierarchy instead of equality, repression not liberty, uniformity not diversity, secrecy not candor, propaganda not information."[41]

What can finally be stated about SDS's "democratic distemper" opposition to the Vietnam War and the "warrior state" that prompted such a "crisis of democracy"? Tom Hayden concludes that SDS achieved much, as it was part of a movement that "forced our government to abandon its policies in Vietnam and the nation to reconsider the Cold War." It and the larger New Left "fostered . . . a moral view of human beings, 'ordinary people' in the process of history." This required an "active citizenship [that] in turn required a society of citizens, or a democracy of participation, where individuals had a direct voice in the making of decisions about their own lives."[42] Hayden's comments go to the heart of an activist civic literacy that created nightmares for Samuel Huntington and his ruling class benefactors.

Kirkpatrick Sale concludes that although SDS "achieved none of its long-range goals, though it ended in disarray and disappointment . . . it shaped a generation, revived an American left . . . [and] played an important part in molding public opinion against the war in Southeast Asia and increasing public understanding of the imperialistic nature of that war." It also produced "a pool of people, many of them of the finest minds and talents, who have forever lost their allegiance to the myths and institutions of capitalist America and who will be among those seeking to transform this country."[43] The tumultuous decade of the 1960s in which SDS arose was "notable for setting a considerable part of its youth against a system that bore them, against its traditions and values, its authorities and its way of life."[44] It was a decade of "democratic distemper" that deepened the "crisis of democracy" that confronts us in the twenty-first century.

A Matter of Conflicting Interests?: Problematizing the Traditional Role of Schools

Sandra Jackson

> In most modern societies, the education of most people is conducted by institutions run by the government. Education is therefore, in the political domain.
> —Charles Taylor[1]

INTRODUCTION

In the United States, education is a political issue. Since the latter half of the twentieth century, several waves of politically driven school reform tied to "national security issues" have swept the nation. Blaming schools for such a breech in national security, politicians berated public schools for having allowed the Soviets to beat the United States into space with the launch of Sputnik in 1957. Politicians used this "security threat" to create a mandate for public schools to provide rigorous academic training, especially in math and science, imperative to produce the brainpower necessary to put the country ahead of the Russians. Almost three decades later, *A Nation at Risk* (1983), the report by the National Commission on Excellence in Education in the mid-1980s, again argued for change on the basis of national security and the need to sustain economic growth and maintain superiority in the world. It asserted that the United States was at risk of losing preeminence in the world as a consequence of slippage in its competitive edge in the global society because of an educational system fraught with inadequate standards that had failed to produce the quality of workers, as well as the science and technology, necessary to remain number one. This line of criticism argued that the root of the problem lay with public schools—their loss of clear direction, lack of quality curricula with far too many electives, inadequate graduation requirements, as well as divergence from their traditional roles. Recommendations proposed five new basics: English, mathematics, science, social studies, and computer science. These were to serve as the antidote to restore schools to their rightful role in the production of highly skilled and technologically competent workers who would assure that the United States would restore its supremacy in the world market.

Approximately twenty years later, President Bush enacted his No Child Left Behind policy, which echoed many of the arguments of the previous report and went further to propose public policy initiatives to implement thoroughgoing reform of education in the United States. Again, the presumption was that schools needed to return to their traditional roles. Yet what this means remains highly contested. The reforms that have focused on standards, high-stakes testing, and choice, spearheaded by the president and supported by conservative politicians and powerful business interests, stand in sharp contrast to the more populist agendas for change. The latter focus on addressing persistent inequalities (e.g., the gap between highly funded and underfunded schools, the gap between high-performing and underachieving schools, and the differential rates of achievement among racially, culturally, and linguistically diverse students), as well as issues related to the very nature of education itself—ideals, core values, and notions about what is most worth knowing.

The major fault line in these frameworks has been a focus on individual achievement and schools that produce students who test well, and a contrasting emphasis on examining structural barriers not only for individuals but also for groups regarding the ways in which race and ethnicity, gender, language, and culture have affected education and schooling for different population groups. As a consequence, debates about education in the United States have been quite contentious and politically charged because of competing interests: the government espousing a given set of priorities to ensure worldwide hegemony; ongoing differences between liberals and conservatives—politicians as well as ordinary citizens; supporters of the Civil Rights movement advocating racial equality and equal opportunity; advocates of the women's movement as well as feminists seeking to redress gender inequalities and sexism; and proponents among communities of color and immigrant communities, as well as educators supporting bilingual/bicultural, and multicultural education to promote cultural and linguistic diversity.

In examining the historical issues of cultural and linguistic genocide, and educational segregation in the United States, Joel Spring contends, "The problem is the inherent tendency of nation-states to use their educational systems to create uniform culture and language usage as a way of maintaining social order and control.[2] In this regard, the "traditional" role of public education has been to socialize individuals to the norms of the dominant culture, forge assimilation of immigrants, and engage in the production of individuals who have internalized the values of obedience, punctuality, efficiency, self-discipline, high-achievement motivation, individualism, competition, and a belief in meritocracy—all of which have promised success and social mobility. Individuals of color and women, who find many of the promises of equity, freedom, and justice yet unfulfilled, have organized, demonstrated, and struggled in pursuit of these illusive ideals in the public sphere, especially in educational contexts, through social movements and legal actions.

The Civil Rights movement and the women's movement have agitated for intervention by the federal government to remedy inequalities and discrimination based on race and sex, and supporters of bilingual and bicultural education have also engaged in legal battles and organized to challenge attempts by cultural purists to make English the official language of the United States and install an English-only orthodoxy. As a consequence of this exercise of agency, changes have been made in public institutions—unsettling a status quo of entitlement based on white skin, class, and gender privilege. In reaction, according to Foner, "conservative rhetoric has depicted the federal government as an alien and menacing presence rather than an embodiment of the popular will."[3]

This chapter will argue that the struggle between a majority population and its dominant culture, imposed on others, and resistance from various ethnic, cultural, and linguistic groups, inclusive of women, is at the heart of the "crisis of democracy" and hence a crisis in education in the United States. The culture wars manifesting themselves in curricular reform regarding race and gender, and struggles over language as in the case of the English Only movement versus the movement for bilingual, bicultural, and multicultural education, among others, reflect profound differences and values in this country. In public debates, conservative rhetoric in reaction to claims related to equity, inclusiveness, and diversity often couches the problem in terms of a nation under siege from within by "special" interest groups whose demands are at odds with the interests of "the people"[4] Within this context, when the struggle for social justice in the broader society is characterized as a crisis, then it should be no surprise that public institutions such as schools become contested terrains, emanating from conflicts of interest and inequality in power.

BACKGROUND

In the United States, "[d]emocracy is an ideal that is filled with possibilities, but also an ideal that is part of the ongoing struggle for equality, freedom and human dignity . . . that promotes the highest aspirations, dreams, and values of individual persons, not only in the U.S. but also throughout the global community."[5] These deeply humanistic values stand in sharp

juxtaposition to a market ideology that is predicated on defining human behavior as essentially unchangeable, perceiving society as an aggregate of individuals exercising individual choices, privileging self-interest as the primary
motivator of choice with personal material-reward as the primary goal, and
protecting and maximizing *individual* freedom of choice.[6] This framework
makes group rights problematic in that they are juxtaposed against individual
rights in a mutually exclusive way. The government accordingly is to look
out for the interests of individuals and their individual pursuits. Within this
context, based upon the notion that the market will self-correct and adjust
accordingly, there are two criteria for government involvement: (1) the extent to which education enhances national sovereignty and security, and (2)
the extent to which education can produce specific, tangible, and quantifi-
able benefits to the smooth functioning of the market economy itself.[7] These
principles undergird reforms advocated by the government as well as conservative forces that seek to limit government involvement and resist any
attempts to use education as a political instrument for extending democracy.[8]
Educational initiatives that do not advance these interests are suspect and
hence ensues a continuing debate about government's proper role in advancing goals for education. Thus, according to Kliebard, "For one thing, what
goes on in schools can hardly remain unaffected by national debates and
. . . professional influences. For another, these expressions emanating from
political business and professional sources are themselves indicators of how
certain elements in society seek to define the world in which they live as well
as what a society's children should know."[9] In the United Stated, the discursive milieu surrounding education includes issues related to race, gender,
class, language, and culture, in addition to other dimensions of difference.
Race, for example, is an autonomous concept, independent and yet intersecting with issues of gender and class.[10] As such, based on physical appear-
ances and characteristics related to skin color, hair texture, facial features, and
other features, it cannot be reduced to or conflated with class based upon
economics and status, which manifests itself in inequality of resources, social
capital, and power. Gender also remains a basis for inequality, which critiqued
through the lens of feminism predicates social change on an analysis of
sexism, patriarchy, and gender stereotyping, as well as a critique of the
traditional disciplines and their inattentiveness to women's issues, as well
as omissions and biases often shaped by biological determinism and essen-
tialism.[11]

   To the discussion about the roles of education and schooling, given differential experiences and achievement, individuals from different ethnic,
cultural, and linguistic groups, as well as women, often bring particularities
of interest regarding education—its aims, purposes, and challenges. Regarding praxis, when we consider the nature of elementary and secondary education, as well as that of higher education, we must ask ourselves whose
heritage and values will be included in curricula and in what manner.[12]

Given the gains of the Civil Rights movement and its legal advances regarding challenges to inequality, racism, segregation and discrimination, and remedies designed to create equal access (e.g., education, housing, work, health care), as well as those of the women's movement regarding issues related to gender and gender equity, curricular reforms as well as pedagogical practices have brought about changes that have manifested themselves in changes in terms of knowledge consumption and knowledge production. This has meant that issues of race and gender previously ignored and missing from the curriculum have been included, challenging Eurocentric content and perspectives, as a consequence of criticism and scrutiny from individuals of color as well as women.

In reaction, those who champion the status quo have asserted that the inclusion of content and material by individuals of color, as well as women, is a departure from studying the best (traditionally defined as the classics most worthy of consideration produced by the West), resulting in substituting work and material of lesser quality and engaging in identity politics, which in their view undermines the quality of education, thereby indulging students in a feel-good curriculum that lacks rigor and substance. Some critics such as Sandra Stotsky, who believe that the contemporary curriculum for high schools is dangerous, argue that multiculturalism in English literature courses is the cause of illiteracy in contemporary America.[13] She and others of like mind argue for a return to the basics—tried and true classics—eschewing inclusion of works by women and people of color. And what we have heard from this sector is that "We have gone astray in what we expect of our educational system. . . . [T]hat it must be redirected to become an integral part of our economic system. Its job is to supply to the world of employment the human skills that are and will be necessary."[14] Those who counter these ideas espouse a very different idea about education in the United States:

> A vision of education that takes democracy seriously cannot but be at odds with educational reforms, which espouse the language and values of market forces and treat education as a commodity to be purchased and consumed. In stead, it will regard it as self-evident that education is a public good rather than a private utility and acknowledge that in a democracy, education has to be constantly reformed as a part of a broader process of social change aimed at empowering more and more people consciously to participate in the life of their society.[15]

A deeply contested notion of the good society thus involves a question of values regarding whether the ideas of democratic citizenship are rooted in equal rights, opportunities, and responsibilities for individuals, or whether such permits inequalities to be perpetuated on the basis of such things as class, race, ethnicity, gender, language, or nationality.[16] Furthermore, when individual identities and collective identities coalesce, resulting in organizing and challenges to existing conditions, identity politics enters the picture. And when interests emanating from diverse group perspectives are articulated, then the differences that become manifest are seen as either important dynamics of a democratic process or as symptoms of a crisis, as in the case of what has been named the "culture wars,"[17] wherein Western culture and civilizations are presented as under siege from those who question and challenge their hegemonic and exclusionary practices. And when it comes to individuals and groups seeking to bring about change in terms of educational policies and practices, curriculum and pedagogy, because they are labeled as not representative of the mainstream, then they are often painted as fringe, special-interest oriented, making illegitimate demands and wanting special treatment, which if addressed would undermine fairness.

As a consequence, people of color, various cultural and ethnic groups, as well as women and others have been put in the position of having to defend their right to be included, and at times when they have voiced their concerns, organized, and engaged in social activism, they have been accused of making things political, whereas the things that they criticize and challenge are normalized and taken for granted as merely the ways that things are—givens, neutral and apolitical. With these dynamics at work in the political landscape in the United States, it should be no surprise that contentions in the political sphere also permeate social institutions.

Whatever understandings about democracy and democratic practices prevail, they necessarily influence the nature of education. Carr and Hartnett argue that "since the system of education in a democratic society always reflects and refracts the definition of democracy that that society accepts as legitimate and true, then educational change occurring in a democracy at any time will reveal how that democratic society has interpreted itself in the past and how it intends to interpret itself in the future."[18] The values implicit in how a given society sees itself and how it practices a democratic ethos will also be reflected in the nature of education, the content of its curriculum and pedagogical practices. With an increasingly diverse population—one in which individuals of color will be in the majority—how will the United States respond to difference and negotiate the terrain of multiplicity regarding culture, race, gender, class, and language as they impact upon education? How will current debates resolve "existing patterns of political, economic and cultural life—[making decisions] which ought to be reproduced and which ought to be modified or transformed?"[19]

CURRENT CONDITIONS

Western societies have been forced to confront the cultural contradictions that refuse to be swept under the rug . . . Multiculturalism simply is. [It] is a condition of the end-of-the century Western life we live in multicultural societies.[20]

Scholars such as Charles Taylor argue that issues of diversity are reconcilable with democratic ideals in that "connecting the democratic value of expanding the cultural, intellectual, and spiritual horizons of all individuals enriches our world by exposing us to different cultural and intellectual perspectives and thereby increasing our possibilities for intellectual and spiritual growth, exploration, enlightenment, and enhancement of life and learning."[21] Within this context, issues related to the experiences of different groups are not "special," nor should they be presented in contradistinction to the mainstream, which is hardly monolithic. Instead, they and their interests are integral to the body politic of the nation, how we perceive our society and ourselves, and how we perceive others and interact with them.

When African-Americans, other people of color, women, and other marginalized groups organized for educational reform during the 1960s and, subsequently, to advocate equal educational opportunity as well as curricular reform, they were participating in a tradition whose principles were based on "promoting the idea that schools should take an active and positive role in shaping their society."[22] In particular, the landmark *Brown vs. Board of Education* ruling that separate education was inherently unequal went far beyond the interests of black people and had implications for other minority groups such as Latinos, Asian Americans, Native Americans, and other ethnic and cultural groups, as well as women, in challenging and proposing remedies to historic problems of discrimination and segregation.[23] Hence, different cultural, ethnic, and ethnic groups, as well as women, have demanded inclusion and acknowledgment of their contributions to society, which has meant not only that they be recognized, but also that their experiences, perspectives, and contributions to society and humanity be treated as valid and valuable regarding understanding human experiences.[24] As a consequence, the curriculum, its content and pedagogical processes, have been the subject of discussion and debate in terms of necessary changes to create curricula that more adequately reflect the breadth of human experiences regarding issues of race and ethnicity, gender, culture, and language.

While for the advocates of reform, these things have been signs of necessary and long overdo changes, the critics have responded differently. Conservatives, political and academic, have gone on the offensive to "protect Western civilization from attacks by African-Americans, members of other ethnic, cultural, and linguistic groups as well as women, as well as the political Left."[25] Those who have challenged Eurocentrism, racism, sexism, linguicism, as well as class biases have been labeled as the new barbarians, who are promoting special interests that are at odds with the majority. What can we make of this argument when women, for example, account for more than 50 percent of the population and individuals of color, Latinos in particular, are ever increasing their numbers (in some states like California and Florida), representing an emergent majority if not significant parts of the population?

According to scholars such as Pinar, "antiracist and antisexist values should reside as core principles at the heart of education and require commitment to social justices, freedom, and diversity to be enacted in the context of daily institutional life rather than murmured as a litany for a world yet to come."[26] Changing the curriculum and how we teach issues of race and gender, in particular, is important for a number of reasons: Being inclusive and addressing difference is not just healthy for a democratic society but it also serves to counteract negative perceptions, images, and stereotypes that perpetuate false ideas and ignorance about others, as well as those that are internalized by individuals and groups about themselves, which are themselves forms of oppression.[27] Here, a critical multiculturalism that focuses on race, ethnicity, and cultural diversity, and draws upon multiple perspectives, argues against a modernist Eurocentrism with its scientific epistemology as the only way to make meaning in the world. The ideals that such a perspective promotes are contrary to those avowed and supported by those who see education designed ideally to produce "independent operators who rise above the values of special interests, secure in their objectivity and detachment from biases."[28]

Regarding the centrality of sex and gender in terms of curriculum, knowledge consumption, and knowledge production, Women's Studies has emerged as a force for change in the academy with implications for the larger society. Feminism has provided a critique of patriarchy and sexism and their impact upon society, beliefs, and practices, and has advocated for change in society as well as its institutions. In higher education, Women's Studies rests on the premise that knowledge in the traditional academic disciplines is partial, incomplete, and distorted because they have excluded women. Goals have included developing and incorporating knowledge in the curriculum produced by women and about the experiences of women, which presents women as agents of change and producers of knowledge[29] and not as passive bystanders and victims in the tableau of history.

The matter of language, not only learning modern languages but also maintenance of one's first tongue that is not English, is also a topic of fierce debate. Regarding the former, certain languages have been privileged over others in the American school curriculum. Initially, the languages of choice were classical—Latin and Greek for the children of aristocrats and elites. Then Romance languages followed and were added to secondary and university-level curricula, with recognition of modern languages as important for education, commerce, and careers. The emphasis has always been on learning English—the presence of Latin, Polish, German, and Russian schools in some communities notwithstanding. The focus has rarely been to equip students to learn a language to facilitate their abilities to relate to and work with others within the society, such as Spanish-speaking individuals within the United States. Instead, Spanish has been deemed useful primarily for those majoring in such fields as Romance Languages, literature, or music at the university level. Otherwise, learning Spanish has not been promoted. And those for whom Spanish is their first language should be obliged to learn English if they have any hope of being successful citizens and enjoying the full benefits of citizenship. The intent is not to maintain the first language but to substitute it with English. Hence, resistance to bilingual and bicultural education, which has sought to maintain competence in a first language, facilitates the learning of English and ultimately cultivates competence in both languages.

Race, cultural diversity, gender, and language continue to be the focus of ongoing debates about education—what is worth knowing, what should be included in the curriculum, content, treatment of issues and ideas, and teaching methods. Whether it be people of color and matters of race and ethnicity; women and issues of sex, gender, and sexism; or groups advocating bilingual/bicultural education, those who support reforms in education and take these issues into account are stigmatized by those who do not share their views and are viewed as pushing particular agendas based upon special interests, wanting special treatment, and wanting things at the expense of others whose needs are more legitimate.

Let us briefly examine how these things have played out in recent debates about education.

SPECIFICITIES: THE CURRICULUM AS A SITE OF CONTEST

> The curriculum . . . can be extraordinarily revealing about the values a given society or some segment therefore cherishes. As such it bestows power on certain social bodies as opposed to others. The curriculum thus becomes one of those arenas in which various interest groups struggle for dominance and control . . . reflecting their ideologies, and . . . expressions of what schools should teach.[30]

Diverse Interests: Civil Rights, Black Studies, Ethnic Studies, Multiculturalism, Women's Studies, and Bilingual Education

Struggles regarding racial equality in education, work, and housing by African-Americans (students, their parents, as well as community activists, other groups in solidarity, and members of organizations like the National Association for the Advancement of Colored People) focused on redressing inequality in education, changing a biased curriculum, and improving student achievement. In addition to challenging segregated and inferior schools, blacks also challenged tracking and steering of students into the lower tracks and special education courses, in which they were overrepresented; whereas they were underrepresented in college preparatory, Advanced Placement, gifted and talented, and honors programs.[31] Even when black students have been in the same classes with white students, they often experienced racism and differential treatment regarding teacher expectations that at times has had serious implications for student achievement and disciplinary practices, which have affected black males in particular.

During the 1960s, not only inferior schools but also biased and at times blatantly racist curricula came under increased sharp scrutiny with demands for change in terms of course content and materials. History and literature were among the first programs to be examined in terms of their omission and/or limited treatment of the experiences of black people. At the same time that black people made demands that material (particularly history, culture, and the arts) about their contributions be included in the curriculum, they also demanded the creation of Black Studies courses and programs. At the secondary level, this resulted in the creation of courses in Black History/African-American History and Black/African-American Literature, among others. At the university level, student and faculty activism resulted in undergraduate and graduate programs in Black and African-American Studies, drawing upon diverse disciplines and fields, primarily from the social sciences, the humanities, and the arts. These things led to demands to hire more black teachers and college professors. In this regard, in an environment in which resistance—individual as well as institutional—against change was often adamant, affirmative action was invoked as a means of rectifying the situation. This, however, was not without its own discontents. Whites, males in particular, claimed that they suffered from "reverse discrimination" and filed suits regarding college admissions (e.g., the Bakke case). Heated debates about the qualifications of black teachers and professors raged in institutions across the country as attempts to address competing claims—equality, redress for past (as well as ongoing wrongs), and fairness. With issues of merit and qualifications raised in terms of their worthiness to enter the profession, the interests of a "minority" ethnic group were pitted against those of the majority and, as a consequence, when school districts, schools, and colleges and universities acquiesced and began to hire individuals of color, they were accused of caving in to special interest groups.

Some attention to the issue of textbooks is warranted here, given the almost singular reliance on them in history and social studies courses. "The teaching of history more than any other discipline is dominated by textbooks."[32] In their study of history textbooks used in schools, Sleeter and Grant found that information and material on different ethnic groups was often missing and, if not missing altogether, quite limited, not only in the scope but also in the amount of space allocated and the number of pages devoted to discussion of relevant topics.[33] The result has been not only a Eurocentric curriculum, which privileged the experiences and perspectives of whites, but also one that eclipsed, if not marginalized, the experiences of various ethnic and cultural groups.

Other scholars have argued that "the absence of African-Americans in many school curricula represents "willful . . . ignorance and aggression toward Blacks, resulting in student mis-education" with harmful effects for not only black students but also white and other students who are given the impression that the experiences of black people are not important and do not matter.[34] This also relates to the experiences of other non-European Americans, and messages in the curriculum and courses that "your ancestors have not done much of importance in the past," from which one can then draw conclusions that "non-European Americans are not important today,"[35] with implications that the same will apply in the future. Furthermore, when material is biased with stereotypes and negative characterizations of a group, this "incessant depiction of the group [in question] as lazy, stupid and hypersexual—or ornamental [or exotic] for that matter— alters social reality so that the members of that group are always one down, this is to say, disadvantaged, the bearers of stigma and lower expectations."[36] It reduces such groups to second-class citizenship and hampers their participation in this society.

Similarly, other ethnic and cultural groups of color (Latino/Latina, Native American, Asian American) have also experienced discrimination. They have also organized and challenged curricula that either omitted their experiences or presented material in limited and biased ways. In the wake of the Civil Rights movement spearheaded by African-Americans, other ethnic and cultural groups and organizations likewise demanded curricula that were inclusive. They too demanded ethnic studies courses and programs. As a consequence, in high schools, new courses in Asian American, Latino/Latina, and Native American history, among others, were included. And at universities, there are programs at both the undergraduate and graduate levels in Latino/Latina Studies and Chicano Studies, Asian American Studies, and Native American and/or Indigenous Studies.

As in the case of African-Americans, in addition to challenges to biased and exclusive curricula, groups within various communities of color have organized to demand the hiring of teachers and faculty members in schools and colleges. Here, depending upon the context, affirmative action has been deployed to ensure the hiring of racially diverse faculty. Hiring them has been at odds with hiring practices that in the past have not brought about diversity. Here too the specter of "special interests" has loomed, and conflicts— at times fierce—have emerged regarding hiring practices, with predominantly white faculties acting in outright antagonism if not reluctance regarding the entrée of people of color into the ranks.

With the advent of what Sleeter and Grant have called single-group studies[37]—one of several strands of multiculturalism they have identified—came changes in high school as well as university curricula, at times manifested in new courses and new programs. As these programs evolved, incorporating new scholarship and research, these single-group studies courses and programs often became more sophisticated and nuanced. For example, instead of just focusing on one aspect of a group's experiences, such as race or ethnicity, they would look at the intersections of different dimensions of difference, such as race and gender, race and class, or a more complex combination of these dynamics, as well as issues regarding sexuality, age, language, nationality, religion, and disability. In this way, these various approaches to ethnic studies, with attention not only to a particular group's experiences but also issues of difference within a given group and interrelationships between groups with either similar or different experiences, has led to the development of an interdisciplinary and multicultural discourse.

Although multiculturalism as a discourse has different meanings based upon different ideological assumptions, at the core is an acknowledgement that the United States and other countries are *de facto* multicultural. Hence, what students learn in school, how individuals are prepared for the world of work, and how corporations do business must necessarily address cultural and ethnic diversity. Among the several strands of multiculturalism, the one that has the most salience for me is Critical Multiculturalism, which not only argues for the recognition of diversity and inclusion in curricula but also provides a "critique of injustice along the axis of white supremacy, racism, patriarchy, class privilege and heterosexism, in pursuit of egalitarianism and the elimination of human suffering."[38] Educators who embrace this framework are encouraged to actively work for social justice, in the classroom, the school, within the profession, as well as in the broader community and society.

Inequalities based on sex and gender and the experiences of women have been the focus of work by feminist scholars and activists. Here too, curricular reform has been the outgrowth of organizing for more accurate and inclusive curricula. Women's Studies is now a full-blown field, having begun much like early approaches to ethnic studies, focusing primarily on sex inequality and the experiences of white, middle-class, Western women at that. Over time, courses and programs that looked at issues of sex and gender have been transformed so that they also consider multiple aspects of women's identities and the ways in which these things intersect and influence the experiences of women: gender, race/ethnicity, class, sexual orientation, nationality, language, religion, disability, and age, to name a few. Early on, advocates of courses and programs that examined the experiences of women were challenged by others who questioned the academic legitimacy of the enterprise, and new approaches to teaching and learning that they introduced often met staunch resistance, because they critiqued traditional disciplinary content and went against the grain of established fields. For example, consider Gerda Lerner's typology categorizing five phases in the development of women's history: (1) recognition that women have a history (in fact, multiple histories); (2) conceptualization of women as a group; (3) affirmation that women [scholars] asked new questions about history and compiled new information about women; (4) challenges to the periodization schemes of historians that were centered on the historical experiences of men; and (5) redefinition of the categories and values of androcentric history through consideration of women's past and present.[39] Other disciplines and fields, such as English, Anthropology, Political Science, Sociology, Art, Music, and Philosophy, have also been transformed by new scholarship and research on women, which has enhanced the curriculum and led to the development of new courses and programs.

Language use and issues of literacy have also been controversial issues regarding education in the United States. Bilingual education affirms cultural and language distinctiveness of different cultures. It is also designed to develop in individuals the literacy skills and social capital to be successful in this society, without being at the expense of their own language(s), but rather in addition to them. This approach to language instruction is quite different from the English as a Second Language (ESL) approach, which focuses on the acquisition of a new language and not on the maintenance of the first language.

Experience has shown that, where no bilingual education program exists,

> [Latino/Latina] parents are less likely to approach the school and talk with teachers, that students are neglected by their teachers and tend to drop out, and that little effort is made to teach them English, preferring instead to classify them as slow learners or retarded. Indeed, these and other evils provided the impetus for bilingual education in the first place.[40]

The goals of bilingual programs, whose aims are to promote literacy in a first language as well as in a second language—in this case English—regarding the United States, are in sharp contrast with current public opinion and individuals and groups who have argued for English only and English as the Official Language policies, which assert that assimilation, hastened by the development of proficiency in English among immigrant groups, is not only "for their own good, but also for the good of the nation."[41] This approach is based upon an either/or dynamic wherein immigrant and resident children and youth have to choose one language over another. If they choose to speak in their mother tongue, then they will have limited opportunity for social mobility in this society because their options for work will be limited; if they choose English, then their lives will be open to a world of possibilities regarding social mobility. Being successful in school will increase their status in society, or so the reasoning goes. However, proponents of bilingualism argue that, while for immigrants, residents, and others for whom English is not their first language, learning English is clearly important, it should not be at "the cost of their own languages (and cultures), but instead in addition to them."[42] Furthermore, research on bilingualism, to date, "indicates that in both the cognitive and affective domains, maintenance bilingual programs or two-way enrichment programs of longer duration (at least six years) would be far superior to transitional bilingual programs," which "do not guarantee English mastery and also prevent children from attaining fluency in either their native languages or in English."[43]

In spite of these findings, linguistic diversity is still not perceived as a value in this society. Instead, what is important is an attempt to forge a homogenized American identity through a coercive requirement to learn English. And yet, the mere learning of how to speak, read, and write English competently is not a panacea for overcoming the structural barriers that face many immigrant and resident students, youth, and adults. One needs to question the assumptions that, if only one learns English well, one would necessarily have a ticket to high paying, high-status jobs, when in reality the employment structure of this economy is based on an increasingly bimodal dynamic, requiring both large numbers of low-paying service sector jobs and increasing numbers of highly skilled, technical workers.

Those genuinely interested in the education of children and youth for whom English is not the first language need to continue to look at education and schooling, the curriculum and teaching methods, as well as the opportunity structure of the job market, issues of race, class, and gender as dynamics that affect individuals, groups, and their life choices. Proponents of Linguistic Human Rights argue that "first people need linguistic human rights in order to prevent their linguistic repertoire from either becoming a problem or from causing them problems"[44] in civil, political, and cultural dimensions of their lives, given that "becoming at least bilingual is in most cases necessary for minorities to exercise other fundamental human rights, including the fulfillment of basic needs."[45] In this context, suppose we considered educating all students in more than one language? What if we advocated that everyone in the United States become bilingual, if not multilingual? Would this not serve individuals and the nation well? This question is posed not for the matter to be resolved, given the debates that would follow; rather, the purpose is to have us think more broadly about the matter of interests, using a framework that would move us beyond seeing others among us as *them*, and disrupting a we/they framework in looking at educational policies, practices, and reforms.

A MATTER OF CONFLICTING INTERESTS?

When we consider issues of race, ethnicity, sex, gender, language, and the ways in which these things intersect and impinge upon the lives of individuals and groups, focusing on issues related to education, we can choose to see these as emanating from different interests or we can choose to see them as interrelated and not inherently at cross-purposes—among themselves or in relationship to the broader society and its interests. According to some critics, educational reforms of recent years "have been formulated outside of the wider cultural and political concerns for empathy. As the politicians mandate test-driven curricula, they create new forms of educational pathology and social injustice that once again punish those outside of the mainstream"[46] and blame them for the conditions in which they find themselves. In my view, if we are to move more fruitfully in the direction of promoting more democratic education, one of the things that would be more serviceable would be to stop engaging in the rhetoric of divide and conquer, or reproducing the notion of irreconcilable differences, when we pay attention to the interests of different population groups and specific issues regarding their experiences in education in the United States. Members of different cultural, ethnic, linguistic groups, and women are constituents of the public and, hence, public education and, as such, its institutions, which have historically catered to the majority and, in the interest of the nation, must find viable ways of incorporating the interests of different groups into the fabric of their mission.

A legacy of free public education is derived from beliefs that public schools could serve to achieve the following: development of citizens by inculcating in them a common denominator of nonsectarian and nonpartisan values in terms of the public good for society and its institutions.[47] Within this framework, it makes sense to define the interests of different cultural, ethnic, and linguistic groups and women as complementary and reaffirmative of values regarding respect for individuals and groups in this society. Public schools are where the majority of children are educated and inculcated with ideals, values, and expectations, as well as ideas about themselves and others. I argue in defense of public education that not only espouses democratic beliefs but also strives to practice them in its daily and lived experiences, incorporating differences in a way that honors diversity beyond the rhetoric of the rainbow.

This means promoting social justice and equality, affirming difference, and being inclusive in multiple dimensions: goals, content, pedagogy, staffing, policies, and procedures. In the contemporary United States, some of the most salient challenges in this regard are issues related to race and ethnicity, gender/sex, culture, language, and class. Among the various interests at play are those of the state, the people—aggregate and disaggregated into different population groups—educators, public officials, students, parents, and business. Depending upon the context, the politics may be fluid, reflecting changes in priorities and alliances. Yet race (and ethnicity) continues to matter, given persistent inequality in educational achievement, income, housing, health care, and quality of life. Inequality because of sex, especially in terms of income and representation in different careers and fields, still persists. Literacy in speaking, reading, and writing English also continues as a divide between the haves and the have-nots. When these things intersect and affect the experiences of individuals and groups, the effects are often adverse, limiting opportunity, stifling development, and limiting one's power to engage in the political arena and struggle for change.

Though public schools are but one of many powerful institutions in society, they have the potential to become agents of change and transformation. Making our public schools places where issues of difference are defined as resources and not problems, where children and youth learn not only about themselves and their own cultures but also about others in respectful and nonstereotypical ways, has the promise of educating the next generations for life and work in a world where the boundaries of we/they can begin to be dissolved. If we are willing to reconsider how we frame issues beyond either/or binaries—the majority versus minorities, men versus women, English speakers and non-English speakers, those who share our religious or spiritual beliefs and those who do not, those who share our particular cultural traditions and those who do not, those who are able and those with disabilities—then perhaps we can begin a process whereby we redefine our interests and create new priorities that work to forge more meaningful ways of addressing individual and collective rights and responsibilities in ways that transcend pitting one against another, negotiating between redressing past wrongs, current inequalities, so that the future can provide greater social justice.

Redefining our interests to include those of others with whom we work and live can become a way of political, social, and economic engagement wherein our collective interests include attention to different groups among us and their particular interests. Perhaps, then, our different interests will not necessarily be seen as in conflict, with one of us winning and the other losing. As it now stands, until we redefine how we look at things and use language, we will be locked into a dance of my interests versus yours, with few willing to really listen to and hear the other and work to accommodate multiple interests for fear of losing something. I hope that in the ongoing conversations and debates about education, that when confronted with issues emanating from the experiences of different groups, more of us will challenge a paradigm of thinking that automatically defines our interests in collision with those of others. Yet I fear that the cult of individualism coupled with privileges and a sense of entitlement that have been derived from an unjust system that has discriminated against individuals and groups on the basis of their race, ethnicity, sex/gender, and language clouds our vision and impedes our ability to move beyond particularity. Too many of us take inequality for granted, see it as the way that things are (and have been) and thus do not question the structural barriers that others face. This perhaps enables us to turn a deaf ear to the voices of others who remind us that the democratic dream has not become a reality for many. I have mine; we have ours; let them get theirs.

I hope that we will choose not to be mean spirited, self-interested, and without empathy. We can begin to change by changing the way that we rear our children and how they are educated in schools. We can further advocate an education that develops the whole person; transcends training and technique; values more than test scores and the consumption of facts and information; engenders reflectiveness and critical and creative thinking; and instills a sense of interconnectedness and interdependence with others as well as the environment. This is a tradition that I would hope we would embrace for our children and youth, one that is forward looking and not one looking back nostalgically at some halcyon good old days that were that for just a few.

— III —

Security Measures:
Defending Public Education
from the Public

A Nation at Risk— RELOADED: The Security State and the New World Order

David A. Gabbard

Students of political economy share familiarity with Max Weber's description of the state as exercising a monopoly over the use of violence. To be more precise, Weber actually contended that "the state is a human community that (successfully) claims the monopoly of the legitimate use of *force* within a given territory"[1] (emphasis added). Some of those same students may also be aware that Plato had earlier ascribed another monopoly to the state that holds tremendous relevance for educational policy analysts' reflections on *A Nation at Risk*, which "celebrated" its twentieth anniversary in 2003. Writing in *The Republic* (Book 3), Plato spends considerable time rehashing Socrates' defense of censorship before he goes on to claim that "we must prize truth." "Lay persons," he says, "have no business lying." Like doctors in charge of the health of the republic, however, the rulers of a just society should recognize that there are times when "lies are useful . . . as a kind of medicine or remedy. Only the rulers of the city—and no others— may tell lies. And their lies, whether directed to enemies or citizens, will be legitimate only if their purpose is to serve the public interest."[2] In addition to the state's monopoly over violence/force described by Weber, we can see how Plato's *Republic* (frequently cited by neoconservatives like former Secretary of Education William Bennett and Alan Bloom [author of *The Closing of the American Mind*] as one the "Great Books" and an intellectual cornerstone of modern democracies), grants the state a monopoly over lies.

As I previously have written, we should consider *A Nation at Risk* to be the greatest lie that the state has ever produced regarding America's public schools. *Risk* was more than a document.[3] In the first place, it was the most efficacious educational report ever issued by the federal government, judged in terms of the scope and scale of educational reforms that it engendered over the past twenty years. It was also a well-designed and orchestrated propaganda campaign that actually began eighteen months prior to its release when Secretary of Education Terrel Bell established the National Commission for Excellence in Education (NCEE). If we examine the tactics of the NCEE as they are described by the Commission's executive director, Milton Goldberg, and senior research associate, James Harvey, and if we even minimally analyze the verbiage used in their descriptions of those tactics, we recognize some rather disturbing patterns in their work.

Goldberg and Harvey report that they and the other commissioners conducted their activities leading up the release of their final report, *A Nation at Risk: The Imperative for Educational Reform*, in "an extraordinarily open manner." Not only did the Commission assume a high profile throughout the eighteen months leading up to its report, wherein Commission members participated in a public event somewhere in the United States every three weeks, but it also maintained that profile for a considerable time afterward. Goldberg and Harvey admit that this rate of high-profile activity was conducted in order to "create a national audience for the Commission's work." They do not report, but we might suspect, that the high profile of their activities was one of the many lessons that they learned after having "examined the methods that other distinguished national panels had used to generate public and governmental reactions."[4]

Neither do Goldberg and Harvey reveal which "other distinguished national panels" they borrowed their methods from. Elements of their arguments, however, reflect the rhetorical style of those involved in formulating and promulgating the policies contained in National Security Council Memorandum No. 68 (NSC-68), the document that came to define U.S. Cold War doctrine. For example, in listing the more publicly admissible lessons that they gleaned from examining other methods for generating public and governmental reactions (dare we say "proper" reactions?), the commissioners explain that "effective reports concentrated on essential messages, described them in clear and unmistakable prose, and drew the public's attention to the national consequences of continuing on with business as usual." This statement bears a startling resemblance to Dean Acheson's account of the rhetorical maneuvers that he and other "hard-liners" in and around the National Security Council deployed to "bludgeon the mass mind of 'top government'" into believing that the Soviets were a military threat to the United States and to world security. Acheson recalls how

> In the State Department we used to discuss how much time that mythical "average American citizen" put in each day listening, reading, and arguing about the world outside his own country. . . . It seemed to us that ten minutes a day

would be a high average. If this were anywhere near right, points to be understandable had to be clear. If we made our points *clearer than truth*, we did not differ from most other educators and could hardly do otherwise (emphasis added).[5]

In addition to making their "essential messages" clearer than truth, the members of the NCEE found that other distinguished panels had framed those messages so as to draw "the public's attention to the national consequences of continuing on with business as usual." On this matter, they could have taken their cue from a 1980 report that Goldberg and Harvey cite from the President's Commission for a National Agenda for the Eighties. The authors of this earlier report had warned that "The continued failure of the schools to perform their traditional role adequately may have disastrous consequences for this nation."[6] On the other hand, further evidence could be ushered in to support the conclusion that the methods adopted by the NCEE to generate a public and governmental response were taken from those associated with NSC-68 and the Cold War hysteria used to promote its underlying agenda.

For example, the self-congratulatory tone taken by Goldberg and Harvey in reporting their success in generating the desired public and governmental response reaches its crescendo with their claim that "Not since the heady days following the launching of *Sputnik I* has education been accorded so much attention."[7] Given the emergence of the New Right and the resurgence of the traditional Cold War conservative bloc in the Republican Party that led to Reagan's electoral victory in 1980, it is not surprising that the discourses surrounding *A Nation at Risk* would reflect the rhetoric of Cold War militarism. This reference to the attention that education received as the result of *Sputnik I* alludes to the rising Cold War hysteria during the 1950s that blamed professional educators for having failed "national security" interests by allowing the schools to deteriorate into bastions of anti-intellectualism—the same essential message delivered in *A Nation at Risk*.

In 1981, Reagan administration officials declared that a new threat to national security had arisen, and alerting the nation to this threat constituted the first "essential message" that Goldberg, Harvey, and other members of the NCEE had to make clearer than truth in the public mind. Though the Soviet menace was still serious enough to elicit mass public concern in the opinions of Reagan's elite planners, the threat of Soviet world domination was now coupled with the risk of the United States losing its preeminence in world markets. "Competitors throughout the world," Goldberg and Harvey explain, "are overtaking our once unchallenged lead in commerce, industry, science, and technological innovation."[8] Although the NCEE attempted to attribute that "once unchallenged lead" to some mythical golden age in the history of American education—the 1950s—even a cursory understanding of WWII and the devastation it wrought on the industrial infrastructures of Japan and the imperial powers of Europe would enable us to gain a clearer understanding of how the United States acquired its "once unchallenged lead."

"OUR ONCE UNCHALLENGED LEAD"

America's elite planning community had predicted as early as 1939 that WWII would leave the industrial infrastructures of the colonial powers of Europe in ruin. Anticipating a German victory, members of this elite, business-dominated policy network set out to determine and enunciate to the federal executive "the political, military, territorial and economic requirements of the United States in its potential leadership of the non-German world."[9]

By July 1941, they had arrived at a conclusion regarding the territorial requirements for their ever-expanding economic interests, which they equated with "national interests." In July, the scope of those requirements, which they had designated as the "Grand Area," included "the Western hemisphere, the United Kingdom, the remainder of the British Commonwealth and Empire, the Dutch East Indies, China, and Japan."[10] By the middle of December, however, after the Japanese invasion of Pearl Harbor pushed America into the war, the Council on Foreign Relations and the government committed themselves to the defeat of the Axis powers and the formation of "*a new world order* with international political and economic institutions . . . which would join and integrate *all of the earth's nations under the leadership of the United States*"[11] (emphasis added).[12] (Note the dramatic similarities between this statement and the foreign policy strategy outlined in the Project for the New American Century and described in the official national security policy of the current Bush administration.)

American entry into the war, then, expanded the territorial vision of the Grand Area as the United States positioned itself to create the world's first truly global empire—a *pax Americana*. As Council of Foreign Affairs Director Isaiah Bowman wrote just a week after U.S. entry into war: "The measure of our victory will be the measure of our domination after victory."[13] The question of how that domination could be maintained had yet to be determined.

With no small measure of foresight, the American policy-planning community recognized that achieving this level of global hegemony could not be easily secured if presented to the American people and the world in such crass terms. As early as April 1941, the Economic and Financial Group of the Council on Foreign Relations warned that "If war aims are to be stated which seem to be concerned solely with Anglo-American imperialism, they will offer little to people in the rest of the world, and will be vulnerable to Nazi counter-promises. . . . The interests of other peoples should be stressed, not only those of Europe, but also of Asia, Africa, and Latin America. This would have a better propaganda effect."[14]

In acknowledgment that the "formulation of a statement of war aims for propaganda purposes" differs "from the formulation of one defining the true national interest,"[15] these elite planners committed themselves to developing a war statement that would "cultivate a mental view toward world settlement after this war which will enable us to impose our own terms, amounting perhaps to a pax-Americana."[16] In August 1941, that statement arrived in the form of the Atlantic Charter, which portrayed Britain and the allies, later including the United States, as combatants in a noble struggle to preserve and extend what Roosevelt identified as the Four Freedoms: freedom of speech, freedom of worship, freedom from want, and freedom from fear. Framed as elements of a more general anti-imperialist commitment in U.S. foreign policy, the spirit of the Four Freedoms carried over into the postwar era with the Truman Doctrine of 1947.

While the plans for an expanded Grand Area established the territorial requirements of the *pax Americana,* the Atlantic Charter and the Truman Doctrine combined to establish the political framework necessary to legitimatize U.S. dominance in the "new world order." That framework provided an image of the United States as the defender of democracy and of the right of all people to national self-determination. Determining and acquiring the level of military force required to enforce its global hegemony stood as the last requirements that the U.S. foreign policy establishment would have to meet in realizing its vision of the new world order.

We must remember that the U.S. policy elite laid its postwar plans under the assumption of a German victory, well before that period we have come to know as the Cold War. They did not anticipate the survival of the Soviet Union. Though the survival of the Soviet Union did partially impede their global designs, the fact that the structures of the Soviet political economy endured Hitler's invasion proved to be rather fortuitous as far as U.S. interests were concerned. Casting the Soviets as a military threat to the preservation of the Four Freedoms, as a threat to the national sovereignty of countries throughout the world, and as an evil force intent on world domination provided the pretext for maintaining and expanding the war economy to meet the military requirements of *pax Americana* and the economic requirements of the dominant elements within the American foreign policy establishment.

At the end of the war, thousands of SS soldiers and other elements of Hitler's armies within the Ukraine and Eastern Europe received U.S. support to continue fighting within the Soviet realm. The United States even employed the services of the head of Nazi intelligence on the Eastern front, Reinhard Gehlen, to coordinate the efforts of those forces under close CIA supervision. On the home front, traditional conservative elements in the

United States continued to express their fears of the Soviet Union as a political or ideological threat. Recognizing that the Soviets were "by far the weaker force," George Kennan, director of policy planning in the U.S State Department, argued that "it is not Russian military power that is threatening us, it is Russian political power."[17] It was under his assumption of the Soviet political threat that Kennan formulated the original U.S. "containment" policy.

As conceived under Kennan, "containment" meant conceding those areas occupied by the Red Army during WWII to Soviet domination while protecting the rest of the Grand Area from the political threat, that is, preventing other nations from achieving independence from the global political economy that subordinates the needs of indigenous populations to the demands of U.S. and multinational corporations. As Gaddis points out, however, what we have come to know as

> containment has been the product, not so much of what the Russians have done, or of what has happened elsewhere in the world, but of internal forces operating within the United States. . . . What is surprising is the *primacy* that has been accorded economic considerations in shaping strategies of containment, *to the exclusion of other considerations* (Gaddis's emphasis).[18]

Those internal forces giving primacy to economic considerations in shaping what we have come to know as containment include the right-wing of the foreign policy establishment and the military contractors, agribusiness, and nationally based oil companies whose economic and political clout grew enormously during the economic recovery provided by WWII. In their view, Kennan's conceptualization of containment, which portrayed the Soviet Union as a political or ideological threat, failed to evoke the necessary sense of crisis or national emergency that could justify the level of military buildup required to either enforce the new world order of 1945 or, in the case of military contractors especially, to ensure their continued long-term profitability. In order to ensure these things, they needed to develop a different portrayal of the Soviet Union and the nature of the threat that it posed to the United States and the world. Working through the Council on Foreign Relations and the National Security Council, these forces developed that alternative vision of the Soviet threat in a secret internal planning document known as NSC-68 (National Security Memorandum No. 68).

Written by Paul Nitze, NSC-68 sought to make it perfectly "clear that a substantial and rapid building up of strength in the free world is necessary to support a firm policy intended to check and roll back the Kremlin's drive for world domination."[19] Though Acheson and Nitze knew, as did Kennan and others within the foreign policy establishment, that the Soviets did not possess the capacity for "world domination," facts hold no relevance where matters of elite policy formation are concerned. Following Plato's advice, the pursuit of elite interests under the guise of "national security" or "the national interest" often demands "useful lies" to effect the implementation of appropriate policies for the "common good." As Jerry W. Sanders explains:

> While the vision of a Pax Americana constructed on the foundation of militarism was accepted within the foreign policy establishment . . . it was not so extensively held outside those rarefied circles. The wider business community and the wider political community would have to be persuaded of the wisdom of tripling military expenditures, bankrolling Europe's rearmament, and garrisoning American troops abroad to ensure the success of such an ambitious undertaking.[20]

NSC-68 was designed to affect that persuasion at the executive level of the federal government. As Dean Acheson would later recall, "the purpose of NSC-68 was to so bludgeon the mass mind of 'top government' that not only could the President make a decision but so that the decision could be carried out."[21] Secret internal planning documents, however, do not suffice to affect policy, especially where federal budgets are concerned. And "bludgeoning the mass mind of 'top government'" only went part way toward that end. Advocates of "rollback" or "containment militarism" would also have to generate a consensus in Congress and a sufficient level of public support in order to transform their secret document into an active policy. Chester Barnard, chairman of the Rockefeller Foundation, predicted to other members of the State Defense Policy Review Committee (which conducted the review leading to NSC-68) that, in order to push the increase in military expenditures that rollback strategy demanded (from $13.5 billion to $50 billion) through Congress, "the government is going to need assistance in getting public support."[22] Or as Robert Lovett, an investment banker with strong ties to the foreign policy elite, claimed: "We must have a much vaster propaganda machine to tell our story at home and abroad."[23]

Toward these ends, Barnard recommended the formation of a private citizen's lobby that could "then translate NSC-68 into public discourse under the guise of extraordinary bipartisan concern transcending ordinary politics to meet the national crisis."[24] These concerns led to the formation of the Committee on the Present Danger (CPD), a private group drawn together by top officials in the State and Defense Department for the sole purpose of gaining support for the policy recommendations contained in NSC-68 from members of Congress and the general public.

Editorials in the *Washington Times-Herald* described the CPD as "a group of citizens supporting the interventionism of the Truman administration," charging that the members of CPD were "all prominent internationalists" who were on the Committee for the Marshall Plan and "profited handsomely from the spending under the Marshall aid program." This account predicted, further, that "they will also profit from spending under the defense program."[25] Quite prophetically, Senator Robert Taft warned that the militaristic policies advanced by the CPD would create "great deficits and inflation, and bring on 'the garrison state.'"[26] Even in the face of this opposition, the CPD was largely successful in creating an image of the Soviet Union as a military threat with aspirations for global domination, thus legitimating both the maintenance of a huge public subsidy to advanced industry through the military system and the now familiar patterns of U.S. intervention in maintaining its global economic hegemony.[27]

Waging the Cold War as a pretext for the huge levels of military spending required to maintain its global empire exacted a heavy toll on the domestic economy of the United States. Though space renders a full accounting of those costs prohibitive here, we only need to consider how the demands of the military-industrial complex for federal research and development funding allowed Germany and Japan to become far more competitive in consumer markets. Given the levels of military spending that the Reagan administration was to initiate in the process of renewing Cold War tensions, however, any linkage between the economic hemorrhaging that military spending had inflicted on U.S. society in years past and the recessionary patterns of the 1970s had to be avoided. This understanding provides some context for grasping the second essential message that the NCEE had to make clearer than truth in the public mind.

CREATING A DOMESTIC THREAT

Just as they had blamed the schools for allowing the nation's educational standards to deteriorate and allowing the Soviets to beat the United States into space in the 1950s, advocates of containment militarism were now blaming the schools for the increasing inability of the United States to compete in international markets and the concomitant recessionary tendencies of the domestic economy. Once again reflective of the hysterical militarism of the Cold War rhetoricians who inspired the language of this report, the authors of *A Nation at Risk* complained that "If an unfriendly foreign power had attempted to impose on America the mediocre educational performance that exists today, we might well have viewed it as an act of war."[28] The prerogatives of business that dominate foreign and domestic policy exclude the possibility that this decline could be related to the Trade Act of 1963 that provided tax subsidies for U.S. firms that relocated or established new production facilities in foreign countries. Also excluded as a contributing factor to the economic plight of American workers, the Maquiladora Agreement that the federal government established with Mexico in 1965 allowed

> U.S. companies to import materials into Mexico duty-free for further processing or final assembly. These products are then transported back to the U.S., where the company pays only a small tariff on the value added in Mexico (labor,

materials, and overhead). Since the labor is main cost and is so inexpensive ($.50 an hour), the tariff is minimal.[29]

Other implicit, though nonetheless "essential," messages that the NCEE was to impart to the public included the assertion that, had the schools provided students with better skills and more knowledge, the thousands of industrial jobs that left America between 1965 and 1980 could have been saved. After all, it was owing to the terrible education of those students that American business had to seek refuge among the more highly skilled and trained masses in nations like Mexico, Thailand, and Haiti. Naturally, the questions of wages, safety standards, and environmental regulations, all the product of the meddlesome American public's interference with the imperatives of business, never entered into the decisions to export U.S. manufacturing plants and jobs overseas. In the final analysis, the "clearer than truth" reality conveyed in *A Nation at Risk* sought to convince the American public that they, because of their poor job skills, were responsible for the downturn in the American economy, which would only worsen under "the continued failure of the schools to perform their traditional role adequately."[30]

Returning to the "extraordinarily open manner" in which the Commission conducted its work, Goldberg and Harvey state that the numerous public events held during the eighteen months leading up to the release of their report afforded the opportunity for "administrators, teachers, parents, and others to . . . discuss their perceptions of the problems and accomplishments of American education."[31] Given that *A Nation at Risk* delivered the same message contained in both the 1980 report from the President's Commission for a National Agenda for the Eighties and the 1983 report from the National Governors Association's Task Force on Education for Economic Growth ("Action for Excellence"), we can only conclude that this message was formulated long before the public was actually "consulted." If that were the case, then the high profile of the NCEE's work can be seen as an effort to manufacture public consent to the education policies that the Reagan administration sought to enact; namely, returning, education to its "traditional role" of providing adequately processed human capital to advanced industry—all at public expense, of course—maintaining the traditional patterns.

All of this conforms to the practices of public diplomacy conducted by the CPD in the early 1950s, the period of time that we commonly associate with the rise of the *security state*—the start of the Cold War. Once the CPD had accomplished its mission of shifting U.S. foreign policy from "containment" to "rollback," it disbanded in 1953. Not inconsequentially, many of its original members and some new ones resurrected the CPD during the Reagan era—Paul Nitze, author of NSC-68, included. The presence of these elements undoubtedly affected the formation of the Office for Domestic Diplomacy (OPD) to help initiate the Reagan administration's second wave of Cold War hysteria to justify the huge budgetary increase in defense spending that contributed so heavily to our current deficit crisis. Holly Sklar cites a senior U.S. official who described the efforts of the OPD as "a huge psychological operation of the kind the military conducts to influence a population in denied or enemy territory."[32] Demonstrating the general sentiments that elite policymakers hold toward the public (the domestic enemy), the OPD also instructed administration officials "to refuse to appear in public forums with well-versed opponents."[33] While most of the OPD's activities were geared toward manufacturing jingoist hysteria over the fear of a massive Nicaraguan invasion of the United States and protecting the "Teflon President" from criticism, we should expect that all of Reagan's cabinet officials were briefed on such strategies and that the NCEE was not excluded from the conversation.

Public diplomacy, such as that carried out by the National Commission for Excellence in Education, represents nothing less than an effectively organized and operated propaganda campaign, serving the function of what Walter Lippmann called the "manufacture of consent."[34] Writing in the 1920s, Lippmann observed that propaganda had already become "a self-conscious art and a regular organ of popular government" aimed at mobilizing public support for policies established by ruling elites. During the same era, Edward Bernays explained further that "the very essence of the democratic process" is "the freedom to persuade and suggest. . . . The conscious and intelligent manipulation of the organized habits and opinions of the masses is an important element in democratic society. . . . It is the intelligent minorities which need to make use of propaganda continuously and systematically." Thus, as Noam Chomsky comments, "If the freedom to persuade and suggest happens to be concentrated in a few hands [e.g., Goldberg and Harvey] we must recognize that such is the nature of a free society."[35]

In retrospect, the NCEE manufactured a sufficient level of consent to allow its educational policy recommendations to be carried forward throughout the Reagan, Bush I, Clinton, and, now, the Bush II administrations. Reflective of the business class's contempt for professional educators, who might have funny ideas about education serving aims other than those specified by the school's "traditional role" (selecting for obedience and conformity), the first Bush administration did not entrust the task of developing an educational policy to carry the nation into the twenty-first century to the Department of Education. Rather, the Bush I team took a more direct route toward casting educational policy to meet the demands of business, charging the U.S Department of Labor with the task of formalizing the NCEE's recommendations into formal policy and, eventually, federal legislation. Though no educational legislation was passed under Bush, the Labor Department did succeed in creating a sort of vision statement called "America 2000," which Bill Clinton and the Democrats embellished and enacted into legislation as the GOALS 2000: Educate America Act.

THE CLINTON TEAM TAKES CHARGE

Lest we should be duped into believing that the other half of the Business Party operates under different imperatives, the Clinton administration's approach to educational reform did not significantly differ from the approach taken under Reagan and Bush. The rhetoric surrounding GOALS 2000, however, demonstrated less of the nationalist flavor of *A Nation at Risk*, preferring a more global approach to convincing the American public of their need for these reforms.

To begin with, GOALS 2000 shared certain characteristics with the North American Free Trade Agreement (NAFTA) and the General Agreement on Tariffs and Trade (GATT) treaty. In the first place, Clinton inherited all three measures from the Reagan and Bush administrations. Secondly, NAFTA, GATT, and GOALS 2000 each represents an element of a more general pattern of structural adjustment related to the postindustrialization process that is redefining America's role in the global economy. One of the most important sources for exploring the relations between GOALS 2000 and America's new role under increased economic globalization is Robert Reich's *The Work of Nations: Preparing Ourselves for 21st Century Capitalism.* According to Reich, former labor secretary in the Clinton administration, any portrayal of American educational policy as serving the interests of corporate America is imprecise. Such claims assume that corporations still function according to the rules of "economic nationalism," wherein American workers, American corporations, and the American government participate in a collective unity of purpose. According to Reich, this fragile unity of purpose could only hold the nation together provided that, "in return for prosperity," American society [accept] the legitimacy and permanence of the American core corporation. Clearly, as Reich relates, U.S. "government officials" accepted these terms, taking "as one of their primary responsibilities the continued profitability of American core corporations."[36] This meant, as Reich admits, that corporate interests dominated the formation of U.S. foreign and domestic policy, to include educational policy.

During the era of economic nationalism, high-volume, standardized production characterized the strength of the domestic U.S. economy. Under these conditions, Reich explains, contributing to "the continued profitability of America's core corporations" by "preparing America's children for gainful employment" was not a "terribly burdensome" responsibility for government officials to meet. "The only prerequisites for most jobs were an ability to comprehend simple oral and written directives and sufficient self-control to implement them." How such training may have translated into civics and social studies courses, Reich does not comment. Turning briefly to his response to a critic of Clinton's educational policies, however, we hear Reich argue that the educational goal of "preparing young people for jobs" is "complementary, not contradictory" to the goal of "preparing responsible citizens with a strong sense of community purpose."[37] Situating his earlier remarks on the responsibility demonstrated by government officials toward maintaining the "continued profitability of American core corporations," we can easily determine which community's purpose responsible citizens should have a sense of.

The only criticism that Reich directs toward our contemporary schools pertains to their failure to respond appropriately or adequately to the shift in economic realities as America moved from an industrial national economy to a postindustrial society within a global economy. Reich is fond of repeating what has become his standard line for diagnosing the ills of America's schools: "The problems with our educational system is not that schools changed for the worse, they simply did not change for the better."[38]

For Reich, it no longer made sense to speak of an American economy. In the new world order, economic nationalism is dead. There remains but one economy, and it is global. Similarly, Reich contended that the high-volume production core corporation is also a relic of our past; the high-value production transnational corporation has displaced it. The only element in any nation's economic structure to have retained its national identity is its workforce and this only because of its relative immobility internationally. The point of Reich's obituary rested in convincing individual Americans that they should no longer perceive their economic fortunes rising and falling together as if they were all in the same big economic boat. Contemporary and future members of the American workforce must recognize that they drift alone, as rugged economic individualists, across the waters of the global economy. Whether they sink or swim depends no longer on the health of the American economy, but solely upon how valuable they can make themselves to the transnational corporations that determine which jobs will wash upon whose shores. The only manner in which they can attract the high-paying jobs that Reich associated with "symbolic-analytic services" is through an improved system of public education.

In an open letter to President Clinton appearing in *Tikkun* magazine, Svi Shapiro lamented "the greatly increased emphasis" that Clinton's educational policy places "on the notion that public education exists to serve the needs of corporate America, *that education is preeminently about preparing kids for the job market*" (original emphasis).[39] This, he contended, is an approach to education "without heart or soul, a discourse about education that accepts liberalism's excision from it of moral and spiritual concerns. It is a language that reduces the education of the young to skills, knowledge, and competencies, one that endorses a disastrously limited view of what it means to nurture a new generation for a world in crisis and pain."[40] If our schools are to play a role in healing this blighted world, Shapiro argues, the political leadership in our country must adopt "a different American tradition and language concerning the purpose and meaning of education—one that connects people, especially the young, to the making of a democratic culture."[41]

In direct response to Shapiro's critique, Reich argued that "While corporate America will benefit from the administration's reforms, the real winners will be the future workers and the current workforce."[42] Given that Reich projected that only 20 percent of the future jobs in the United States will qualify as high-paying, symbolic-analytic positions, the likelihood that future and current workers will actually derive any benefit from the current educational reforms seems rather small.

The death knell that Reich sounded for economic nationalism should be regarded as highly ominous. We have already heard this former member of the federal cabinet admit that corporate interests have long dominated U.S. foreign and domestic policy, and that government officials have taken the continued profitability of U.S. core corporations as one of their primary responsibilities. He even provides some insights into the lengths that those officials were willing to go in preserving and expanding corporate profits. He cites, for example, the CIA's involvement in the overthrow of Iranian Prime Minister Mohammed Mossadegh in 1953 that returned the Shah to power and restored U.S. control of Iranian oil. He also cites the land reform initiated in Guatemala under President Jacobo Arbenz Guzman that "confiscated" the plantations of the United Fruit Company as having prompted a similar response from the U.S. government on behalf of the interests of American core corporations. What he does not tell us is that what Mossadegh and Guzman, as well as Fidel Castro, Ho Chi Minh, Daniel Ortega, and others recognized as "official enemies" in U.S. doctrine, share in common is having committed the crime of economic nationalism.

As State Department officials explained in 1945, "The philosophy of the New Nationalism embraces policies designed to bring about a broader distribution of wealth and to raise the standard of living of the masses." Advocates of economic nationalism, they continue, "are convinced that the first beneficiaries of the development of a country's resources should be the people of that country."[43] It could be added that economic nationalism might also advocate the participation of a country's people in determining the direction that such development takes. The U.S. government's position has, of course, been opposed to this brand of radical thought, believing that U.S. investors should be the first beneficiaries as well as the planners of development wherever, whenever, and however they decide it should occur. Trickle-down effects of U.S. investments that might actually benefit the masses, at home or abroad, have always been regarded as an incident, not an end, of American policy. Further expectations are regarded as heretical to standard doctrine.

It is interesting that Reich should undertake to convince Americans that economic nationalism is now a relic of our own past. Given the extent to which elite U.S. planners have held economic nationalism to be anathema with regard to other nations within their domain, we could read Reich's book as an official declaration of the third-worldization of the United States, wherein the United States is regarded as one among many colonies of a new state structure that transcends national borders.

"In the *Financial Times*, BBC economics correspondent James Morgan describes a 'de facto world government' that is taking shape: the IMF, World Bank, G-7, GATT, and other structures designed to serve the interests of TNCs, banks, and investment firms in a 'new imperial age.'"[44] It has been noted that such *de facto* governing institutions are immune from popular influence or even popular awareness. Even before NAFTA was signed into law, its architects demonstrated the usual contempt for democracy. The Labor Advisory Committee (LAC), based in the unions and established under the Trade Act of 1974, is legally bound to advise and inform the executive branch of government before any trade agreement is made. In the case of NAFTA, the LAC was informed that its report on the Agreement was due to President Bush I on September 9, though the Committee was not provided a copy of the document until September 8. When the LAC finally did release its report, it reached some frightening conclusions regarding the likely consequences of NAFTA and called for the agreement to be renegotiated. Most important, they noted, "'NAFTA will have the effect of prohibiting democratically elected bodies at [federal, state, and local] levels of government from enacting measures deemed inconsistent with the provisions of the agreement,' including measures on the environment, workers' rights, health and safety, etc."[45]

In an important book dealing with the antidemocratic and environmentally dangerous tendencies within the new wave of free trade agreements, Tim Lang and Colin Hines point out that in the case of the Canada-USA Free Trade Agreement, the prototype for NAFTA, "government subsidies to encourage energy efficiency and [natural resource] conservation," for example, "are given no immunity from trade challenge." Among the many cases that they cite to support their concerns is that of British Columbia, which was forced to "abandon reforestation programs when it was challenged by the U.S. forestry industry as an unfair subsidy, and hence contrary to free trade."[46] In a similar case, Mexico brought a case before GATT decrying the U.S. Marine Mammal Protection Act (1972) as an unfair trade barrier when it was used to embargo imports of Mexican and Venezuelan yellow fin tuna because of the damage to dolphin populations incurred as the result of those nations' fishing methods. GATT ruled in favor of Mexico; Americans will just have to live with their impotency to affect policy where it threatens the prerogatives of trade.

Numerous other cases can be cited to justify concern that under the imperatives of "free trade" "it is a violation of natural liberty and even science to deceive people into thinking that they have some rights beyond what they can gain by selling their labor power,"[47] a point that returns us to Reich's response to Shapiro that the educational goal of "preparing young people for jobs" is "complementary, not contradictory" to the goal of "preparing responsible citizens with a strong sense of community purpose."

At first glance, there would appear to be a contradiction in Reich's promotion of an educational mission that would develop "responsible citizens with a strong sense of community purpose" and his support of "investor rights" agreements such as NAFTA and GATT that would effectively supersede any national policy decision affected through citizen initiative if that decision threatened the prerogatives of free trade. The contradiction is removed, however, when we realize that Reich's definition of a "responsible citizen" differs from our own and after we question just which community's purpose these responsible citizens are to have a sense of.

In the case of elected officials, it is quite easy for us to determine how Reich perceives their roles as responsible citizens. As cited previously, Reich readily admits that, under the old economic order, government officials took "as one of their primary responsibilities the continued profitability of America's core corporations." With no evidence to support a conclusion that these responsible citizens have undergone any kind of religious conversion since the time those corporations became transnational, we can logically discern from Reich's analysis that it is the transnational corporate community's purposes that government officials, including federally commissioned educational reformers and other responsible citizens, should now sense, protect, and extend.

The Hegemony of Accountability: The Corporate-Political Alliance for Control of Schools

SANDRA MATHISON AND E. WAYNE ROSS

The current accountability strategies of school reform rely heavily on measuring outcomes, especially student achievement, and attaching consequences, either positive or negative, to various levels of performance. These accountability strategies affect everyone and every aspect of schools and schooling at local, regional, national, and international levels.

In most states and across the United States, *outcome-based bureaucratic accountability* prevails. This form of accountability holds teachers and schools accountable to state education authorities for producing improvements in student learning outcomes. Such an accountability strategy focuses teachers, administrators, schools, parents, and students on specific forms of limited knowledge and skills. Government agencies create guides for common content and standards that are manifest in performance on mandated student tests.

Since *A Nation at Risk* was published in the early 1980s, the emphasis in K–12 school reform has been the development of a world-class school system that can be directly linked to increased international economic production and prominence. In other words, corporate interests that have been promulgated by the business community have driven school reform efforts. There are many contexts in which this special interest is manifest, although one of the most prominent has been the four National Education Summits, controlled and dominated by corporate CEOs and governors.

In this environment of corporate influence in school reform, many interventions are promoted. Some examples are school choice plans (voucher systems, charter schools), comprehensive school designs based on business principles (such as economies of scale, standardization, cost efficiency, production line strategies), management of schools by noneducators, back to basics curricula, teacher merit pay, and strong systems of accountability. These interventions reflect what Michael Apple describes as "conservative modernization" in his analysis of the politically right agenda for school reform.[1]

In this chapter, we will look specifically at the increased and increasing emphasis on accountability in schools, which has become the means of enforcement and control used by states and businesses. This is so because those who declare that schools ought to be a certain way cannot themselves make schools be that way. States and corporations can only demand that others remake schools, and the authority to carry out this mission is delegated, although not the authority to decide on the mission. The delegation takes the form of uniform outcome measures of productivity, for example, scores on standardized tests or graduation rates, which provide evidence that the authority delegated to teachers or professors is being properly exercised. We will explore this hegemony of accountability, its origins, meanings, and consequences, as it has developed in K–12 education.

THE MEANING OF ACCOUNTABILITY

Accountability is a means of interaction in hierarchical, often bureaucratic systems, between those who have power and those who do not. Accountability is "a state of being in which persons are *obligated* to answer to others"[2] (emphasis added). Complex hierarchical systems do not permit those in power to be everywhere and do everything at the same time to achieve what they consider to be desirable outcomes. Consequently, authority must be delegated to others, which disperses power to lower levels of the hierarchical system. Those who receive this authority do not receive it in full, however. Power flows through them, but not from them. For example, the authority of accountable persons is limited to establishing the means by which the ends of power shall be achieved.

Specifically, accountability is an economic means of interaction. When power is delegated and dispersed to those within a hierarchical system, there is an expected return from the investment of that power in others. Those to whom power has been delegated are obligated to answer or render an account of the degree of success in accomplishing the outcomes desired by those in power. Because of the diffuse nature of many hierarchical systems, accountability depends on both surveillance and self-regulation. The power of surveillance is born out in part by the spectacle that may result from accounting by those to whom power has been delegated. In other words, the powerful in small numbers are surveying the performance of many (through means such as standardized tests), which in turn become spectacles observed by the many (as in when school test scores are reported on the front page of the newspaper).[3] Self-regulation, that is, the faithful exercise of delegated authority, is in part based on surveillance and the concomitant possibility of spectacle, but also on the perception of the legitimacy of those delegating power.

This perceived legitimacy is key to the hegemony of accountability. Hegemony is based on a projection by a dominant group (such as governments and corporate leaders) of their own way of seeing the world so that those who are subordinated by it (such as school administrators, teachers, students, parents) accept it as "common sense" or "natural."[4] These groups subordinated in the hegemony of accountability thus live their subordination, and this subordination is sustained through everyday discourse and practice, as well as in the popular media.

Within systems of accountability, delegates of power must answer to some higher authority, but the identity of this authority is obfuscated when the interests of the public (for example, "the American people") are used to obscure the special interests of the few. Additionally, the obfuscation of the identity of those in power and its purpose (i.e., being in the greater good) also serves to convince the many of the value of the interests of the few. The implication is that teachers, administrators, and public schools are accountable to the public, but the higher authority is more specifically the interests of the capitalist state, an inextricable conglomeration of business and government interests.

THE MANIFESTATION OF ACCOUNTABILITY IN K–12 SCHOOLS

Historically, forces external to schools have controlled them. For example, the Sputnik era brought massive curricular reforms, such as *Man a Course of Study* (MACOS), *Biological Sciences Curriculum Study* (BSCS), and others, and even accountability schemes such as the spelling tests proposed by Joseph Rice in Boston early in the 1900s to rid schools of headmasters were considered to be undesirable. Still, the power of accountability in K–12 schools increased dramatically in the early 1980s with the publication of *A Nation at Risk*. That report linked American educational performance to the decline in the "once unchallenged preeminence [of the United States] in commerce, industry, science, and technological innovation." Whether this is really true is debatable, but the report created a powerful rhetoric from which the current accountability movement derives.

The era of big curriculum reform lacked any widespread and sustained change on schools, in large part because local conditions mitigated efforts to create standardized content, pedagogy, and classroom processes. The curriculum reform era has been replaced by a standards-based reform era focusing primarily on outcomes, a basic utilitarian approach that focuses more on ends (e.g., test scores) than means, but that affects both. Much of the impetus and continued support for standards-based educational reform comes not from educators, educational researchers, or the public, but rather from corporate business. In fact, a main current in the history of education in the United States is the effort of corporate leaders and their allies in government to shape public education to the ends of business.[5] The four National Education Summits held since 1989 have been key events in the rise of the accountability movement in schools and intensified efforts to transform schools to meet the corporate expectations.

The National Education Summits

In 1989, President George H. W. Bush called the nation's governors together for the first National Education Summit in Charlottesville, Virginia. They set goals and developed ways to measure progress, but were stymied by resistance to federal interference in local school decisions. Seven years later, governors and top corporate leaders met at IBM's conference center in Palisades, New York, and developed an approach for states to accomplish what had eluded participants in the first summit, namely, defining what should be taught in local schools and enforcing curriculum standardization through state--mandated tests—what is called the "standards movement." The most recent summits (in 1999 and 2001) have aimed at consolidating "gains" that have been made in the corporate/state regulation of knowledge in public schools, including the successful adoption of a national testing plan, which was President George W. Bush's top domestic priority when he took office in 2001. The 2002 reauthorization of the Elementary and Secondary School Act (ESEA) is the most dramatic change in the federal role in local education since the early 1960s. Ironically, the Republican Party, which has argued for the abolition of the U.S. Department of Education, is now responsible for the greatest federal involvement in local schools.

This business-government alliance has, however, encountered public resistance to its agenda. At the 1999 Summit, Public Agenda—a public opinion research organization—reported to participants that the movement to raise standards in public schools strikes a responsive chord with the public, but also warned that the issue of standards is not immune to the "normal controversies and complications that accompany any large-scale policy change."

What is noteworthy about their report, *Standards and Accountability: Where the Public Stands*, is its straightforward description of the agenda that must be pursued if the economic and political elite is to maintain legitimacy— and respond to opposition—as they define the curriculum and pedagogy of public schools. The number one task according to Public Agenda is effective propaganda, or as they put it:

> Experts and decision-makers often must concentrate on the labyrinth of details needed to make a policy work in real life. But to sustain change . . . that touches

people's families and daily lives, leaders need to take time periodically to re-state the basic rationale, to remind people of the beliefs and values that under-lie reform. When the going gets a bit rough, people need to be reminded of why we're here.

It is important to note that the "we" in this case refers to the summiteers and other opinion makers like Public Agenda and *Education Week*, the trade weekly that is an ardent proponent of the standards movement and which collaborated with Public Agenda on its survey of public opinion regarding the standards movement.

Although the authors of *Standards and Accountability: Where the Public Stands* make much of the "established and remarkably stable" support for standards-based educational reform in the United States, they are mindful of "pitfalls that could derail or unsettle support." First, the report warns that standards advocates should expect unhappiness when the rubber hits the road and students are retained in grade or denied diplomas. Pointing to the dra-matic shift in public support for managed health care as people experienced drive-by surgery and denial of treatment options, Public Agenda warns stan-dards advocates that delivering test score increases must be accompanied by the "appearance of fairness" in managing the reform effort. Now that thou-sands of students are being forced to repeat a grade or denied a diploma, it is likely that the mere appearance of fairness will not be enough to stave off opposition to standards and the high-stakes tests that accompany them. Par-ents and teachers are the two groups most likely to derail the standards train.

The Public Agenda report—in a somewhat quixotic claim—declares that parents are insignificant players in the standards movement. Although par-ents generally support standards-based reform, Public Agenda says, "most are not especially well-informed or vigilant consumers, even concerning their own child's progress." This claim conflicts with reports that the once-sporadic resistance to standards-based educational reforms is blossoming into a broader rebellion. For example, as a result of parent protests, Los Angeles school officials recently backed off a plan to end "social promotions," and in Massachusetts, officials were forced to redefine cut scores on state tests that otherwise would have prevented as many as 83 percent of Latino and 80 percent of African-American students from receiving high school diplomas.

Although Public Agenda—and perhaps the corporate leadership of the movement—considers parents to be little or no threat to standards-based educational reform, politicians appear more sensitive to the growing anti-standards, antitesting pressures. Test boycotts and other forms of resistance have moved the governors of Michigan and California to offer students money ("scholarships" of up to $2,500) for taking or scoring well on state-mandated tests. Indiana politicians are bracing for an enormous backlash against the state graduation test, which threatens to keep 50 percent of the seniors in urban districts and a quarter of seniors statewide from graduating this year.

Teachers are the most significant potential pitfall to the standards movement, according to the Public Agenda report. Although many school administrators and the top leaders of the teacher unions are solidly on the standards bandwagon, rank-and-file teachers' pivotal role is rightly acknowledged:

> If teachers believe that standards policies are important and well thought out, they can sustain and nourish parental support. If teachers are convinced that standards policies are unfair or destructive, they can undercut parental support with extraordinary speed. . . . District directives are often ridiculed or resented, and experienced teachers have already been through waves of reform, which in their minds produced very little of value. Public Agenda's research strongly suggests that bringing the nation's teacher corps firmly inside the movement to raise standards could be the most pivotal challenge of all.

Following the lead of Public Agenda, the top agenda item at the summit was teaching, in particular, devising ways in which teacher preparation and pay can be tied directly to the standardized curriculum and tests developed by states.

The influence of dissenting voices, other than parents and teachers, was evident during the most recent summit when Kurt Landgraf, CEO of ETS, issued a press release that was a direct attack on Fairtest, a group advocating fairness in testing and also supporting a demonstration at the summit in Palisades, New York.

In the end, the National Education Summits are yet another portrait of power relations in neoliberal democracy. It represents our hierarchical society, where citizens are made to be passive spectators, disconnected from one another and alienated from their own desires, learning, and work. The spectacle of standards, test scores, and summits obscures the role of parents, teachers, and students in decision making in public education. This spectacle expresses what society can do, but this expression also communicates what is permitted with regard to teaching and learning, and limits what is possible.

The Liberal-Conservative Alliance

The National Education Summits and the standards-based educational reforms they have nurtured should be understood both within the context of neoliberalism and coalescing of historically liberal and conservative political and economic principles. A hallmark of the standardization movement is its remarkable capacity to unite seemingly disparate individuals and interests around the "necessity" of national and/or state educational standards—the standardization imperative. Ostensibly strange bedfellows, including for instance E. D. Hirsch, Diane Ravitch, Chester Finn, Gary Nash, Bill Clinton, Edward Kennedy, both President Bushes, IBM Chairman Lou Gerstner, the leaders of the American Federation of Teachers (AFT) and National Education Association (NEA), forty-nine state departments of education, and nearly all governors (Democratic and Republican), they join to support standards-based reform and its concomitant "need" to implement systems of mandated, high-stakes testing. Somehow, these "divergent" educational leaders manage to pull together around standards-based reform as the medium for "real" public school improvement.

In the past several years, the Education Excellence Partnership, which includes the AFT, NEA, The Business Roundtable, U.S. Chamber of Commerce, National Alliance of Business, Achieve Inc., National Governor's Association, and the U.S. Department of Education, has sponsored over fifty full-page advertisements in *The New York Times* promoting the standards agenda and, in particular, the use of high-stakes tests as means to both "motivate achievement" and retain children in grade. (We should note that the use of tests in these ways contradicts what we know from a large body of educational research, which tells us that high-stakes testing reduces students' motivation to learn, and grade retention damages children's chances to succeed educationally.)

Education policy is being crafted in a milieu distinguished by the pro-standards consensus among an array of both liberal and conservative players and exemplifies how elites manufacture crises (e.g., the widespread failure of public education) and consent (e.g., the way to save public education is through standardized schooling driven by high-stakes tests). Accordingly, the commitments of the political-pedagogical right—public school privatization, the reduction of national financial support for public education, the promotion of U.S. global corporate hegemony, "creationism," sociocultural homogenization around a few dominant "moral" themes, anti-immigration, the assault on organized labor, school prayer, and so on—blend with those of the left—equality, expanded democracy, economic opportunity, social justice, diversity, and so on—to create a clever though fundamentally confusing admixture of multiple contradictions and inconsistencies.

At its core, the pro-standards consensus can be characterized by its commitment to a relatively few defining principles. Advocates argue first that standards-based reform is necessary vis-à-vis school improvement because the current educational "crisis" is rooted in the inability or unwillingness of "failing" schools to offer the same "high quality" programs provided by more "successful" schools. Because the identified purposes, selected content, teachers, and modes of evaluation must be better in some (usually wealthy and majority white) schools than in others (usually less wealthy and majority Latino/Latina and African-American), the implications are unmistakable. Elite educational leaders and policymakers are saying that "other" schools can indeed improve, but only to the extent that they become more like "our" schools, hence, the one-sided standardization imperative and the subsequent normalization of whiteness, wealth, and exclusionary forms of knowledge.

In short, the standardization alliance argues, in most cases without any evidence, that (1) today's students do not "know enough" (no matter how "knowing enough" is defined); (2) curriculum and assessment standards will lead to higher achievement (although arguably many students achieve highly now—they just do so differently or in ways not easily quantified); (3) national and state standards are crucial in terms of successful USA-corporate-global economic competition; (4) standards-based reform should occur with federal guidance yet be implemented under local control (thus keeping both big government liberals and New Federalist conservatives happy); and (5) "higher" standards/standardization will promote equal educational, thus economic and political, opportunity.

Some Specific Effects on Schools and Schooling

The National Education Summits and the standards-based reform movement as a whole are quintessential examples of how neoliberal democracy works to thwart meaningful participation of the many by allowing the few to speak for all. The objective appearance of standards-based reforms, which aim to reform schools by focusing on test scores, conceals (partially) the fact that these reforms are the result of the deepening economic inequality and racial segregation that are typically coupled with authoritarianism. For example, in Chicago, public schools have been militarized—six schools have been turned into military academies and over 7,000 students in 41 schools are in Junior ROTC—and teachers have been given scripted lessons, keyed to tests, to guide their instruction. In a dramatic shift away from local control, urban schools systems are being taken over by states. In Detroit, a Democratic mayor and Republican governor disbanded the elected school board and appointed a new board—whose members represent corporate interests and of whom only one is a city resident. In December 2001, another partnership between a Democratic mayor and Republican governor resulted in a state take-over of the 200,000-student Philadelphia school system with the intention of giving Edison Schools, Inc., the largest for-profit manager of public schools in the United States, a six-year, $101 million contract to become a district consultant and run forty–five of the city's schools.

The primary justification for the seizure or closing of schools and/or the imposition of standardized curriculum has been poor test scores and high dropout rates. But standardized test scores are less a reflection of ability or achievement than measures of parental income. Bolon's study of student scores on the Massachusetts Comprehensive Assessment System demonstrates a very strong positive correlation between student test scores and average community income.[6] He concludes, "Once community income was included in models, other factors—including percentages of students in disadvantaged populations, percentages receiving special education, percentages eligible for free or reduced price lunch, percentages with limited English proficiency, school sizes, school spending levels, and property values—all failed to associate substantial additional variance." Analysis of student scores on the Ohio Proficiency Test also illustrates this finding.[7] Other recent data show that someone taking the SAT can expect to score an extra thirty test points for every $10,000 in parental yearly income. Dropout rates are directly related to poverty, and none of the powers demanding the school seizure or standardization is prepared to address the question of poverty.

The standards-based education reform movement and its dependence on standardized testing is not only good for business, but also good business. While we have argued that a sociopolitical agenda (of mixed perspectives) drives these reforms in education, they also present the opportunity for much enhanced profit-making in textbooks, educational materials, and test sales and increased stock values. These are corporate business interests intertwined with government officials in no less significant ways than other aspects of public life, such as energy or the environment. There are three major textbook/standardized testing companies in the United States (McGraw-Hill, Harcourt, and Houghton Mifflin), and all will see sales and profits skyrocket as the new ESEA is implemented. George W. Bush's entanglement with Enron is rivaled by his entanglement with McGraw-Hill, one based on several generations of mutual support between a family of politicians and a family of publishers. Even not-for-profit organizations such as the Educational Testing Service (ETS) have ousted their academic CEO (Nancy Cole), replaced her with a marketing executive (Kurt Landgraf), and created a for-profit subsidiary, *ETS K–12 Works*, which will sell tests and testing services to elementary and secondary schools.

CONCLUSION

Standards-based reform is an effort on the part of some external, although not necessarily official, body to define and establish a holistic system of pedagogical purpose (like Goals 2000), content selection (like state curriculum standards), teaching methodology (like the promotion of phonics), and assessment (like state-mandated tests). These intents combine such that (1) the various components of classroom practice are interrelated and mutually reinforcing to the extent they coalesce around the others and are perceived as inextricable, and (2) performance is completely subsumed by the assessment component, which serves as the indicator of relative success or failure.

These external bodies are often official entities, such as governmental agencies (the federal government and its newly passed Elementary and Secondary Education Act) or professional associations (the National Council for the Teachers of Mathematics and its Standards for Mathematics) or unions (the American Federation of Teachers and its support for the ESEA). These bodies can also be unofficial, such as the Business Roundtable and other special-interest groups. The formal status of these external bodies is irrelevant. What matters is that they have power and authority, not necessarily direct means of control, of schools and schooling. Herein lies the necessity for accountability, and from the singularity of perspective that advantages the political-corporate interests rises hegemony.

Accountability, as we described at the beginning of this chapter, is about authority—who has it, who does not, and how it is exercised. We have described the ways in which authority is manifest and has become centered in demands by business and political alliances for standardization of processes, outcomes, and the measurement and reporting on these in elementary and secondary education. The hegemony of accountability derives from the use of standardization to promote the interests of corporate-political elites, although often under the guise of the public good.

Neoliberalism and Schooling in the United States: How State and Federal Government Education Policies Perpetuate Inequality

David W. Hursh and Camille Anne Martina

Over the last decade, education in the United States has undergone the largest transformation within its history. In New York, policymakers have created standards for all the subject areas and have instituted standardized tests in a variety of subject areas and grade levels. High school students take standardized exams at the culmination of most courses but must pass the exams in five subject areas to graduate from high school. Data from New York indicate that this testing and accountability system has resulted in increased inequality.

Similarly, the No Child Left Behind (NCLB) Act extends governmental intervention into education by "steering from a distance."[1] Previous to NCLB, elementary and secondary school education policies were the responsibility of the state and local governments. However, with NCLB, the federal government determines which subject areas take precedence, limits the ways in which they may be taught, and designates what reform options are available to schools and districts that fail to improve sufficiently their test scores. NCLB extends testing and accountability to all states.

The United States, like many countries, is transforming its educational system within the context of the changing global economic system. Internationally, education increasingly focuses on those subjects and dispositions that increase citizens' economic productivity. Susan Robertson describes the changing mandate as requiring "educational systems, through creating appropriately skilled and entrepreneurial citizens and workers able to generate new and added economic values, will enable nations to be responsive to changing conditions within the international marketplace."[2] In the United States, policymakers have initiated accountability systems in which standardized tests are used to determine whether students are to graduate or be promoted from one grade to another and to evaluate schools and school districts. Further, the federal government and some states are transforming education into a market system through charter (publicly funded, privately governed) schools, vouchers (public funding that students can use for private school tuition) and school choice (permitting students to choose between schools within and across school districts). Jill Blackmore describes these changes as shifting "from the liberal to the vocational, from education's intrinsic value to its instrumental value, and from qualitative to quantitative measures of success."[3] Schools are decreasingly concerned with developing thoughtful informed citizens and more concerned with raising test scores and preparing economically productive employees.

In this chapter, we will undertake a critical policy analysis in which we place educational reform within the context of the social structure and examine its implications for social inequality. In particular, we situate our analysis within the rise of increased global economic competition and neoliberal policies in which the government seeks to retain legitimacy by instituting reforms to improve education while reducing education funding as part of the overall plan to reduce governmental expenditures on social services and, if possible, to privatize them. As evidence, we will draw primarily on the federal government's implementation of NCLB and New York State's new testing and graduation requirements.

Over the last decade, education in the United States has undergone the largest transformation within its history. While the federal government provides less than 10 percent of public school funding, it has intervened to an unprecedented degree, through NCLB, in elementary and secondary education.[4] Before the passage of NCLB, elementary and secondary school education policies were the responsibility of the state and local governments. However, with NCLB, the federal government has determined which subject areas take precedence, limits the ways in which they may be taught, and designates what reform options are available to schools and districts that fail to improve sufficiently their aggregated test scores. The federal government now requires standardized testing in math and reading (and later science), which are to be used to determine whether schools or districts are making "adequate yearly progress" (AYP). Students in schools that are designated as failing for two consecutive years (and in some states this is 90 percent of the schools) are given the option of enrolling in a successful school in their district or, if there are no successful schools in their district, in another district. NCLB, along with charter schools and voucher systems, introduces markets into education, therefore introducing a market system into public education. Although previous to NCLB, some states[5] were using standardized tests to hold students, teachers, and schools accountable, NCLB extends testing and accountability to all states.

One state that had already initiated a system of testing and accountability is New York. The State Education Department (SED) and the Board of Regents have created standards for all the subject areas and have instituted standardized tests in a variety of subject areas and grade levels. Elementary students are required to take standardized tests in grades four, five, six, and eight.[6] High school students take standardized Regents exams at the culmination of most courses but must pass the exams in five subject areas in order to earn a high school diploma.[7] Because these exams are used to compare teachers, students, schools, and school districts, and passing the exams is required for high school graduation, these have become high-stakes exams.

A variety of data indicates that the emphasis on testing and accountability has not resulted in improved education. Numerous reports reveal that the emphasis on raising test scores is leading to students being pushed out of schools so that their low or failing score will not harm the school's passing rate or aggregate score.[8] In New York, the new requirements have resulted in an increased dropout rate, especially for students of color, students for whom English is a second language, students living in poverty, and students with disabilities.[9] Elementary teachers report that they are pressured to spend more time preparing students for the tests given at their own or subsequent grade levels and less time teaching those subject areas not tested. For example, fourth-grade teachers are pressured to prepare students not only to do well on the English Language Arts exam, the first standardized exam given to elementary students, but also to prepare fourth graders for the social studies exam given in the fall of fifth grade. The pressure placed on fourth-grade schoolteachers is causing many of them to request transfers to other grades or to resign from teaching.[10] Furthermore, secondary school teachers report that they devote increased time to teaching toward the test.[11]

One group of students, in particular, has been harmed by the standardized testing requirements. Previous to this year, many English as a Second Language (ESL) students excelled in their courses and were accepted by a university but did not graduate because they could pass all but their English Regents exam. This year the ESL students face an additional problem. Because the ESL exam, an exam that they must pass to be waived from ESL courses, was made significantly more difficult, few have been able to pass the exam, even though they could pass the English Regents exam required for graduation. Although no statewide figures are available, schools reported that less than 10 percent of students passed the ESL test, essentially relegating them to less academic courses.[12] Students of color, living in poverty, and for whom English is a second language are facing more, not fewer, education barriers. The exams are exacerbating, not lessening, inequality.

High-stakes testing and accountability has had a negative effect on teachers and students by narrowing the curriculum and increasing the number of students dropping out and teachers leaving schools. How is it, then, that the tests have received such widespread support and are only recently receiving public resistance and critical commentary?

In order to answer that question, we need to place the rise of high-stakes tests and accountability systems within the context of the changing economic, political, and cultural policies of the last three decades.[13] In particular, we will situate schooling within the demise of Keynesian and the rise of neoliberal policies, the denigration of collective social responsibility and the rise of individualism, and the implementation of systems of auditing and accountability.

Beginning in the 1970s, neoliberal policies began replacing Keynesian policies in North American, Europe, and much of the rest of the world. Post–World War II Keynesian economic policies focused on providing a stable and growing economy through government intervention in the economic cycle and support of social services such as education, health, and welfare. In contrast, neoliberal policies focus on reducing tax revenues and, consequently, social spending. The federal government, particularly under the current Bush administration, has vastly increased military spending and reduced corporate and individual taxes, creating a budget deficit that forces social service cuts.[14] As the federal government has shifted social spending to states, states, which also compete with one another to reduce taxes and thus create a "favorable business climate," spend the least that is politically feasible on social services.[15]

In order to reduce resistance to cuts in social services, neoliberal governments have attempted to retain legitimacy by shifting social responsibility from society to the individual and by using auditing and accounting procedures to improve education efficiency. Conservative leaders in both the United States and England have embarked on an ideological crusade to shift social responsibility from the community to the individual, thereby transforming the relationship between the individual and society. Margaret Thatcher portrayed this ideology most succinctly when she stated, "There is no such thing as society. . . There are individual men and women, and there are families. And no government can do anything except through people, and people must look to themselves first."[16] Thatcher's statement shifts responsibility for success or failure entirely onto the individual and family. Thatcher, Gillborn, and Youdell note, "perfectly encapsulated an ideological drive that reduced everything to individualized relationships between providers and consumers, and understood inequality variously as a sign of personal/community deficit or part of the necessary spur to achievement in a meritocracy."[17]

By reducing success to individual merit, schooling becomes one more consumer choice where one benefits by choosing wisely. Consequently, both England's and the U.S.'s educational policies increasingly focus on developing educational markets in which schools compete for students and families. In England, each school's students' aggregated performance on a variety of exams is published yearly in what are commonly referred to as "league tables." Gillborn and Youdell state that "according to the rhetoric of the market place, the tables are meant to provide 'objective' indicators of quality so that consumers can discriminate between the competing institutions."[18] Similarly, in the United States, NCLB legislation requires that states post the test results for each school and identify schools as either achieving or failing to achieve "adequate yearly progress," (AYP) with students given the option to leave failing for passing schools. (However, given the high percentage of schools designated as failing in a district and state, the number of openings for students is a small percentage of the students eligible to transfer.)

While collective responsibility is denigrated and education is reduced to a system where everyone competes for the best schools, government must still be seen as supporting education. As neoliberal governments reduce social welfare expenditures, they must be careful to retain the legitimacy of the economic system and policies. While inequality is exacerbated and funding for education is reduced, neoliberal governments must develop strategies that legitimate its policymaking.[19] Therefore, governments need to appear to be concerned with and supporting education even as they reduce funding.

Further, because neoliberals have condemned previous liberal governments for their intervention into the everyday lives of citizens—either through welfare programs or regulations, neoliberals must implement these reforms without direct intervention. Consequently, governments in many countries have resolved this dilemma by "steering at a distance."[20] Rather than enacting coercive or prescriptive control, governments replace constraints with incentives. Auditing and accountability replace intervention, therefore lessening resistance. "Prescription is replaced by *ex post* accountability based on quality or outcome assessments. Coercion is replaced by self-steering—the appearance of autonomy. Opposition or resistance is side-stepped, displaced."[21]

Lastly, neoliberal governments must adopt discourses that convince the public of the necessity of these reforms. They therefore embed their educational policies within a discourse of fairness and objectivity. As we will show, in the United States, the state and federal governments claim that the reforms will result in improved education for all. Further, NCLB's assessment of AYP is intended to "give them [parents and communities] objective data" through standardized testing.[22] In England, the "league tables" are meant to provide "objective indicators" of quality.

In the remainder of this chapter, we will first briefly describe the shift from Keynesian to neoliberal economic policies and demonstrate that the state, in order to retain legitimacy while reducing social services such as education, implements educational policies that indirectly control education "from a distance," which they justify as improving education for all and providing objective assessments. We will then critique the policy claims of promoting fairness and objectivity and argue that, in fact, the outcomes are the opposite of the claims.

THE RISE OF NEOLIBERALISM AND EDUCATION'S ROLE IN DEVELOPING PRODUCTIVE WORKERS AND LEGITIMATING THE GOVERNMENT

Neoliberalism arose as a corporate and political response to the Keynesian accommodation that existed to different degrees in Europe and North America after World War II. In contrast to the years preceding the war, an unusual level of agreement between corporations and workers marked the first two decades after the war. During this period, workers consented to capital's right not only to control the workplace but also to allow capitalist control of investment and growth, primarily through the growth of multinational corporations. In exchange, workers, women, and people of color struggled for and were able to extend their personal and political rights for education, housing, health, workplace safety, and to vote.[23] This same period was marked by unusually rapid and stable economic growth, fueled in large part because of the growing wages of workers. However, while workers were earning and spending more, businesses' net rate of profit fell by more than 50 percent between 1965 and 1974.[24] Profits fell primarily because cost pressures from labor could not be passed on to consumers in the increasingly competitive and open world economy.[25]

In order to restore higher rates of profit, the United States and other developed countries implemented monetarist and neoliberal policies[26] that would support corporations over workers. In the United States, monetarist policies restored the power of capital by inducing a recession to deflate wage demands, escalate the scarcity of jobs, and reverse the growth of social spending. Such policies were instituted with the intent of reducing the living standards of all but wealthy Americans. In 1979, Paul Volcker, Federal Reserve Board chairman, provided the following rationale for the recession: "The standard of living of the average American has to decline. I don't think you can escape that."[27]

Such monetarist policies were soon linked with neoliberal policies that emphasize "the deregulation of the economy, trade liberalization, the dismantling of the public sector [such as education, health, and social welfare], and the predominance of the financial sector of the economy over production and commerce."[28] In particular, the consequences for education are similar to that for all public goods and services. Tabb writes that neoliberalism stresses the privatization of the public provision of goods and services—moving their provision from the public sector to the private—along with deregulating how private producers can behave, giving greater scope to the single-minded pursuit of profit and showing significantly less regard for the need to limit social costs or for redistribution based on nonmarket criteria. The aim of neoliberalism is to put into question all collective structures capable of obstructing the logic of the pure market.[29]

Efforts to privatize public services, then, are occurring worldwide, partly in response to the U.S.-dominated World Bank and International Monetary Fund requirement that national governments develop economic policies that emphasize economic growth and property rights over social welfare and personal rights. In some countries, such a Chile, social security, health care, higher education and, to some extent, elementary and secondary education have been highly privatized.[30] Such global changes led Stephen Gill to conclude that "[t]he social settlements and forms of state created after World War II have been transformed and in some respects destroyed."[31]

Efforts to dismantle the public sector have significant implications for educational policy. While some policymakers may desire to reduce funding for education, education remains significant as a means of developing productive workers and legitimizing current inequalities. As Roger Dale notes, government policies need to support continued economic expansion while "providing a basis for legitimation of the system as a whole."[32]

INCREASING EDUCATIONAL OPPORTUNITY OR REIFYING INEQUALITY?

A system of standards, high-stakes testing, and accountability has been implemented partly because it draws on continuing frustrations over public schools. Progressives have criticized schools for reproducing inequality through tracking working-class students and students of color into academically inferior courses and unequal funding.[33] Conservatives have criticized schools for their lack of standards and rigor and economic inefficiency.[34] Critics continually point out that the United States spends more per student than other countries but is not highly ranked when its academic results are compared with other countries. For example, Secretary of Education Paige recently used the newly released Organization of Economic Cooperation and Development report "Education at a Glance" to note, "[T]his report documents how little we receive in return for our national investment. This report also reminds us that we are battling two achievement gaps. One is between those being served well by our system and those being left behind. The other is between the U.S. and many of our higher achieving friends around the world. By closing the first gap, we will also close the second."[35]

Consequently, U.S. policymakers at the state and federal levels have called for reforms, such as standards, standardized testing, and accountability, as a way to improve educational efficiency and ensure that all students learn. Secretary of Education Paige describes NCLB as striving "to provide every boy and girl in America with a high quality of education—regardless of his or her income, ability or background."[36] In this section, we will examine the official claims that testing and accountability are improving education and argue that the evidence shows that the quality of schooling for most students is declining.

The first rationale—that these reforms are necessary to ensure that all students learn—is reflected in policy statements at the state and federal levels. In New York, the state's educational policymakers, including the past Chancellor Carl Hayden and present Commissioner of Education Richard Mills, justify the testing and accountability regime on the grounds that standards and standardized testing are the only way to ensure that all students, including students of color and those living in poverty, have an opportunity to learn. They argue that it is these same students who, because of the end of industrialization and the rise of globalization, can no longer be permitted to fail. All students must succeed educationally to ensure that the individual and the nation succeed economically.

They also point out, as progressives have, that our educational system has better served those students who are already advantaged. In New York State, the Regents exams originated in the mid-1800s, as both a college entrance exam and as one means of standardizing the curriculum.[37] However, over the last century, the New York State educational system evolved into a two-track system, with Regents exams and curricula for college-bound students and non-Regents courses for non–college bound students, with the latter courses dominated by working-class students and students of color.

In order, ostensibly, to reduce the disparity between working-class and middle-class students, the State Education Department eliminated the non-Regents or local diplomas. Students can only be in the Regents track, and if they fail to earn a Regents diploma, which requires passing the five Regents exams, they cannot receive a high school degree. Carl Hayden, the New York Chancellor of Education from 1996 to 2002, draws on the discourse of fairness to justify this development:

> The requirement that *every* child be brought to a Regents level of performance is revolutionary. It is a powerful lever for education equity. It is changing for the better the life prospects of millions of young people, particularly poor and minority children who in the past would have been relegated to a low standards path. Too often, these children emerged from school without the skills and knowledge needed for success in an increasingly complex economy.[38]

Similarly, the federal government has promoted NCLB as improving the education for all children. Secretary of Education Rod Paige recently argued that NCLB is especially important for African-American students.

> We have an educational emergency in the United States of America. Nationally, blacks score lower on reading and math tests than their white peers. But it doesn't have to be that way. We need to collectively focus our attention on the problem. . . . We have to make sure that every single child gets our best attention. We also need to help African-American parents understand how this historic new education law can specifically help them and their children.[39]

The second rationale—that we can improve education efficiency through standards and standardized testing—is also reflected at both the state and federal levels. In New York State, proponents of standards and standardized testing argued that the curriculum standards have been objectively determined and that standardized tests provide a valid and reliable means of assessing student learning. Such objective methods are required, they state, because teachers and administrators cannot be trusted to assess student learning objectively and accurately. Therefore, teacher-generated assessment protocols and instruments are dismissed, within this discourse, as subjective and unreliable. However, testing proponents ignore that the standardized tests assess only a small percentage of the state's standards and have questionable validity and reliability. Testing proponents imply that to adopt other means of assessment results automatically in a lowering of standards, as can be seen in Chancellor Hayden's response to the possibility of retaining performance assessment:

> There is an even greater danger. The least rigorous, the least valid, the least reliable approved alternative [assessment] is then available to any school. Which schools will be first in the race to the lowest common denominator? Those having the most trouble bringing all children to a Regents level of performance. Those keen to reacquire the low standard option lost when the RCT [Regents Competency Test for those in the non-Regents track] and the local diploma were abolished. Those that never believed that all children can reach high standards. Were this to occur, it is all too apparent that poor and minority children would disproportionately bear the burden of diminished expectations.[40]

Similarly, NCLB claims that the standards have been objectively determined, that standardized tests provide a valid and reliable means of assessing student learning, and this approach improves on teacher-generated assessments. The *Parents' Guide to No Child Left Behind* informs parents that NCLB "will give them objective data" through standardized testing.[41] Further, objective data from tests are necessary because, in the past, "[m]any parents have children who are getting straight A's, but find out too late that their child is not prepared for college. That's just one reason why NCLB give parents objective data about how their children are doing."[42] Teachers, they imply, have not rigorously enforced standards nor accurately assessed students, therefore covering up their own and their students' failures. Further, test scores will be useful to parents because "[p]arents will know how well learning is occurring in their child's class. They will know information on how their child is progressing compared to other children."[43]

Because teachers, NCLB claims, have relied too often on their own assessments, test scores will also benefit teachers. NCLB "provides teachers with independent information about each child's strengths and weaknesses. With this knowledge, teachers can craft lessons to make sure each student meets or exceeds the standards."[44] Moreover, not only have teachers relied on subjective assessments, they have relied on "education fads," "bad ideas," and "untested curricula." Therefore, NCLB "puts a special focus on doing what works," as demonstrated by "scientifically based research" using the "medical model."[45]

However, we can question whether the tests increase fairness or are objective. What have been the consequences of eliminating the non-Regents track and diploma on the quality of courses and student graduation rates? Do students' test scores on the Regents exams lead us to believe that the assessments are more objective than teacher evaluations?

Although the stated goal of eliminating the non-Regents track and diploma was to bring "*every* child . . . to a Regents level of performance" (emphasis in original),[46] the reality has been somewhat different. First, the Regents courses and some of the standardized exams have been made easier so as to reduce the number of students dropping out who would otherwise not pass the courses required for graduation. This has led to a lowering rather than a raising of standards. Second, many of the students who have typically been in the Regents courses have opted for enrolling in Honors and Advanced Placement courses (courses that are sometimes accepted as course credit by universities) and International Baccalaureate Program as a way of maintaining academic distinction from the average students. Therefore, the two-track system has been maintained with former non-Regents students enrolling in the easier Regents courses, and former Regents students enrolling in Honors and other advanced courses. Students are still receiving unequal opportunities to learn.

Although some of the Regents courses and exams have been made easier, some students are failing to pass all five of the exams required for graduation and dropping out of school. Students for whom English is a second language have difficulties with the English exam, and students with disabilities are having difficulties with all the exams. Further, as we will explain, some of the exams are constructed so poorly that many students fail them. Sixty-three percent of high school students failed the recent Math A exam (the math exam most students take to meet the Regents requirements).[47] Consequently, in New York, the gap in performance between the advantaged white, middle-class students and disadvantaged working-class students and students of color has increased, as has the dropout rate for students in the poorer urban schools.

In 2001, students for whom English is a second language left school at a 12 percent higher rate than the previous year.[48] This year, because of the increased difficulty of the ESL exam, as stated earlier, students for whom English is a second language are *more* rather than *less* likely to be retained in ESL and relegated to less academic courses. The passing rates on the ESL exam are only a small fraction of what they have been in the past.[49]

Further, we should ask whether the effort placed on improving schools though testing and accountability is intended to cover up inequalities in funding between school districts and the increasing poverty rate, which negatively affect student learning. Currently, New York State's schools are the most segregated and the second most unequally funded in the United States. Because of the current economic slowdown, the state's urban schools have received significant reductions in revenue. In the 2001–2002 school year, the New York City public schools received $1 billion less than the previous year.[50] New York State's highest court, the Court of Appeals, recently (June 26, 2003) "ordered reform of the entire statewide funding formula to ensure that all schools have sufficient resources to give their students the opportunity to meet the Regents Learning Standards."[51] The remedy was ordered in part because the Court observed "tens of thousands of students placed on overcrowded classrooms, taught by unqualified teachers, and provided with inadequate facilities and equipment. The number of children in these straits is large enough to represent a systemic failure."[52] The Court rules that the state cannot require students to achieve certain standards with providing the means to do so.

The most recent census report reveals that the percentage of children living in poverty has increased for the second straight year.[53] Further, "the gap between the rich and the poor more than doubled from 1979 to 2000," which is the "greatest economic disparity between the rich and the poor of any year since 1979, the year the budget office began collecting this data" and probably since 1929.[54] Although the United States may spend the most per student (while it spends a smaller percentage of its gross domestic product than many countries), the inequalities in family income and high rates of child poverty are likely to explain the discrepancy between education spending and academic results.

Not only might a system of high-stakes exams and accountability lead to a higher student failure rate and not remedy the underlying causes of academic failure, standardized exams may provide less, not more, accurate information about student learning. We have already suggested through the sharp increase in the failure rate for the Math A and ESL exams that questions can be raised regarding the exams' construction, objectivity, validity, and reliability. Such inconsistency between exams not only spells trouble for the claims of New York's education policymakers that the exams provide evaluations that can be used to improve students' education, but also negatively impacts NCLB, which relies on state exams to measure AYP. Therefore, if New York's exams fail as assessment measures for the state, they also fail as measures for the federal government.

SMOKE AND MIRRORS: PROVIDING
OBJECTIVE EVALUATION OR MANIPULATING
ACHIEVEMENT DATA?

First, the average score on various exams varies so greatly that passing or failing an exam tells us little about the student's learning. As stated earlier, students in New York are currently required to pass five Regents exams (one each in English, math, and science and two in social studies) to earn a high school diploma. The degree of difficulty for these exams has varied, critics argue, depending on whether the State Education Department (SED) wants to increase the graduation rate and therefore makes the exam easier or wants to appear rigorous and tough and therefore makes the exam more difficult. Exam passing rates can be increased or decreased simply by adjusting the cut score. Such manipulation can turn a low percentage of correct answers into a pass and a high percentage of correct answers into a failure. For example, in the recent "Living environments" exam, the science exam most often used to satisfy the Regents science requirement, students needed to answer only 39 percent of the questions correctly to earn a passing grade of 55 percent. Conversely, the exams for the advanced, nonrequired courses, such as physics and chemistry, have been made more difficult. Thirty-nine percent of students failed the most recent physics exam[55] in order, critics charge, to make Regents testing appear more rigorous. Moreover, for no apparent reason other than incompetence, the most recent (June 2003) Regents Math A exam (also the one students are most likely to take to meet the Regents requirement) was so poorly constructed that the test scores had to be discarded. Only 37 percent of the students passed statewide.[56] At Rochester's Wilson Magnet High School, a school ranked 49th in the nation by *Newsweek*, all 300 students who took the exam failed. A panel convened by the SED to examine the test concluded that the test poorly matched the standards teachers were directed to address in their courses and that early field tests indicated that there would be a high failure rate. NCLB's claim that standardized testing provides the objective assessment that teachers have lacked does not stand up to scrutiny. The best predictor of students' future academic success continues to be that resulting from teacher-constructed assessments.

Second, it is unlikely to be the case that, as NCLB claims, the exams will provide "independent information about each child's strengths and weaknesses."[57] either teachers or parents. In New York State, teachers are not even permitted to see the test questions for the exams given in grades four through eight. Teachers do receive their students' test scores but not how they did on each question. Further, while NCLB claims that it will "give parents objective data about how their children are doing,"[58] parents are not provided with their child's test score except on the high school Regents exams, a score that was already available to them.

Third, the determination of whether a school is making AYP tells us little about whether a school is succeeding. Not only can we question the test scores on which the determination is made, but the determination of success or failure may have little to do with whether the school is improving. Schools and districts are to measure whether students are learning through standardized tests with the scores indicating whether the student is or is not achieving proficiency in subject area standards. Students' aggregated scores need to improve each year, and all students are required to achieve proficiency by the year 2014. In the United States, state education commissioners set, with the approval of the federal Department of Education, what counts as proficiency in each subject area and the minimal level of improvement schools and districts must achieve each year to attain "adequate yearly progress." Each school and district is required to both aggregate student test scores and disaggregate test results "into groups of students who are economically disadvantaged, from racial and ethnic minority groups, have disabilities or have limited English proficiency."[59] The aggregated and disaggregated test scores must all demonstrate adequate yearly progress for the school to be labeled successful. Because states develop their own tests and determine what counts as proficiency and the minimal standard or rate of improvement schools must achieve in order to demonstrate that they are making AYP, states' results can vary greatly.

For example, contrary to a commonsense interpretation of AYP, in New York, schools are *not* evaluated based on whether their test scores are improving but whether their aggregated and disaggregated test scores exceed a minimum yearly threshold that gradually increases over the next decade. Consequently, a school is considered to be passing as long as its scores exceed the threshold, *even if its scores fall.* Similarly, schools that begin with initially low test scores *may be considered failing even if they significantly increase their test scores*, as long as those scores remain below the threshold. Therefore, achieving AYP has nothing to do with whether a school's test scores rise or fall, only whether its scores for that year exceed or fail to meet the minimum threshold.

Because test scores strongly correlate to a student's family income, a school's score is likely to reflect its students' average family income, not teaching practices or curriculum. Consequently, the largest percentage of failing schools in New York is found in urban and poor school districts. Almost all (83 percent) of the failing schools are located in the big five urban districts: NYC, Buffalo, Rochester, Syracuse, and Yonkers.

To NCLB's testing requirements that schools demonstrate improvement for all disaggregated groups of students on all the tests, Florida added the further draconian stipulation that no school that has been assigned a grade of a D or an F (per the annual rating of A through F) could meet AYP requirements. Not surprisingly, 90 percent of Florida's public schools were designated as failing to meet AYP, and 100 percent of districts failed.[60]

In New York State, where urban schools with rising scores are likely to be "failing" to make AYP and suburban schools with falling scores are likely to be "succeeding" to make AYP, urban teachers working hard at improving their schools and demonstrating success are likely to be discouraged, if not defeated. In Florida, with 100 percent of the districts failing, we might conclude that this is meant as a condemnation of the public school system.

Historically, U.S. public schools have not served well students who are not white or middle to upper class. Schools in wealthier communities typically receive substantially more funding to educate students than schools in poorer urban (i.e., nonwhite) and rural communities. Students in urban schools are much more likely to be in overcrowded classrooms with inadequate supplies and unprepared teachers. Consequently, in most urban districts, fewer than half the students graduate from high school. Further, even when students from different backgrounds are in the same school, the school is likely to track wealthier students into more challenging and advanced courses.

However, the educational reforms of the last decade focus not on improving the classroom conditions but increasing teacher and classroom accountability through standardized testing and increasing competition between schools through school choice (charters, vouchers, and, in NCLB, transferring students from "failing" to "passing" schools). Such efforts, we have argued, are a consequence of globalization and the dominant neoliberal policies in which education is to prepare skilled workers able to generate economic value. Further, education is not only required to further economic productivity but to be economically efficient. Schools must do more with less.

State and federal governments have succeeded in adopting these reforms because they situate them within the discourses of objectivity and fairness. Moreover, they have not directly intervened into the lives of teachers and students but "steer at a distance."[61] By giving educators the appearance of autonomy, resistance from teachers, parents, and students has been reduced.

Education systems in the United States and elsewhere are being transformed without widespread public debate. Yet, as we have shown, the system of testing and accountability is even less objective and fair than the present system. It is crucial that questions be raised about the future of schooling for all citizens.

State Theory and Urban School Reform I: A Reconsideration from Detroit

Barry M. Franklin

The decade of the 1970s onward has seen important changes in large U.S. cities and their schools that call for a rethinking and recalibration of our understanding of how such schools are governed and, more broadly, how they interact with other sectors, including other elements of the state and civil society. Within these cities, there have been major demographic changes that have resulted in the movement of whites, including substantial numbers of the white middle class, to the suburbs and beyond. At the same time, these cities also experienced the growth of minority populations, largely African-Americans but also Latinos and Asians, that are, on balance, less well educated, less gainfully employed, and less economically well-off than the whites whom they replaced. The most complete instance of this change has been the emergence of the black-led city where African-Americans not only constitute the majority of the population but also control the city's political apparatus, including the schools. In other cases, this change has been less extensive. Blacks or other minorities may or may not represent the majority of the city's total population, but they often constitute a majority or close to a majority of the school-age population. And they may or may not dominate the political life of these cities, but they clearly constitute emerging power blocks with increasing degrees of influence and authority over schools and other matters.[1]

More broadly, there has been another important change that both underpins the demographic shift noted earlier and also has had its own independent effects on urban America: the array of social and economic transformations collectively labeled as globalization. Most important of these changes has been the emergence of worldwide communication and transportation systems. Other changes, all of which require global communication and transportation networks, include the expansion of trade and investment across national borders, the growth of international financial markets, the immediate impact of distant events, the global effects of local political and economic decisions, and the redistribution of power among nation-states, local entities within nations, and within regions that span national boundaries.[2]

The most immediate impact of globalization on American cities has been that of economic disinvestment or deindustrialization. The increased mobility of capital globally, which is an outgrowth of the international expansion of financial markets and resulting investment opportunities, subjects national and local economies to global capital dynamics that, in the United States context, have tended to undermine economic growth and promote foreign over domestic investment. In many U.S. cities, the result has been a pattern of plant relocation, downsizing, job loss, and capital flight. Coupled with the demographic changes noted earlier, the impact on many cities has been the destruction of their manufacturing infrastructure, the erosion of their tax base, persistent poverty, and economic dependency.[3] Such changes have not left urban schools unaffected, bringing with them racial segregation, the lack of financial resources, a deterioration in school physical plants, and a pattern of persistent low achievement and low school completion rates among students.[4]

During the last decade, the idea of the state has become an increasingly important conceptual lens that critically oriented educational scholars have used to better understand the interplay between schools and society under these conditions. In part, their interest can be explained by the attractiveness that the concept of the state has recently come to enjoy among social scientists of all stripes who have sought a corrective to its absence or, at best, its passive and reactive presence in their society-centered interpretations of politics and government.[5]

More particularly, critical scholars of education have embraced the notion of the state as a way to move beyond simple reproductionist interpretations of the role of schooling as a social institution. Such reproductionist explanations did give birth to efforts during the 1970s to move educational scholarship beyond a celebratory understanding of schooling as the handmaiden of democracy and progress. It enabled these scholars to begin to explain how schools serve as agencies of social control to perpetuate existing social relations, thereby maintaining an unequal society.[6] Yet, pursuing this analysis, a second generation of educational researchers soon began to recognize that a focus on reproduction alone offered an inadequate understanding of how schools and those within them worked. Schools, they argued, were not passive agencies that simply reproduced the social order as dictated by political and economic interests. Rather, they were sites of contestation where an array of actors reflecting different class, race, and gender roles struggled for political, economic, and cultural control. At the end of the day, those with the most power and privilege often won, but it was truly a battle, and within it were the seeds for different and more egalitarian outcomes.[7]

In this chapter, the notion of the state will be used as a conceptual framework for interpreting urban school reform, particularly as globalization has affected the character and conditions of cities and their schools. This approach will look at urban school reform as a process of state building, and will situate contemporary urban school reform in the context of the demographic and economic shifts that have affected large U.S. cities since the 1970s. I will begin by describing the theory of the state that I think is most fruitful for interpreting present-day reform in city schools. I will then look at a number of twentieth-century state-building initiatives to consider how this theory explicates reform, both political and educational. I will next offer a case study involving the mayoral takeover of the Detroit Board of Education that illustrates the applicability of this theory for interpreting efforts to improve urban schools. Finally, I will conclude by considering how this state-centered theory moves us along further in our understanding of educational change.

STATE BUILDING IN TWENTIETH-CENTURY AMERICA

The notion of the state (in this chapter) comes from Rueschemeyer and Evans and refers to those "organizations with the authority to make binding decisions for people and organizations juridically located in a particular territory."[8] In developing an understanding of the state, it is important to avoid the kind of reproductionist view that sees schools as passive sites whose destiny is determined solely by external actors. The central feature of the state is its relative autonomy. It is an actor in its own right that often operates at its own behest, independently of other groups and classes. The state, in other words, can possess its own goals and take its own initiative to attain those ends. Although its programs and policies often support the long-term interests of dominant social classes, the state is not simply a vehicle through which those groups pursue their policies.[9]

A major characteristic of twentieth-century American political reform has been *state building*. Many of the legislative initiatives associated with the Progressive era at the turn of the century were designed to provide an array of incipient bureaucratic organizations, local, regional, and national, with the administrative capacities to cope with the changed conditions that urbanization and industrialization had brought to the nation.[10] One good example of this kind of state building can be seen in the attempts of three Progressive era presidents (Theodore Roosevelt, William Howard Taft, and Woodrow Wilson) to reform the Interstate Commerce Commission (ICC).

Their efforts on this score between 1904 and 1920 were designed to enhance the commission's power to regulate the railroads beyond that contained in the 1887 Interstate Commerce Act. By expanding the rate-making authority of the ICC and giving it new power to supervise the operation of the railroads, they enhanced the federal executive's capacity to regulate transportation over and against that of Congress and the courts.[11]

The creation of the Wisconsin Industrial Commission in 1911 represents a similar example of state building, but this time at a regional level. By establishing the commission, the Wisconsin legislature shifted the regulation of employment from the courts to the executive branch, thereby enhancing the capacity of the state to deal with a number of diverse matters affecting labor, including arbitration, child labor, women's working hours, and apprenticeships. Over time, solidifying responsibility for employment policy in one regulatory agency had the effect of further increasing the administrative capacity of Wisconsin's state government. By the 1920s, for example, the Wisconsin Commission was able to enact a host of rules promoting workplace safety and to conduct studies for new social provisions, including unemployment compensation.[12]

The decade of the 1920s saw similar undertakings, such as the provision of federal funds to support infant and maternal health programs, as a means of strengthening the administrative capacity of the U.S. Children's Bureau.[13] The establishment of an array of New Deal agencies during the 1930s provides additional illustrations of how the state can act to change the driving force behind public policy. The Agricultural Adjustment Administration (AAA) and the National Recovery Administration (NRA), both created during the early days of the Roosevelt administration, represented good examples of how the state augmented its ability to manage the economic dislocations of the depression by introducing regulative policies in place of voluntary appeals.[14]

In their study of state building during the New Deal, Finegold and Skocpol point to two factors that drove these initiatives forward. One had to do with the administrative capacity that agencies undertaking initiatives already possessed. They argued that the government agencies most successful in implementing state-building initiatives were those that possessed the most administrative capacity with which to begin.[15]

They illustrate this point by comparing two Depression era agencies, the AAA and the NRA. Both agencies possessed similar leadership and pursued the same general objectives of raising prices in the midst of an economic depression through the use of production controls. Notwithstanding their similarities, the efforts of the AAA were successful while those of the NRA were less so. What distinguishes these two agencies and their ultimate impact, according to Finegold and Skocpol, were their differing capacities. The AAA was part of the U.S. Department of Agriculture, which was one of the most powerful agencies in what was a relatively weak American state. It was an organization staffed by agricultural economists whose education in the nation's land grant colleges and government experience had prepared them to initiate policy on behalf of the state, even when their views differed from those of the nation's farmers. The Department of Agriculture, then, had acquired the bureaucratic expertise that provided the agency with the capacity necessary to use the provisions of the Agricultural Adjustment Act to further enhance its authority.[16]

The NRA, on the other hand, did not have a corps of trained professionals to provide it with expertise and leadership. It had instead to rely on political appointees who were borrowed on a temporary basis from the very industries that the agency was responsible for regulating. The economists who worked for the NRA never possessed the power and influence that their counterparts at the AAA enjoyed. The result was an agency that lacked the capacity to undertake its charge.[17]

A second factor that Finegold and Skocpol argue affects state initiative is that of party alignment. When faced with demands from the citizenry, state actors can respond in a number of ways. They can yield to these demands, reject them, or simply ignore them. What these demands entail, who makes them, and the responses of state managers are in large part determined by the political parties and within-party factions into which these actors are divided. Beyond winning elections, political parties devote their attention to attempting to create the kind of party alignments that will empower them to influence the policy initiatives of the state. Finegold and Skocpol argue that the shift from an industrial policy based on voluntary restraints on the part of business and labor to the regulative policies of the NRA was due in part to a transition in national politics from a Republican to Democratic majority. Likewise, they maintain that the same change in party alignment made possible the advent of an agricultural policy based on production controls.[18]

The introduction of curriculum differentiation during the early years of the twentieth century points to how an understanding of the state and the process of state building can account for instances of educational reform. The prevailing explanations that educational scholars have offered for differentiating the curriculum do not seem to recognize the role that schools and school leaders have played as actors in this practice. Early twentieth-century school reformers, according to one such interpretation, enamored as were many Americans of the day of the efficiency orientation of business, embraced what were the most popular of those practices, the principles of scientific management. Adapting such procedures as the time and motion study and job analysis to the task of selecting and organizing the curriculum, they created a school program composed of numerous specialized courses of study.[19]

In a clearly reproductionist variation of this interpretation, other scholars have attributed the movement for curriculum differentiation to the efforts of business elites. By introducing vocational education, they sought to produce a workforce that mirrored the class divisions of modern American society and that spurred forward industrial growth.

According to this view, curriculum differentiation made the schools an instrument of social control to meet the labor requirements of American industry and thereby to preserve the political and economic power of the nation's business classes.[20]

The problem with these types of explanations is that they view the schools solely as sites where external parties or issues play themselves out. Schools and those who participate in them are seen only as passive observers of the workings and struggles of others, not real participants. What these interpretations of curriculum differentiation fail to do is to account for the role that school administrators and teachers played in promoting and instituting curriculum differentiation.

The key players in establishing curriculum differentiation in the nation's schools were not business or other external interests. The support for this innovation, instead, came largely from school administrators themselves, who saw this proposal as providing them with the capacities that they required to resolve immediate problems that they faced in governing schools. These managers, then, were acting to a large degree at their own behest to augment the effectiveness of the sector of the state in which they worked. A critical concern for these educational leaders was how to reconcile their long-standing belief in the common school ideal, namely, the view that schooling should be accessible to all children in the same setting, with the reality of enrollment growth and the increasingly diverse student population that such expansion had brought with it. Their solution was to admit virtually all children into the school and, once there, to channel them to different curriculum programs, some vocational and terminal and others academic and preparatory, on the basis of their presumed abilities, interests, backgrounds, and inclinations.

A second problem facing these school leaders was that, as occupants of the emerging profession of educational administration, they had to find a way to legitimate their expertise and professional status. By calling for the introduction of curriculum differentiation, they were providing that justification. In promoting this practice, these administrators were to a certain extent creating an ideology celebrating the technical expertise that could justify their standing as a distinct professional specialty within the schools. Policies such as curriculum differentiation provided the symbolic trappings of incipient professionalism. Promoting curriculum differentiation, however, served more than an ideological function. Once school systems introduced this practice, they had to go out and hire teachers who had the expertise in educating the children who would fit into these different curricular programs. And having such teachers in their employ required these school systems to hire specialized administrative personnel as supervisors. The initiatives that school leaders put forth for differentiating the curriculum not only legitimated school administration as a profession. They actually were central to the building of the profession.[21] Curriculum differentiation, therefore, was a state-building effort that was to a significant degree initiated by school administrators to enhance not only the effectiveness of their organization but their own professional efficacy.

DETROIT'S MAYORAL TAKEOVER AS A STATE INITIATIVE

Earlier it was suggested that this theory of the state is useful in interpreting and understanding current issues of urban school reform. The recent struggle for mayoral control of the board of education in Detroit, Michigan, serves as an illustration. On May 4, 2000, Detroit's reform school board selected Kenneth Burnely, the then superintendent of the Colorado Springs Public Schools, as its choice for the city schools' first permanent chief executive officer (CEO). His appointment marked the culmination of a year and a half struggle, modeled in large part after the 1995 mayoral takeover of the Chicago Public Schools, to replace the city's elected school board with one appointed by the mayor and to replace the superintendent with the new and more powerful position of CEO. The year before in his State of the State Address, Michigan's Republican governor, John Engler, had called for a state takeover of failing school districts. As he saw it, such legislation would bring the same benefits that he claimed had occurred in Chicago, namely, higher test scores, increased attendance, higher standards, better graduation rates, the end of social promotion, and the reduction of waste, fraud, and corruption in the management of the city's schools.

In proposing the takeover, Engler was addressing a two-pronged criticism of the city's schools. There was the widely held view, more prominent outside the city than inside, that the schools had failed academically as evidenced by a pattern of low achievement, poor state proficiency test scores, low graduation rates, and high dropout rates. At the same time, the district was depicted as inept in its administration of the schools, particularly the management of its fiscal affairs. Neither the board of education nor the school administration was viewed as capable of addressing either problem. This was a viewpoint that many Detroiters challenged as an inaccurate and racially motivated attack on the state's largest black-led city and its school system. As they saw it, the proposal paid no attention to the ongoing efforts on the part of Detroit to improve its schools and ignored similar problems that existed in majority white school districts throughout the state.

The actual takeover legislation was drafted by Michigan's Republican-controlled Senate during the next several months. The initial proposal called for mayors in school districts enrolling at least 100,000 students, the only one in Michigan being Detroit, to appoint a reform school board composed of five members, each of whom would serve a four-year term. It would be the board's responsibility to employ a CEO who would serve at their pleasure. Once this legislation was enacted, the duties and the powers of the elected school board and its officers would be suspended. The proposal was to be in effect for five years, after which time Detroit voters could petition for a referendum on the continuation of the mayoral appointed board of education. In the final version of the bill, the size of the reform board was changed to seven members, six appointed by the mayor with the seventh seat given to the state school superintendent or his designee. In the final legislation, the elected board was not disbanded but kept on in an advisory capacity.

Detroit's elected board and the superintendent did not simply accept the takeover proposal. Both Daryl Redmond, the board president, and Superintendent Eddie Green challenged Engler's assessment of the state of the city's schools. The board also put forth its own reform initiative that called on the city's employers to allow parents to take half a day a month to work as volunteers in their children's school, authorized the use of its current budget surplus on low-performing schools, and shifted oversight of contracts and bids from the board to the superintendent.

Detroit's black Democratic mayor, Dennis Archer, was, at least initially, a reluctant player in these events. At first, he seemed to support the takeover, but once the bill was introduced in the legislature, he reversed his course. Ultimately, however, he became a supporter of the plan. In part, his equivocation was due to the fact that he believed that reform required more than organizational changes. He favored a reduction in class size to seventeen in the early grades, mandatory summer school for low achievers, establishment of citywide afterschool programs, and efforts to recruit additional teachers. A deal brokered by State Senator Virgil Smith, the only African-American member of the Detroit legislative delegation in support of the takeover, to provide the city's schools with an additional $15 million to help pay for the additional initiatives that Archer had requested finally brought him on board.

There were, as it turns out, other reasons for Archer's initial unwillingness to support the takeover. He was in the midst of his own struggle to fend off a recall drive that began six months after his reelection to a second term at the behest of a coalition upset with his policies regarding the awarding of licenses to run the city's new casinos. Although the recall effort would ultimately fail, there were other doubts raised about his leadership ability as a result of a failed effort to deal with snow removal in the wake of a surprise blizzard earlier that year. There were city residents who criticized him for paying more attention to citywide reforms, such as school improvement, at the expense of neighborhood issues, such as the modernization of the fire department, community policing, and the demolition of abandoned buildings.[22]

At the heart of the takeover battle was a struggle between Mayor Archer and Detroit's largely black Democratic delegation to the state legislature, particularly State Representatives Ed Vaughn and Kwame Kilpatrick. In part, this was a battle over how to undertake educational reform in which these legislatures favored efforts to improve the existing system of school organization rather than to change it. Yet the quarrel between Archer and these black Detroit Democrats predates the takeover debate. Ed Vaughn had run for mayor against Archer in 1997 and lost, while both Kilpatrick's parents, Congresswoman Carolyn Kilpatrick and Wayne County Commissioner Bernard Kilpatrick, had at times contemplated running for mayor. Kwame Kilpatrick and his father, in fact were members of the African-American Men's Organization, a group that was organized in 1997 to counter Archer's influence.

The takeover offered Archer's black rivals the perfect opportunity for expressing their antipathy toward him. Archer's ongoing problems, particularly the recall attempt, his botched effort to deal with snow removal, and the criticism of his approach to addressing city problems, had rendered him vulnerable to attacks from his opponents. While Engler's proposal was being debated in the Michigan Senate, these black Detroiters helped secure the passage of an alternative bill in the House of Representatives that called for the governor to appoint a monitor who would run the schools while retaining the elected board of education in an advisory capacity. Their efforts in support of this legislation represented their way of embarrassing the mayor by telling him, in effect, that they preferred to turn the city's schools over to a white Republican governor rather than to their fellow black Democrat.

The takeover dispute was, however, not just about conflict. It also was the vehicle for an alliance between a black Democratic mayor and a white Republican governor. Although Archer and Engler voiced similar criticisms of the Detroit Public Schools, it is not clear to what extent they agreed on educational matters. Engler and Archer's alliance may have had more to do with the politics of the moment than with educational ideology. The success of the takeover proposal was the most recent indication of the fact that Detroit was losing the influence that it once had enjoyed in the state legislature. The city's declining population, Republican control of the state government, and recent term-limit legislation were the culprits behind this change. Between 1950 and 1990, Detroit's population fell from about 1.8 million to just over 1 million. As a result, the city has lost membership in the state House of Representatives from thirty seats in 1950 to twenty in 1970 to thirteen in 1999. Declining population had also affected Detroit's voting power. In the 1958 gubernatorial election, about 25 percent of the votes came from Detroit. In 1978, the city accounted for 11.5 percent of the votes, and in the 1998 election, for 7.5 percent of the votes. And recently passed term-limit legislation would soon force the most senior mem-

bers of the Detroit legislative delegation, whose tenure and experience pro-
vided them with the greatest influence, to leave office. The result was that
Republicans at the state level could act notwithstanding the opposition of
Detroit Democrats.

Seen in this light, Engler may have viewed the takeover as a means of
cementing an alliance with Archer that would divide state Democrats and,
as a result, further diminish Democratic Party power in Michigan. For Engler,
the takeover, if it actually served to improve the schools, offered him the
opportunity to enhance his reputation as a visionary and a leader without
much risk. He could undertake the initiative without worrying about anger-
ing Detroit blacks, since he did not need their votes to get elected. And if
the takeover failed to improve the schools, he could blame Archer. The mayor
was also attracted to the takeover by the prospect of reforming the city's
schools, which would further advance the leadership role that he was assum-
ing in national Democratic Party politics. For Archer, however, the venture
was riskier. If the schools did not improve, he would in all likelihood suffer
increased opposition to his administration.[23]

How, then, does our theory of the state help us to interpret this instance
of urban school reform? First and foremost, it directs our attention to the
role that an array of state actors played in initiating this reform and propelling it forward as well as in attempting to block it. The theory also explains
why the impetus for this reform came from state government. Despite our
long tradition of local control, it is state government that possesses the legal authority for public education. When it came to changing the schools,
Michigan's governor and legislature questioned the capacity of the city to
resolve its educational problem. They evidently believed that the resources
of state government provided them with the administrative capabilities to
address these seemingly intractable problems.

The theory also points to the impact that conflicts and alliances between
and among political parties and politicians have on educational reform. It
leads us to recognize that the outcome of such initiatives as the mayoral takeover hinge on the relative mix of conflict and agreement between and among
individuals of different political persuasions and parties. The theory also alerts
us to the fact that the success of this reform had a lot to do with demographic
changes that had reduced the influence of Detroit on state politics, which
in turn had created a realignment of political parties that favored Republicans over Democrats.

CONCLUSIONS

This chapter attempted to develop a theory of the state to account for
urban school reform in the period after 1970. The starting point was the
idea that the state operates as a relatively autonomous actor in undertaking
initiatives, in this case programs and policies, to reform urban schools. The

theory represents an alternative to the view that schools are passive entities in the process of school reform that serve as venues where other parties outside the state, business and other agents of capital, struggle for control. It cannot be denied that state initiatives often serve reproductive class interests, but such processes are not as predetermined as many educational theorists claim.

The theory of the state does move us along further than we have heretofore been in our understanding of school reform. It enables us to explain how schools and those who work within them initiate change. In that regard, it calls our attention to the twin issues of capacity and political party alignment. The state undertakes initiatives to enhance its administrative capacities to solve the problems that it faces. What propels these initiatives are the existing capacities that the state possesses to act and the existing alignment of the state's political parties.

Yet this interpretation only takes us so far. It works to explain the kind of political and educational initiatives that the state takes when faced with the deteriorating conditions that globalization has brought to cities. Where it fails, however, is to account for the kind of state that has emerged under conditions of globalization and how the reform of city schools proceeds within such a state. Under these circumstances, governments, national, regional, and local, have had increasing difficulties in managing their economies and have instead concentrated their energies on adjusting their policies to the demands of global markets. What this has amounted to, in many instances, are efforts to render their markets more accessible and receptive to international capital by reducing public expenditures, lowering taxes, decreasing regulation, and trimming bureaucracy. It is an attempt, in effect, to reconstruct the state by shifting its role from one of directing policy to enabling it.[24]

In the initial conception of the state as a bureaucratic agency, the regulative mechanisms were to be found in its policies and legislative enactments. These were observable and easily recognized instruments of control. It is less immediately clear, however, how our recalibrated state governs. Actually, the governing instrument is the same. It is the language and discourse through which we frame policies and legislation and, more broadly, through which our modes of thinking and reasoning construct our understanding of the world. The circulation of these discourses through our various cultural practices throughout civil society carries with them the initiatives of the state.[25]

The changed role of the state that is described here is not really new. The impetus for the actions of bureaucratic agencies that have been identified with the initiatives of the state has always been the prevailing patterns of thinking and reasoning and the discourses through which they are carried into cultural practices. The discourses through which state initiatives are framed, in fact, structure the institutional forms that they ultimately take.[26] What is new, however, is the apparent shrinkage of the bureaucratic apparatus that carry these initiatives. As a consequence of these changes, the old public sector, which is taken for granted as the provider of social services, has virtually disappeared. An array of other actors, including families, businesses, churches, voluntary agencies, and individuals themselves make those provisions, thereby redefining the division between the public and the private.

The impact that this new understanding of the state has on policymaking and reform can be seen in the growing popularity of partnerships. Partnerships represent the efforts of groups and individuals, including government, business, the church, the voluntary sector, schools, and individuals themselves, to work together to solve problems. Seen in this way, they constitute an alternative vehicle apart from government for the state to pursue its regulative role. By transferring responsibility for governing to an array of groups, individuals, and agencies throughout civil society, they serve to reduce the cost of regulation, thus meeting the demands of globalization for a reduction in public expenditures.

Regulation under these conditions, however, appears in a different form in which the close involvement of the state in the lives of its citizens is replaced by a different form of governing, one that operates or seems to operate at a distance. As Rose notes:

> The state is no longer to be required to answer all society's needs for order, security, health and productivity. Individuals, firms, organizations, localities, schools, parents, hospitals, housing estates must take on themselves—as "partners"—a portion of the responsibility for resolving these issues—whether this be by permanent retraining for the worker, or neighbourhood watch for the community. This involves a double movement of autonomization and responsibilization. Organizations and other actors that were once enmeshed in the complex and bureaucratic lines of force of the social state are to be set free to find their own destiny. Yet, at the same time, they are to be made responsible for that destiny, and for the destiny of society as a whole, in new ways. Politics is to be returned to society itself, but no longer in a social form: the form of individual morality, organizational responsibility and ethical community.[27]

The locus of responsibility, which once lay in the bureaucratic apparatus of government, is now shifted outward to numerous locations in civil society.

The state as a distinct and visible agency is to some degree displaced by a more diffuse entity, that of community. A murky notion at best, the term refers in this context to the kind of common purposes and shared attachments that bind people together into a whole.[28] What is common and shared among proponents of this view is the notion of responsibility. The rights that are typically bestowed on individuals by the state become under this new arrangement part of one's individual responsibility. The various components of society's safety net—welfare payments, health services, unemployment insurance, and even education—cease to be entitlements and instead require that individuals commit themselves to be self-sufficient. That is, they seek work, accept employment opportunities, and engage in the necessary learning that will maintain and strengthen their economic viability.[29]

We can gauge the impact of holding to this view of the state on educational policy by considering how educational policymakers adhering to this interpretive framework explain the problem of low academic achievement. They tend to eschew structural explanations of school failure that place the blame on poverty, racism, or inequality. Rather, they place responsibility on such factors as deficient families, communities, or teachers who because of their own failings are unable to help low-achieving children master the skills and dispositions that will make them successful in school. When it comes to remedies, they favor schemes that subject these seemingly less than adequate groups to systems of surveillance and accountability that ensure that they perform adequately. For parents, they support home-school contracts, mandatory curfews, and demands that they supervise the homework of their children. They support curriculum standards and competency testing to monitor the work of teachers. And they promote manpower training to improve not only the specific job skills but the self-esteem and motivation of the residents of economically distressed communities.[30] These proposals are rooted in a different theory of the state, one that is beyond the scope of this chapter but represents the subject of the next chapter with a view from Milwaukee.

State Theory and Urban School Reform II: A Reconsideration from Milwaukee

Thomas C. Pedroni

In the previous chapter, the state, in the person of government officials and agencies, was envisioned as a relatively autonomous actor undertaking urban educational reform (e.g., in Detroit) as a reconsolidation of the state's power under conditions of globalization. This chapter extends that analysis through an examination of managerialist state governance practices in relation to urban school reform in Milwaukee, Wisconsin.

Specifically, this chapter indexes the ways in which three policy documents impacting Milwaukee Public Schools—*The Neighborhood Schools Plan*[1], *The Parent/Student Handbook on Rights, Responsibilities, and Discipline*,[2] and *The Wisconsin Model Academic Standards*[3]—reconstruct the key subjects of the home-school relationship as a form of governance. This is done by disciplining the affective inner life of the child, by "bringing the parent in" as a "partner" to the child's education, and by constructing the interaction of the parent with the school as an economic exchange between a consumer and a producer within an educational marketplace.

In relation to this recharacterization of the child and parent in educational policy and reform, Popkewitz and Lindblad write:

> [This] refiguring and "re-making" inscribe particular principles that are to govern the family, parent, and childhood through professional discourses about childhood, parent, and "community" that circulate within social policy about childcare and pedagogy. . . . The interest is a reform that is often phrased as democratizing the school or early childhood systems of care by making these

institutional settings more responsive to their clients. When focusing on the children of the poor and marginalized social groups, the democratization is also phrased as a way to "rescue" the child through rescuing the parent. It is thought that parents with the proper habits, dispositions, and behaviors would enable the success of their children as they develop into adults. Discourses of "community" are attached to this democratization, suggesting that the solution to democratization is localized and flexible strategies in which the new political rationalities are related to the moral and social practices of parents and children.[4]

Popkewitz develops these ideas further in an essay written with Marianne Bloch, entitled "Administering Freedom: A History of the Present. Rescuing the Parent to Rescue the Child for Society."[5] The authors examine the development of social and educational policy in the late nineteenth century as part of the construction of the modern American citizen within a liberal democratic state. The changing principles of governing that these developments represent are conceptualized by Popkewitz and Bloch as the effects of power.[6]

It should be noted that the concept of the state that is mobilized by Popkewitz and Bloch is not that of the state as an entity of government but, rather, the state as sets of relations through which governance practices are constructed. For the authors, the parent and the community have long been part of the historical trajectory of governing practices focused on the "good" child through the governing of his or her parents and community.[7] The technologies of governance in education that Popkewitz and Bloch invoke are the systems of reason that refigure the family, childhood, and the community in fabricating an individual and a citizen who acts through the inscription of "calculated systems of self-inspection and self-consciousness."[8] These technologies emerged in the social sciences as an interventional strategy of the state (conceived here in the traditional sense), infusing educational research and educational policy. "Educators and moralists began to stress the child's need for play, for love and understanding, and for the gradual, gentle unfolding of his [or her] nature. Child rearing became more demanding as a result, and emotional ties between parents and children grew more intense at the same time that ties to relatives outside the immediate family weakened."[9]

Pertaining to the urban poor, the research sought to find better ways of not only reorganizing the conditions of the poor, but also of reconstituting the identities of the poor themselves. Thus, the new social sciences came to the "administration of freedom" through multiple and overlapping ways.[10] These ways included the psychological research of the early twentieth century, which inundated parents, especially mothers, with "expert" advice on the proper training and rearing of children. In these discourses, the minute qualities of individual children were to be compared with others of the same age, inscribing a new meaning to the idea of normal.[11]

In the present moment (the context of the Milwaukee Public Schools documents), reforms embody

> the empowerment of teachers and parents through participation in site-based management, home-school collaboration, parent "choice," vouchers, and the new charter schools initiated by teachers and parents for diverse reasons. While moving to an "active," empowered and decision-making society, the decentralization of the active, collaborative teacher and parent is also steered through centralized federal, state and community standards, examinations, and "outcome based educational" reforms that embody homogeneous objectives and pedagogy necessary for all to achieve, or perform (high standards for everyone).[12]

However, according to Popkewitz and Bloch, these reforms fail to see the effects of power in the ways in which their systems of reasoning construct the identities of the parent, child, and community, producing inclusion or exclusion in their wake.

THE THREE MILWAUKEE PUBLIC SCHOOL DOCUMENTS

The three documents examined in this chapter are each key components of recent reforms in Milwaukee Public Schools. The first, the *Wisconsin Model Academic Standards* (hereafter referred to as "the *Standards*") is a document reflecting the national movement for content and performance-based standards in the primary subject areas (English Language Arts, Math, Science, and Social Studies). Of particular relevance to this case study are the shifting and increasingly specific notions of the "normal, proper" child constructed in this document. The *Standards* are targeted at all elementary and secondary public school systems within the state of Wisconsin, including Milwaukee Public Schools. The document was first introduced and published in 1997 by the Wisconsin Department of Public Instruction.

The second and third documents under consideration were both produced directly by Milwaukee Public Schools. The first of these, the *Parent/Student Handbook on Rights, Responsibilities, and Discipline* (hereafter referred to as "the *Handbook*") is a policy document that will be examined not only for its construction of the "normal" child, but also for its deployment of a parent who is identified both as a "partner" in the child's education and as a "consumer" within an educational marketplace. The final document, the *Milwaukee Public Schools Neighborhood Schools Plan* (hereafter referred to as "the *Neighborhood Schools Plan*" or "the *Plan*") will likewise be explored for its construction of the parent as "partner" and as "consumer," as well as for the specific way in which it deploys the concept of "community" and "neighborhood." Both these latter documents were produced and published in August 2000.

As previously discussed, each of these documents emerges in a local and global context of proliferation of discourses of educational markets, standards, and of parent, child, school, and community partnerships. Specifically regarding Milwaukee's instantiation of this context, these documents must be read in part in relation to the formation of the 1990 Milwaukee Parental Choice Program, which, at the time of its inception, represented one of the most important shifts in the way that education, as a manifestation of the welfare state, was to be conceived. Through a complex amalgamation of forces that resulted in the formation of a citywide voucher program targeted for low-income families, Milwaukee became a key stage for shifts in the character, form, and funding of education in the United States.[13]

THE SHIFTING PRESCRIPTION OF NORMATIVE CHILD BEHAVIOR

In 1997, the Wisconsin Department of Public Instruction produced the *Wisconsin Model Academic Standards* in response to, and in participation with, the national standards movement. Wisconsin organized its standards into two separate categories: "content" standards and "performance" standards. Interestingly, while the performance standards are highly elaborated, detailed, and specific, the content standards are startlingly brief and general. The content standards mention broad areas of study only in passing and are not schematically presented in relation to different age groups.

The significantly more detailed performance standards are calibrated to specific skills, subskills, and behaviors within varying age groups. Performance standards are presented in great detail for the fourth grade, eighth grade, and twelfth grade. Each set of "skills" and "subskills" (behaviors, really) are boldly introduced with the phrase "By the end of [fourth, eighth, or twelfth] grade, students will:".[14]

Many of these behavioral objectives which children must manifest by the specified age are not totally surprising, in that they do not deviate significantly from traditional (if problematic) notions of "what constitutes knowledge." For example, "by the end of grade four, students will . . . distinguish between fact and opinion and provide evidence to support opinions." However, other behavior objectives are quite striking both for their microscopic attention to (and surveillance of) behavioral minutiae, and for the specific *type* of behavior that they demand and incite. Many of the behaviors suggest a breathtakingly panoptic vision of mandated surveillance and self-surveillance of the child. Minutiae including students' fleeting facial expressions and gestures are to be measured and tested; even the internal affective state of the child is to be evaluated and normed.

For example, under the section "Participate effectively in discussion" we have, "By the end of grade four, students will . . . use effective eye contact and other nonverbal cues [and] reflect on the ideas and opinions of others and respond thoughtfully."[15] Here, the way the child is to be known is not limited to the content she or he might be called upon to recall on paper or orally; neither is she or he evaluated solely on the intellectual quality of her or his critical responses; rather the precise positioning of the child's body, and her or his affective relationship to others' opinions, is to be monitored and evaluated. The child must properly invest her or his response with the correct affective qualities; she or he must do so "thoughtfully," implying not only "analytic" thought, but also, we read, consideration of others' feelings in light of the affective nature of her or his response. Regarding questions of inclusion and exclusion, we must ask ourselves whose raced, gendered, and classed mannerisms are being normalized here, and who is being excluded from participation (and success).

By the end of eighth grade, we find students will "[Speak] from notes or an outline, relate an experience in descriptive detail, *with a sense of timing and decorum appropriate to the occasion*" (emphasis added).[16] This performance standard posits and reifies a monolithic notion of appropriate timing and decorum, thus inviting certain identities that conform to "the appropriate," while negating and excluding others. Furthermore, in this section, by the end of grade eight, students must "differentiate between formal and informal contexts and employ an appropriate style of speaking, adjusting language, gestures, rate, and volume according to audience and purpose."[17] The binary categories that the *Standards* mobilize here—formal/informal, appropriate/inappropriate—again produce inclusions and exclusions along sociocultural lines and set the boundary between those who may participate without sanction and those who may not.

As with the fourth-grade performance standards, the minute particularities of the internal affective state of the eighth grader are to be evaluated and normed, as students are required to "[o]bserve the appropriate etiquette when expressing thanks and receiving praise."[18] What the appropriate etiquette is for expressing thanks must be already universally agreed upon, for what this might be is not delineated in this otherwise extraordinarily precise document. Teachers and other evaluators will presumably know it when they see it.

These specific behavioral requirements are not anomalies within the document. Under the section entitled "Participate effectively in discussion," effectiveness is specified in the following manner: "Students will . . . participate in discussion by listening *attentively*, demonstrating *respect* for the opinions of others, and responding *responsibly* and *courteously* to the remarks of others" (emphasis added).[19] Furthermore, the ability to participate effectively in discussion is to be evidenced, as "students will . . . invite ideas and opinions of others into the discussion, responding *clearly* and *tactfully* to questions and comments" (emphasis added).[20] Various "workplace literacies" are amply present in these strings of adverbs, and the affective qualities to be (literally) embodied are to be monitored even more closely as the child matures.[21] For in eighth grade, the student must "Display and maintain [!!] facial expressions, body language, and other response cues that indicate respect for the speaker and attention to the discussion."[22] The amount and the particularity of teacher-policing and self-policing of the child's body and affective state is highly noteworthy here.

Finally, by eighth grade, students must participate in discussion "without dominating," must "establish and maintain an open mind while listening to others' ideas and opinions," and must "accept and use helpful criticism."[23] Again, the particular cultural models that are to serve as standards for each of these behaviors are unnamed and, thus, reified as universal, producing significant inclusions and exclusions as the effects of power.

The *Standards'* penetration of and construction of the twelfth graders' inner life is even more breathtaking. Besides needing to "observe the appropriate etiquette when expressing thanks and receiving praise," students must "demonstrate confidence and poise during presentations, interacting effectively with the audience, and selecting language and gestures mindful of their effect."[24] Poise and confidence are recast as mandated qualities of the maturing American citizen; not only must these qualities exist in the subject's soul, but they must be made manifest. Not only must they be demonstrated as internal static qualities, but they must also be maintained in "effective interaction" with an audience.

In addition to being required to "convey criticism in a respectful and supportive way," the very internal affective self-scrutiny of the twelfth graders is to be laid bare for evaluation, as these young adults are mandated by the *Standards* to "[b]e aware of and try to control *counterproductive emotional responses* to a speaker or ideas conveyed in a discussion" (emphasis added).[25]

If the ways in which these internal qualities of the soul manifest themselves are universal and obvious (as the *Standards* imply by not mentioning them), then one might wonder why they need to be mandated by performance standards at all. Clearly, there are certain populations that are anticipated as not (yet) manifesting these personal competencies. These policies, therefore, embody the idea of *parens patriae* for the targeted populations; that is, the *Standards* deploy the state as a surrogate parent.[26] As these discourses work upon and through children, they exclude and include along particular race, class, gender, and sociocultural lines, among others.

THE SHIFTING PRESCRIPTION OF NORMATIVE PARENTAL BEHAVIOR

However, the policies under examination do not operate in the spirit of *parens patriae* exclusive of the parent, leaving the parent untouched; rather, the scaffolded discourses of these policy documents also seek to "'rescue' the child through rescuing the parent."[27] For example, although the *Parent/*

Student Handbook of Rights, Responsibilities, and Discipline, echoing the *Standards,* works on and through the child, it also extends its formative discursive reach into the identity of the parent as "partner" in the child's subjective formation through education. Therefore, although "[c]hildren will have the opportunity in the school and in the neighborhood to become competent, responsible, and generous, and to belong to a caring community . . . we must have strong and true partnerships with parents and all those in the community who influence and affect our students and family."[28]

The *Handbook* is then quite directive in positioning the parent as an educational "partner": "Parents have the RESPONSIBILITY to . . . communicate to their children that they as parents, as well as the school district, have high academic expectations of them and that they believe in their ability to achieve high academic success" (emphasis in original).[29] Furthermore, "Parents have the RESPONSIBILITY to . . . provide an environment for home study and learning that will help to foster their children's best academic and behavioral performance in school" (emphasis in original).[30] The shifting discourses of the school as enshrined in this policy circulate into the very homes of the children, applying a normalizing gaze to the parent, forming the parent in his or her interactions with the child, and disqualifying or including the parent (and thus the child) based on his or her performance in the prescribed and mandated parenting behaviors.

In Wisconsin, it is worth noting that this incitement of the parent is not simply "rhetorical." It also makes its appearance in "model" devolutionary welfare policy, such as in Wisconsin's Learnfare legislation. As Clarke and Newman argue, "The shift of responsibilities to families has been accompanied by the subjection of households to greater state surveillance, regulation, and intervention."[31] Learnfare is a component of *Wisconsin Works (W-2),* the state-created welfare entity formed at the time that federal legislation under the Welfare Reform Act devolved most aspects of social welfare provision to the fifty states. Under Learnfare, parents who are placed in jobs funded through Wisconsin Works are fined if their school-age children are not enrolled in schools. Learnfare students meet regularly with "Case Managers," who, beyond monitoring enrollment and attendance, provide the following services: "assessment, career development and planning, problem solving and role play, non-traditional counseling, crisis counseling and intervention, supportive services, and referral to community services."[32]

This incitement of the parent continues in the devolutionary discussions of the *Milwaukee Public Schools Neighborhood Schools Plan.* Parents are worked upon and formed by the *Plan's* "primary objective," which is "to create community-rich schools where . . . [p]arents are afforded the greatest possible opportunity to become actively involved in every aspect of a child's education."[33] By "bringing the parent in,"[34] the parent who becomes actively involved in "every aspect" of a child's education is normalized, while those who will not or cannot are excluded, along with their

children. This ostensibly democratizing manifestation of devolution furthermore means that "[p]arents and children have increased opportunities to
make choices and influence the curricula offered at *their* neighborhood
school; communities and families work together to help children succeed"
(emphasis added).[35]

Within the scaffolded discourses of the *Handbook* and the *Plan,* we see
the specter of embattled school officials, attributing the exclusion (literally
through failure, in many examples) of so many students to parents who do
not manifest the same school-related dispositions as their middle-class and
suburban counterparts. Such prescriptions for parental behavior and invita-
tions to parent "partnership" are not commonly made explicit to parents of
the latter, more privileged, social locations. Instead, they surface as an eq-
uity-inspired gesture of inclusion, which nevertheless excludes the very populations it seeks to include by defining those populations outside the scope
of normalcy. The *Handbook* and the *Plan* attest to the notion that the normative parent does not reside within the documents' spatial and geographi-
cal purview. The parents who do reside there must either be reconstituted
(itself a form of exclusion) or be excluded outright.

Although both the *Handbook* and the *Plan* "bring in the parent" as an
educational "partner," they also construct the parent as a "consumer" within
an educational marketplace. As this educational consumer is fabricated, we
must keep in mind the effects of the mobilization around vouchers and educational marketization in the 1990 Milwaukee Parental Choice Program,
discussed earlier.

The discourse of educational marketization and "choice" lies at the cen-
ter of both Milwaukee Public Schools documents. Most of the Milwaukee
Public Schools' thirty-nine-word mission statement, as presented in the
Handbook, addresses itself to the consumer/parent: "Milwaukee Public
Schools will ensure that maximum educational opportunities are provided
for all students to reach their highest potential so that . . . parents choose
Milwaukee Public Schools to educate their children."[36] That such a tauto-
logical accounting of the district's position within an educational market
would dominate its mission statement is a testament to the depth of perme-
ation of market discourse into Milwaukee's educational milieu. Further
evidence of this is apparent in the fact that one of the "three goals" of
Milwaukee Public Schools is defined as improving "family satisfaction, *as
measured by their choices in the education marketplace*" (emphasis added).[37]

The construction of the parent as consumer in an educational marketplace
is even more pronounced in the *Neighborhood Schools Plan.* In the second
paragraph of its introduction, this document appeals to the parent/consumer
by "recognizing" that "choice is limited for many parents." Furthermore,
"The district will have achieved its aims only when each MPS neighborhood
school provides the kind of educational programs and services that will make
those schools as good a choice for parents as [other] schools."[38] The docu-

ment later continues, "The success of this five-year endeavor will be measured by the number of students who choose to attend their neighborhood [public] schools."[39] In managerialist fashion, success is thus measured by the number of customers the *Plan* generates.

The construction of the parent as consumer is again one that is riven with inclusions and exclusions. With the parent postulated as the "empowered" rational consumer competing equally and freely within an educational marketplace, those parents who are not able to, or choose not to, compete equally within the educational market are excluded in the same moment that they are ostensibly included by being so empowered. In effect, they are empowered to exclude themselves, to participate in their own exclusion.

A significant portion of this 122-page document is devoted to expanding "communications efforts." In a section entitled "Increasing Community Awareness and Support," the document states that "the goal of the neighborhood schools communications plan is to communicate to parents, prospective parents, and the community that there are excellent MPS schools within their neighborhoods providing the types of services, curriculum, and overall education they want and need for their children."[40] The *Plan* further envisions "a successful districtwide . . . and localized . . . communications effort . . . to best reach each individual neighborhood," and identifies its "primary, key audience" as "[p]otential MPS parents and [p]otential MPS [s]tudents."[41]

The specific "strategies and tactics" for reaching this audience include "billboard" and "bus board advertisements" in "key neighborhoods." Such advertisements are to be created by "working with a local designer" to develop a "brief and attention-getting slogan and graphics . . . to excite the community about the new MPS neighborhood options."[42] Proposed interventions in the document also include radio and television advertisements, a "school selection catalog," and "ongoing media efforts." This latter suggestion involves contacting media to "highlight stories regarding neighborhood schools recruitment [read: marketing] efforts, . . . new choices for local families, . . . and successes of neighborhood schools . . . . These contacts may consist of offering story ideas [and] coordinating media announcements."[43] Further centering the figure of the parent/consumer within the *Plan's* discourse is this section's conclusion: "The key to a successful Neighborhood Schools Plan is to attract neighborhood children to neighborhood schools."[44] That is, the success of the plan is to be gauged, first and foremost, not by anything to do with learning, but rather by the ability of the schools to attract parents/consumers.

CONCLUSIONS

It has been shown in this chapter how the shifting discourses of the child and parent are manifested in three key policy documents impacting the

Milwaukee Public Schools. These documents reflect new patterns and priorities in identity construction as a form of state governance. Borrowing from the theoretical constructs of Popkewitz and others, it has been shown how the three policy documents, in intersecting and overlapping ways, reconstruct the key subjects of the parent, child, and school nexus by disciplining the affective inner life of the child, by "bringing the parent in" as a "partner" to the child's education, and by constructing the interaction of the parent with the school as an economic exchange between a consumer and a producer within an educational marketplace.

Each of these deployments excludes the very subject population that it ostensibly "empowers" and includes, for the shifted normative categories of parent, child, and community contain within them their own exclusions, which operate most powerfully upon the marginalized populations that the reforms target.

— 11 —

Cooking the Books: Educational Apartheid with No Child Left Behind

Sheila L. Macrine

Education without opportunity is the "devil's gift"

—Noam Chomsky, 1999

On January 8, 2002, with great fanfare and bipartisan support, President George W. Bush signed the No Child Left Behind (NCLB) Act, saying it expressed his "deep belief in our public schools and their mission."

On the two-year anniversary of its enactment, NCLB education reforms continue to garner rock-solid support from a majority of Americans, according to a new national poll released by Americans for Better Education.[1] As the NCLB legislation trickles down to local school districts, its impact is likely to fundamentally alter the relationship between the federal government, the states, and America's 14,500 public school districts. This shift in the balance of power over education, from states and local school districts to big government, is the most significant in a generation. Looming behind the veneer and rhetoric of the Bush education plan is a set of destructive actions that are designed to destroy public education by enabling a huge exodus into risky experimental alternatives.[2] "No Child Left Behind" is much more than a label devised by clever promoters.

The Bush administration has endorsed a doctoring mechanism for misinterpreting standardized test numbers as well as high school dropout rates. Misrepresented as an educational reform effort, NCLB is actually a cynical effort to shift public school funding to a host of private schools, religious schools, and free-market diploma mills or corporate experiments in education.[3]

Probably the grossest example of this type of flagrant abuse of power in education is called the "Texas Miracle." In the academic year 1999–2001, there were no high school dropouts at Houston's Sharpstown High School. The miraculous "zero dropout rate" was said to be an impossible feat by the Houston superintendent, Rod Paige. The so-called "Miracle" also reported that only 1.5 percent of Houston's entire high school student population dropped out of high school that year. Rod Paige said that he accomplished this miracle by holding his principals and administrators directly responsible for students' test scores and student graduation rates. In his new plan, principals who met their goals were rewarded with cash bonuses upward of $5,000, as well as other incentives. Those who did not make the grade, however, were transferred, demoted, or forced out. This seemingly impossible accomplishment not only put Houston's education reform efforts on the map, it also buoyed the then Texas Governor Bush throughout his presidential campaign, eventually making him the "Education President." Accordingly, Rod Paige was named Secretary of Education when Bush became president.

One of the high schools in question, Houston's Sharpstown High School, is populated mostly by underprivileged Mexican immigrants who have historically been prime candidates for dropping out of high school. It also has, as with most inner-city high schools, a history of large dropout rates in the 25 percent to 50 percent range. How did this superintendent turn this large urban city school system around in a matter of a few years? Simply put, he did not.

History will undoubtedly refer to this period of educational reform as the "Texas Scandal"! Those low high school dropout rates for Houston's public high schools, the very ones that Mr. Bush, the "Education President" crowed about, were just not true, according to Robert Kimball, former assistant principal at Houston's Sharpstown High School. Kimball reports, "I had seen many, many students—several hundred a year—go out the door of this high school, and I knew that they were quitting. The students told me they were quitting."[4] The fact is that between 25 and 50 percent of the high school students dropped out or left school that year. Using fuzzy math and statistics—and some creative bookkeeping—some principals earned top accountability ratings for their schools. A recent state audit in Houston, which examined records from sixteen middle and high schools, found that more than half of the 5,500 students who left in the 2000–2001 school year should have been declared dropouts but were not. In some cases, they prevented some students from taking the all-important tenth-grade tests through retention in ninth grade; others did not count large numbers.

The latest statistics suggest that the reading scores have been consistently no better than the national average. Existing research consistently shows that nothing special has been happening in Texas. The Texas State (TAAS) exam results, which were used as the primary basis for exaggerated performance gains, have been criticized in the press and shown to be untrustworthy by two independent research papers published in peer-reviewed journals. Accountability at all costs is a very dear price to pay. "It is a model of inflated achievements through fuzzy math. It is Enron accounting," said Joseph Rodriguez, a former employee of the district's office of research and accountability.

This type of accountability was recently exposed on the CBS television news program *60 Minutes*. After viewing a *60 Minutes* segment, one woman commented that "When confronted with evidence of fraud, deceit and inappropriate bookkeeping, a member of Bush's cabinet (Secretary Rod Paige) has no explanation for something that occurred during his watch. As a veteran teacher of twenty-three years, I fear that my children's children will be the ones forced to deal not only with the ballooning deficit, but also with the damage to our public education system that will be the result of the No Child Left Behind Act and this administration's domestic policy."[5]

A resident of Houston wrote: "When kids drop out, they say they are getting the GED. Many of these children never attended or applied to the school, but the school system does not count them against their dropout rate."[6]

A retired Texas teacher from a small town with a good school district said,

> I am not surprised that Houston "doctored" dropout ratings." If you will check schools around the state, I believe that you will find teachers and administrators pressured into teaching the test in order to have better ratings, because they are expected by the public and school boards to produce a perfect product. Schools are not a business and should not be run as businesses. Every child is different and scores on tests will be different. Teachers should be given the opportunity to teach the child, not the test.[7]

High-stakes, standardized, shallow, discriminatory, meaningless, and underfunded testing cnot only ontinues to deny our children the tools necessary for critical thinking but also takes the much needed monies from public schools.

This corporate managerial model of controlling schools and principals is the very one that Paige has set forth for the rest of the nation. As Bush reported, Texas's education system leads the nation in school accountability. The lessons that should be learned from this is not just to be suspicious of the "tall tales" of Texans but that, more broadly, we should be cautious in drawing sweeping conclusions about large and complex educational endeavors, particularly when big government wants to tell teachers how and what to teach.

TROUBLING TIMES

It has been noted that the idea of No Child Left Behind is a noble one. However, the messages behind it, and its future legacy, will surely be that of abuse of power, fraudulent books, and fuzzy math with little concern left for the future of our children. The current state of educational reform can be traced back to the Elementary and Secondary Education Act of 1965 (ESEA), enacted to provided guidance and funds to K–12 schools. After the ESEA came the report called *A Nation at Risk* in 1983. Its authors argued that American public education was being watered down and that a typical high school graduate in 1982 was less capable of mastering information and technology than the typical graduate from earlier cohorts. Those claims suggested that:

1. The content of public school curricula was not challenging.
2. Expectations for students were set too low.
3. Students spent too little time in school and wasted much of their time while in school.
4. Teachers lacked ability and preparation.

In other words, the report supported a return to the "basics" and "skills and drills."

In order for the schools to get federal monies, they were told to gut their current program and to institute the No Child Left Behind skills and drills, teaching-to-the-test curriculum. On top of that, they had to be accountable. Everything that the principals and teachers did had to have demonstrated results. If not, they would be taken over by the federal government. There has never been a time in the history of education where the risk to individual teachers and principals has been so appallingly under the threat of big government's big stick.

Schools have been told that their "problem" was that they use unreliable and untested methods that can actually impede academic progress. The solution suggested by NCLB was that schools must now convert to use evidence-based or scientifically based practices and materials. Finally, the Parental Options part of the act was presented as a lifeline for parents, giving them information on how their child is achieving academically, as well as how their school and school district perform. This parent piece also allowed parents to shop around for other schools if they deemed that the published scores at their neighborhood schools were not up to par. This amounts to nothing more than testing and publishing results, or outing and punishing under-financed schools, with results in the local newspapers.

Under the new regulations, when measuring Adequate Yearly Progress (AYP), states, school districts, and schools will have to count the "proficient" scores of students with the most significant cognitive disabilities who take assessments based on alternate achievement standards. Under the NCLB legislation, there are serious sanctions to be administered if a school does not make adequate yearly progress. For three to four years following inappropriate progress by schools, in the eyes of the federal Department of Education, the state can take over and run the schools, fire the principal and most of the staff, turn the school over to private management, or make the school a public charter school. For instance, any school or district that receives Title I Part A funding and does not make the AYP target will face a series of interventions and sanctions. In the current versions, only test score gains count—no other factors can be used to take a school off the list. Thus, in a twist of irony, the school that pushes out low-scoring students or repeatedly retains them in their grade would be rewarded if scores went up.

These outrageous manipulations and attacks on the livelihoods of teachers and educators, so severe that they can lose their jobs if they do not get those test scores up, should be illegal. It is no wonder that corruption was rampant in the Houston schools. The unattainable promises that schools must make in order to receive needed monies—that by the year 2012, all children will come to school ready to learn and those in schools will be able to read—is tantamount to a Victorian encumbrance or servitude.

While we witness falsehoods in Houston, Gerald Coles[8] noted that there were also problems with the National Reading Panel. This panel was brought together by Rod Paige and Assistant Secretary of Education Susan Neuman, in an effort to tell the folks what the best reading practices were. The National Reading Panel began its work. It reported that it whittled down a vast database of literature (100,000 studies) to 104 studies considered relevant. The Reading Panel, as the designated arbiters of education, evaluated the work in these studies and concluded that phonics (a skills-oriented approach emphasizing awareness of sounds and the symbols that represent them) was the crucial technique for teaching children how to read. The conclusions were that the logistics of reading were to be emphasized, while the content of material, comprehension, and interpretation of ideas were considered to be of minimal importance. From this perspective, children learn best within a cultural and historical vacuum. Because of the panel's deliberations, phonics is now a very large part of the conservative agenda in the United States is to create a focused climate of ideas, techniques, and policy to reinforce certain reality constructions in the country.

Joanne Yatvin, former superintendent of the Cottrell School District in Boring, Oregon, and later an elementary school principal in the Oregon Trail School District, was the lone dissenter on the panel. She, along with fifteen other members, was called on to produce the seminal document on helping children to read. She was a member of the National Reading Panel authorized by the U.S. Congress and convened under the direction of the National Institute of Child Health and Human Development. She should be given great accolades for her courage to stand up to the group, which was under the political thumb of this administration to support the ideology behind the "back to basics" movement in NCLB. She deserves thanks from every teacher of reading throughout the country. She called the panel's work a deficient process and a contrived report. Yatvin recalls:

> I was very disappointed, as many of my colleagues were, with the product of this auspicious panel. It was as though they were afraid to make any recommendations that could help the teachers and students. Furthermore, they recapitulated all of the politically correct "back to basics" and "phonics approach" rhetoric while never recommending anything more than what one could find in any undergraduate textbook on reading. The Report's focus on beginning reading is a glaring disregard of the fourth-grade slump. Reading for Bush is a utilitarian process of gathering together pieces of information for later performance.[9]

The plan to implement NCLB is just too simple and very dangerous. It places unrealistic demands on the already challenged public schools. It provides too little capacity-building support and too little time to meet new demands. It labels teachers, principals, and schools as failures. It permits the wholesale transfer of corporate models of management and corporate takeovers. It further mandates transfer of the much-needed public funding to charter schools and alternatives, such as private corporation education management companies like Whittle's Edison Schools. It promotes funded education of many previously private schoolchildren with public monies. It is all about "corporatization" and "privatization."[10]

Although it is understandable that some child advocates and school reformers, who in the past have been frustrated with the quality of education for poor students, viewed NCLB as a potential tool to force schools to improve, there are fundamental problems with the law besides underfunding small class sizes, inappropriate testing, and unrealistic school improvement goals.[11] The others are the provisos on improving "teacher quality" and on promoting "scientific" approaches to reading that also deserve attention.[12]

THE NEW MANAGERIALISM

NCLB represents the McDonaldization of our schools, wherein education is served up like food in a fast-food restaurant. George Ritzer suggests that, in the later part of the twentieth century, the socially structured form of the fast-food restaurant has become the organizational force representing and extending the process of rationalization further into the realm of everyday interaction and individual identity.[13] McDonald's serves as the case model of this process . . . McDonaldization . . . is the process by which the principles of the fast-food restaurant are coming to dominate more and more sectors of American society as well as of the rest of the world.[14]

No previous action by the federal government has posed a graver threat to schools, children, teachers, and even librarians than the current ESEA law and its regulations. Given NCLB's radical experimentation and risky, unproven change strategies, McKenzie suggests that it should instead be named "Helter-Skelter." It promotes narrowing curriculum and scripted lessons in order to drive up test scores and avoid the dire consequences of failing at NCLB. It is also marked by the change in the direction of education from efforts toward sound education to a factory-style education that is narrow, undemocratic, and essentially unhealthy for children. This new direction underscores the principles of the fast-food restaurant, where everything is homogenized and packaged.

Under NCLB, we will revert backward to where, as Giroux elegantly posits, teachers in this country are mainly trained to be technicians about their subjects rather than intellectuals.[15] In other words, most teachers—particularly under the NCLB curricula—will be so focused on the scripted content they teach that they will have little time to spend on academic disciplines and the larger world in which they teach. They see teaching as a tool for helping students get better standardized scores and not as a tool for improving the world.

Giroux argues that the role of teachers and administrators is to become "transformative intellectuals who develop counter-hegemonic pedagogies that not only empower students by giving them the knowledge and social skills they will need to be able to function in the larger society as critical agents, but also educate them for transformative action. That means educating them to take risks, to struggle for institutional change, and to fight both 'against' oppression and 'for' democracy outside of schools in other oppositional public spheres and the wider social arena."[16]

Thus, Giroux[17] situates teaching within a true democratic process, whereby the classroom is one of the few public institutions in which an exchange of ideas and utopian visions can take place. However, for this to happen, teachers cannot have their voices silenced, their pedagogy gutted, and their decision-making power thwarted. This type of nonteaching is referred to as a process of deintellectualizing and deskilling of teachers.

Schools and children will suffer from restricted funding even as President Bush tries to divert federal education funds to pay for privatization schemes and charter schools. Funding for education already faces a crisis at the state level as revenues have declined disastrously during the Bush economy. Even as demands for accountability soar, the resources to sustain real change will become constricted.

Giroux explains that teaching has become "apolitical . . . stripped of its . . . ethical imperative to analyze and remediate existing societal and institutional practices" and of its mission to promote "self-empowerment and social transformation." There has been a "devaluing and deskilling of teachers," as they have been "reduced to . . . 'clerks of the empire'" by "the present rush toward accountability schemes, corporate management pedagogies, and state-mandated curricula."[18] Schools "favor the interests of the dominant culture," as "the dominant curriculum separates knowledge from the issue of power," and "the hidden curriculum" favors boys over girls and whites over people of color.

OBSCURE PROVISION

Pick any part of the NCLB document and it reads like a military manual. Interestingly enough, there is a little-known provision of the NCLB Act that is beginning to stir up some controversy. David Goodman[19] writes that his local high school sent the names and phone numbers for all juniors and seniors to U.S. military recruiters. This is more than a back-door assault on student privacy. It may have life-or-death consequences for unwitting kids who are contacted by recruiters.

This student information giveaway was mandated in a little-known provision of NCLB. Although the law went into effect in 2002, many schools only became aware of the obscure military recruiting provision in the last year. Schools risk losing all federal aid if they fail to provide military recruiters full access to their students; the aid is contingent on complying with federal law.[20] This recruiting access provision is different from draft registration. Military conscription ended in 1973, but starting in 1980, eighteen-year-old males have been required to register for possible military call-up.

So, what does military recruiting have to do with education? Nothing. Nevertheless, it has everything to do with eliminating a community's ability to decide how it guards student privacy.

The military recruiting requirement has forced many schools to overturn longstanding policies on protecting student records from prying eyes. Most local high schools carefully guard student directories from the countless businesses and special-interest groups that are itching to tempt impressionable teens.

The No Child Left Behind Act is better suited to be called the No Child Left Untested, Undocumented, Unregimented, Unregulated, Untracked, Unmonitored, Unidentified from Preschool on Upward Act, thereafter leaving the students unqualified, uneducated, unintellectualized, unskilled, unemployed, and unequal.

SCIENTIFIC APARTHEID–DUAL EDUCATIONAL SYSTEM

With its narrow focus on math and reading scores, NCLB threatens to choke off balanced educational programs, especially for our least advantaged students. In the name of "saving" them, NCLB will actually starve them. NCLB condemns them to permanent status in the underclass. It also worsens an already desperate funding crisis for library programs. The school libraries and library programs of urban and disadvantaged children have long endured poor funding in contrast with their suburban peers.

Tragically, NCLB promises that the federal government will label schools as failures; underachieving schools are immediately "punished"; parental choice and supplemental services are "consequences" for underachieving schools; and local control of schools is "reduced." The president's FY2003 education budget provides "less funding than promised" for the No Child Left Behind Act and "ties the hands of teachers," making it even harder for them to do their jobs.

Presently, the promise of education in urban and poor rural schools is a myth. It is a "dirty little secret." That "dirty secret" is the "dual educational system" that exists in this country. It is a school system that promotes apartheid in education and denies educational opportunities. It is a dualistic system that no longer promises a way out but promises a life of poverty. In order to fix that dirty little secret, the Bush administration offered the answer: accountability with full-on management attack. That accountability is managed by financial controls in a quid pro quo manner; do it my way or the highway. The call for scientifically based curriculum, or "scientific" anything, smacks of doublespeak for genetics-based racism, standardized racism, segregation, and apartheid. Yes, we do have a problem in schools, but only in certain schools. The type of skills and drills curriculum that is promoted in the new legislation is devoid of humanity and is completely mechanistic. This is not a curriculum developed to create thinkers and learners. This curriculum is set forth to feed the unskilled labor forces and perpetuate the McDonaldization of the poor with yet another politically driven effort to appease the manufactured outrage over alleged unsuccessful schools.[21]

The shock is that we have become a nation of deskilled teachers teaching deintellectualized curricula in new managerial type schools that institutionalize poverty. The urban curriculum is a bunch of mindless skills and drills that adds little to creativity, to thinking, and, ultimately, to learning. Two school systems and the lower track level of education is the best we can offer urban schools. Sure, Kozol warned us about ignoring it.[22] Yet little has been done, and nothing has really changed. No one wants to bear the blame. None of us wants to think that in America—the glorious incubator of democracy—we are endorsing hidden messages. On one hand, the message is "It is essential to acquire an education in order to attain upward mobility in the modern economy." On the other, democracy and opportunity for the nation's poor women and children is a farce.

Lately, schools are abuzz with talk of the new legislation that will transform American public education. Regrettably, for the principals, the schools, the teachers and the students, this smokescreen is just going to set educational reform back twenty years. Based on false data and promises, schools are already trying to convert to the new managerialism system that comes with this obsession of accountability. It has only been four months since New York City adopted its new citywide reading curriculum, yet New York plans to abandon it in forty-nine troubled elementary schools so it can win $34 million in federal aid that is available only if the city uses a more structured program approved by New York State and the federal Department of Education.[23]

According to the current Chancellor Klein,[24] the city's choice of reading curriculum, a balanced approach, was far superior to the more rigid phonics-only programs endorsed by the Bush administration. He went on to say that, in spite of this, the federal Department of Education insists that schools must use the more traditional skills and drills to assure better standardized-testing scores. He added that recent national testing data showed that New York and San Diego—sites that used a balanced-literacy approach—were making better progress than cities using Washington's so-called "scientifically proven" programs. Actually, the Balanced Literacy Approach is more realistic and develops skills and strategies in authentic texts. It is more in keeping with how children really learn. Nevertheless, the threat of losing $34 million as Chancellor Klein hopes get in federal reading program funding is hard to refuse in his cash-strapped schools. Some school systems are not applying for the Reading First money. Apparently, Boston Public Schools' applications for funding were rejected by the federal Department of Education because Boston refused to completely abandon its balanced reading program. They felt that they would have had to make such major changes to accommodate the Reading First monies that they would have to toss out everything that they had been building. On top of that, if the schools continue to show low scores for consecutive years, they will be put on notice, which may jeopardize all of their funding.

In an October letter to state chief school officers, Paige complained that state plans to "ratchet down their standards in order to remove schools from their lists of low performers" were "nothing less than shameful."[25] Some states proposed complicated statistical techniques for gauging school progress; others back-loaded their predicted progress, with far greater gains toward the end of the twelve-year timeline. Most states noted in a January report by the Education Commission of the States that they had a long way to go. In addition, by the spring of 2003, despite Paige's warning, many states were trying to rework their standards to downgrade their definition of proficiency. Challenging the reasons that NCLB, as currently written, will be unable to fulfill its lofty promises is a key to building a coalition that can force Congress to make changes in the law.

Even Rod Paige was quoted on October 1, 2003, as saying, "There's a two-tiered education system in this country." Mr. Paige told an audience at the National Press Club in Washington on September 24, "For the lucky, their education is the best in the world. However, for others, there is an underperforming system. Students come to school, but they find little education. Effectively," Mr. Paige said, "the educational circumstances for these students are not at all unlike a system of apartheid."[26] This is very curious, because the very system of education that he is promoting acts as a tool of apartheid.

An article in a local New York newspaper begins with a parent lamenting the fact that his child cannot go to the public schools:

> We saw sorrow: dark, run-down buildings; outdated textbooks; overcrowded classrooms; kids being taught in hallways; the inexorable erosion of arts curricula. We came away with an overwhelming sense that everything important to us was disappearing. So after a lot of agonizing, we found a private school that bore an uncanny resemblance to the public schools we'd grown up in, full of light and, equally important, joy. So, we started writing checks. The private schools describe their curriculum as one that inspires a passion for learning through a progressive approach to education. It is one that values intellectual pursuit through creative expression, self-discovery and community involvement.[27]

The parent went on to say that "the school our son and daughter attend now is a bastion—no, a fortress—of privilege, and yes, the wealth factor is daunting. But the most important privilege is learning, with ceaseless encouragement, and the dividends go beyond a faculty devoted to pressing our kids to do their best, not merely adequate, work."

Unfortunately, the underlying messages taken from all these efforts go back to the dirty secret; we do have educational apartheid, and we have paid dearly for all these educational experiments to track kids in low-achieving tracks. Why waste money on kids who do not learn, why waste money on teachers who do not teach, why waste money on administrators who do not carry big sticks? A brutal awareness is emerging, one that scholars such as Henry Giroux, Peter McLaren, Jonathan Kozol, Maxine Greene, Donaldo Macedo, Ken Saltman, and others predicted: we are under siege and our educational system is under attack.

PUBLIC EDUCATION DOES NOT SERVE A PUBLIC—IT CREATES A PUBLIC

Legislation mandating authoritarian and harmful prepackaged reading instruction only serves big corporate interests, textbook companies, testing agencies, and neoliberal political agendas. Neoliberal policies increase inequalities, and the marketization of education has perverted the goals, motivations, methods, standards of excellence, and standards of freedom in education. Neoliberalism is a global phenomenon. Restructuring of schooling and education has taken place internationally under pressure from international capitalist organizations and compliant governments. These dangerous intrusions are being masked in legislative mandates for "evidence-based or scientific" accountability.

With all the talk about the success of the reforms in Texas as well as "scientifically based" reading research, what the politicos and some of the educational reformers have concealed is that these "findings" are scandalously flawed!

"Scientifically based reading instruction" appears nearly fifty times in the legislation and refers to instruction that proceeds stepwise from smaller to larger units of written language: from phonemic sounds (smallest unit of speech sounds) to letter-sound relationships (i.e., phonics) to word identification to reading fluency and eventually to meaningful comprehension. Instruction is direct, explicit, and systematic, conveniently packaged in reading programs that include textbooks and an array of instructional materials, and manufactured by big publishing companies. Teachers, serving as middle managers and adhering to the preplanned lesson sequence in a teacher's manual, lead their students lesson after lesson, skill after skill, day after day. Testing that is heavily skills-based is an ever-present goal and shaper of this instruction.[28]

This attempt to justify federal mandates of curriculum under the guise of science institutionalizes racism. In other words, the curriculum of the urban and poor schools systems is going to be the kind that no good school system would ever adopt without undo pressure. The dual system that Paige referred to is true, but NCLB is part of the problem. It falls short on all fronts while the education legislation and politicians camouflage themselves in cunning apolitical-research-as-final-arbiter stratagem and the National Institute of Child Health and Human Development have fortified these attacks.[29] The phrase "science tells us" makes doctrine based on biased beliefs appear to be objective, independent findings based on impartial pursuits.

Adding to these calls for more and more accountability; we have been met with distortions from the findings of the federally funded National Reading Panel Report. This is a panel of top reading experts who were called together to help direct teachers in best practices. This panel also undergirded the new federal initiatives. There are other federal mandates, past and current, that have also impeded improving reading instruction—and worse, the public education system—through privatization, teacher disempowerment, and a mechanistic and systemic business model.

Many of my colleagues who teach in basic education, both elementary and high schools, have been waging their own little wars, as they try to oppose the legislation mandating the resultant curriculum that comes with these mandates, which are authoritarian and detrimental prepackaged reading instruction. Coles writes, "These teachers are like many who have been learning about the so-called scientific research used to justify restrictive mandates, such as those contained in the educational legislation of George W. Bush. They read books and articles on sound teaching. They share information with colleagues. They support one another. They speak out individually and in groups against these mandates. Most of them continue to insist upon using sound teaching in their classrooms."[30] Unfortunately, this is in direct opposition to the principals in the urban schools who have their own mandates to raise the standardized reading and math scores. I am not so convinced that the monetary rewards are what are motivating the principals. I think their very jobs are on the line.

Teachers should reject this form of oppression, but they need their jobs. I want the teachers to know that there are others who share their horror. In fact, most teachers are taught explicitly not to teach explicit facts; this harms the kids who do not have their basic facts the most. Discovery, integrated and complex, is the opposite of isolated and explicit teaching. Yet, who is there to support these poor teachers who have been bombarded with paradigm wars and now by politicians who are dictating to them whom to teach and what to teach using scripted basal systems? No one. In times like these, each one of us must stand up and bear witness to the lies. Coles suggests that sometimes it means going against the grain, feigning to teach the anemic, scripted lessons but actually providing students rich literacy learning behind the closed classroom door. Moreover, he adds, it sometimes means yielding to the mandated instruction; adding as much sound teaching as possible within compulsory constraints; enduring until the failures of the mandated pedagogy become evident; hoping and working to make sound teaching prevail." Alfie Kohn astutely claims that "Our children are tested to an extent that is unprecedented in our history and unparalleled anywhere else in the world. The result is that most of today's discourse about education has been reduced to a crude series of monosyllables: 'Test scores are too low. Make them go up.'"[31]

Across the nation, legislators and policymakers are dictating the course of literacy education—all in the name of "indisputable scientific evidence." Unchallenged, this research has influenced just about every area of education and reading instruction. This is what Maxine Greene refers to as "gobbly-gook curriculum." Children educated and socialized to develop a sanitized, contentless cognitive style for acquiring new information (such as reading instruction that is focused only on phonics) can more easily be guided toward desired attitudes, values, and behaviors. Complicit institutions (education, as well as mass media and religious groups) will have plenty of incentive, patriotic and monetary, to participate in policies sponsored by the government, legitimating the practice for the majority of people.

Recently, one Pennsylvania school district became the first district in the nation to sue the state education department over No Child Left Behind requirements.[32] The Reading School District's goal in suing the Pennsylvania Department of Education over the federal education law is to protect its schools from what the district believes are unfair sanctions. This one act of courage may have wider implications because it is believed to be the first such action by a local district.

Schools are not seen as sites of struggle over different orders of representation, or as sites that embody particular configurations of power that shape and structure activities of classroom life. On the contrary, schools become reduced to the sterile logic of flowcharts, a growing separation between teachers and administrators, and an increasing tendency toward bureaucratization. The overriding message here is that the logic of technocratic rationality serves to remove teachers from participating in a critical way in the production and evaluation of school curricula.[33]

CONCLUSIONS

It has been noted everywhere that the idea of No Child Left Behind is a noble one. However, the messages behind it and its future legacy will be that of cooking books, fuzzy math, and abuse of power with little concern left for the children. Hidden behind this NCLB program lurks an agenda to shut down public schools and send their clients into the brave new world of corporate schooling, even though there is no convincing evidence that these free-market alternatives will reverse the long-established patterns of poor school performance.[34] We have watched a handful of corporate pioneers try but fail to impress with industrial schools for more than a decade. After two more years of NCLB, parents, teachers, and communities will rise up and demand an end to the interference, the false promises, the gimmickry, and the rash experimentation.

Levidow argues eloquently in his comments that "It is inadequate simply to oppose marketization or to counterpose whatever existed beforehand. Resistance would be strengthened by developing alternative pedagogies, which enhance critical citizenship, e.g., debate over the collective problem-definitions of society."[35] If we advocate educational methods and content along those lines, then we can link "academic freedom with responsibility to public debate over potential and desirable futures."[36] We need to stand up and challenge this gangsterized way in which educational policymaking has over taken education and our teachers, students, and administrators. Each of us must choose our starting point when challenging existing practices of segregated education. We seek to highlight the deep injustice and the damage we have witnessed to individuals, schools, and communities by the perpetuation of "special services." We believe there are no neutral bystanders; we must make no apologies for attempting to end the segregated world of a special educational system.

Even as a war rages in Iraq, another war is being waged against the children, the teachers, and the public schools by politicos who are so intent on pushing their phonics agenda that they will indulge in half-truths, dismiss the findings of well-respected researchers, and try to impose narrow-minded thinking and definitions on the rest of us.[37] These ideologies have stripped teachers of their decision-making role, marketized students as consumers, and comodified the curriculum. Administrators are coerced into being more concerned with standardized test performances and outcomes than with students as thinkers. Neoliberal education is an act of violence against people. If we allow ourselves to passively accept the conditions imposed on us, our schools, and our children by No Child Left Behind and the decisions of the National Reading Panel, the corporate takeover of schools predicted by Gabbard in his introduction to this book is eminent. NCLB promises opportunity but denies access to an educational system that can provide opportunity. These ideologies regulate, control, dominate, and ultimately oppress and silence students, teachers, and schools. I conclude that only with a counternarrative to contrast the emergence and hegemony of governmentality and federally funded mentalities of education can we fight this type of educational and societal oppression. Those mentalities are violent, frightening, and present grave consequences for democracy and education.

— 12 —

The Securitized Student: Meeting the Demands of Neoliberalism

Kenneth J. Saltman

The language of security now dominates the manner in which Americans learn to think about some of the most vital issues of their public and private lives. Speaking before the largest conference ever held on the issue of childhood obesity, Surgeon General Dr. Richard Carmona described obesity among children as a threat to our national security. In January 2003, *The New York Times* cast the U.S. Supreme Court case over affirmative action at the University of Michigan as a matter of national security. I want to focus here not only on the increasing prominence of the language of security as it appears to influence educational policy and school culture, but also on how this language has facilitated a shift in how the neoliberal agenda is being justified by its proponents.

As the dominant ideology of the present moment, neoliberalism exerts the greatest ideological and material influence over schooling at every level. Broadly, proponents of neoliberal ideology celebrate market solutions to all individual and social problems, advocate privatization of goods and services and liberalization of trade, and call for dismantling regulatory and social service dimensions of the state, which only interfere with the natural tendency of the market to benefit everybody. In the purview of neoliberal ideology, such public institutions as public schools, public utilities, public healthcare programs, and social security should be subject to privatization. As Chomsky points out, despite the rhetoric of free trade, advocates of

A version of this chapter appeared in the journal *Workplace* 5.2 July 2003.

neoliberal ideology seldom want to dismantle those aspects of state bureau-cracy responsible for public subsidies of private industries, such as agricul-ture or military, nor do they want to subject artificially supported industries to genuine competition.[1]

The central aspects of neoliberalism in U.S. education involve three in-tertwined phenomena:

1. Structural transformations in terms of funding and resource allocations: the privatization of public schools, including voucher schemes, for-profit charter schools, school commercialism initiatives.
2. The framing of educational policy reform debates and public discourse about education in market terms rather than public terms: the nearly total shift to busi-ness language of "choice," "monopoly," "competition," "accountability," "ef-ficiency," "delivery," and so on. The intensified corporate control over mean-ing-making technologies generally has played a large part in reshaping the public discourse about education.
3. The ideology of corporate culture in schools. This is characterized by the tech-nology fetish, the emphasis on accountability-based methodological reforms, such as testing, and the standardization of curriculum.

The framing of 9/11 enabled not only a more open admission of violent power politics and defiant U.S. unilateralism, but also an intensified fram-ing of democracy as consumer capitalism. Who can forget the September 12 government and corporate calls for the public to demonstrate their patrio-tism by going shopping? The neoliberal dictate to understand citizenship as consumerism could not have been clearer. But what should not be missed in the invocation to embrace the market as a form of social recovery following 9/11 is an intensified articulation of the market as an issue of national se-curity defined openly through patriotism. This is different from Clinton's Secretary of Defense Richard Cohen justifying the bombing of Iraq for the benefits to consumers at the gas pump. In that case, the equating of democ-racy as consumerism was clear, but it was not really linked to the discourse of national security.

Because our political language has been so heavily corrupted, it needs to be explained that neoliberalism does not separate our two dominant politi-cal parties. The Democrats and Republicans differ only in the matter of how to impose neoliberal economic policies. On this matter, we have witnessed a significant shift since the Bush administration came to power. The old neoliberalism of Clinton was tied more closely to economic triumphalism during a period in the 1990s that saw great economic growth though the vast majority of that wealth was distributed to the top of the economy. Within economic growth, the failures of the market to provide universally were framed as the failings of individuals—the working class, the poor, and crimi-nals. For example, television in the 1990s did important ideological work in such police reality shows as *Cops*, *America's Most Wanted*, and *America's Wildest Police Videos* by making working-class and poor citizens appear as criminals and portraying this alleged criminality as the social problem itself. The economics, politics, and history informing the experiences and choices made by those citizens tackled by police officers was absent from the narrative. A metaphor for the disappearing public under neoliberalism, these shows produced a viewing community that was rewarded morally for not being the focus of the indicting camera lens. The same period saw the drastic rise in imprisonment of roughly two million Americans, a disproportionate number of them nonwhite.

The new neoliberalism under George W. Bush makes economic failure a racialized policing problem in a different and possibly expanded way—a problem with national and international security. Within the intensified articulation of economic growth and consumerism as issues of patriotism and national security following 9/11, the economic recession could be blamed on Osama Bin Laden. Under the neoliberal model of Reagan through Clinton, only the domestic poor themselves could assume the blame for any failure of the market to provide nationwide prosperity. The new neoliberalism is defined, as before, by the American poor within the nation, with their criminal economic dependency and moral failure to consume at proper levels. But now, as well, the new neoliberalism is defined by the foreign poor, both inside and outside the nation, with their failure to successfully embrace the market. The ideological effectiveness of the strategy involves making the failure of markets no longer strictly the enemy within, that is, the American, but rather making the failures of the market the enemy outside, the foreign poor—the Muslim poor in particular. In old neoliberalism, the domestic criminal figure causes the damage to the economy. In the new neoliberalism, the criminal state or criminal extra-state actor (the terrorist) does. In both cases, the virtue of the market is upheld and the framing justifies the continued use of the state for expansion of its repressive and punitive functions simultaneous with the dismantling of its supportive functions (e.g., Aid to Dependent Families, attempts to cut or privatize social security, Medicaid). The old neoliberalism may have been riding on market triumphalism but, as now, it stigmatized the poor as morally failing for needing or wanting state support. The argument is not that the neoliberal discourse of discipline is no longer relevant in the domestic context. In fact, it could not be more relevant, as school reform is organized around disciplinary language and the logic of accountability[2] with the discipline-based knowledge policies of standardized curriculum and high-stakes testing being imposed along with the prisonization or militarization of the space of the school itself in the form of zero tolerance policies, metal detectors, surveillance systems, and police presence. Rather, I am pointing to the ways that the coercive goals of U.S. foreign policy to actually discipline populations converge with the representation of market failings as disciplinary problems posed by foreign nations and populations and how this disciplinary logic pervades educational reform as well.

In what follows, I show how the discourse of security is being used to unite educational policy reform with other U.S. foreign and domestic policies that foster repression and the amassing of corporate wealth and power at the expense of democracy. I also describe how the language of security frames students as securities themselves (i.e., commodities and investment opportunities) and how this same language increasingly subjects students to overzealous security measures, such as zero tolerance policies, surveillance, searches, and police presence. At the same time, ironically, neoliberal economic policies render students less secure by gutting the caregiving and social support role of the public sphere. My discussion also includes an examination of how the language of security increasingly defines students in terms of their future capacities to serve the nation's military as it undertakes a more overt imperial mission. I conclude by discussing the rise of student resistance that links the challenge to educational policy to the challenge to U.S. foreign and domestic policy.

In 2000, the U.S. Commission on National Security, also known as the Hart-Rudman Commission, affirmed the national security role of public schooling openly declared in 1983 by *A Nation at Risk*: "If an unfriendly foreign power had attempted to impose on America the mediocre educational performance that exists today, we might well have viewed it as an act of war." Education has been defined through the discourse of national security from the Cold War to the rise of neoliberalism with the end of the Cold War to the Hart-Rudman U.S. Commission on National Security in 2000 to the No Child Left Behind legislation and the State Department's antiterrorism pedagogy following 9/11. The defining of public schooling through national security has consistently been a matter of subjugating the democratic possibilities of public education to the material and cultural interests of an economic elite. Hart-Rudman made this quite explicit, calling for increased attention to the role of education for national security by suggesting an increased role of the private sector and making explicit that although labor and environmental concerns should be considered, they should not be allowed to block or reverse free-trade policy. However, the ways that public schooling has been defined through national security has changed markedly, in particular with regard to the rising culture of militarism, in which the newest incarnation participates. Current attempts to redefine public schooling as a security matter participate in the broader attack on public space and public participation as corporate media propagates an individualizing culture of fear. The importance of highlighting these changes involves both challenging the idea that new militaristic school reform initiatives are merely a response to 9/11 and, more important, providing the groundwork to challenge the ways that education for national security undermines the democratic possibilities of public schooling and the public sector more broadly.

MAKING KIDS INTO SECURITIES, MAKING KIDS INSECURE

The neoliberal ideal of making an enterprise of oneself is tied to dismantling the security of state provisions for kids. Put another way, the entrepreneurial-self championed by neoliberal ideology supports and is supported by the undermining of social—that is, collective—security by shifting security to the individual. Educational reforms of the late 1990s and early 2000s share the same goals as that of Welfare to Workfare. The rise of homelessness resulting from the dismantling of welfare has fallen hardest on children. The average age of a homeless person in America is nine years old. The undermining of social forms of security takes shape in the attempts to privatize the social security program, the continued privatization of public schools, the discursive framing in corporate media of the public good as the private accumulation of profit and the health of the stock market. In what Zygmunt Bauman refers to as the "individualized society,"[3] politics is rendered at best a privatized affair and at worst, impossible. Moreover, as Bauman points out, neoliberalism results in the privatization of the means of collective security.

Bauman suggests that corporate globalization (the global neoliberal agenda) with its unchecked liberalization of trade, privatization of public services, "flexible" labor, and capital in constant flight renders individuals in a state of constant insecurity about the future.[4] For Bauman, the possibility of the kind of political struggle that could expand democratic public values and would provide the necessary solidarity that forms the preconditions of social security has been imperiled by such a thorough commodification of social life that even thinking about the public, let alone working to strengthen it, has become difficult. Mass-mediated representations found in such varied locations as on nightly news and marginal sports translate economic insecurity into privatized concerns with public safety, such as street crime, school dangers, viruses, and, of course, terrorism. As well, mass media channels this anxiety into private preoccupations with controlling and ordering the body, its fitness, its appearance, its fluids, its pressure, its caloric intake. Both the material and representational assault on the public sphere produce anxiety, insecurity, and uncertainty about a future filled with flexible labor, capital flight, and political cynicism. The dismantling of social safety nets and other public infrastructure (such as social security, public schools and universities, welfare, public transportation, social services, health care, public legal defense, public parks, and public support for the arts) intensifies and accelerates this insecurity. The widespread insecurity resulting from the dismantling of the public sector undermines the kind of collective action that could address the very causes of insecurity. As Bauman insightfully writes,

> The need for global action tends to disappear from public view, and the persisting anxiety, which the free-floating global powers give rise to in ever growing quantity and in more vicious varieties, does not spell its re-entry into the public agenda. Once that anxiety has been diverted into the demand to lock the doors and shut the windows, to install a computer checking system at the border posts, electronic surveillance in prisons, vigilante patrols in the streets and burglar alarms in the homes, the chances of getting to the roots of insecurity and control the forces that feed it are all but evaporating. Attention focused on the "defense of community" makes the global flow of power freer than ever before. The less constrained that flow is, the deeper becomes the feeling of insecurity. The more overwhelming is the sense of insecurity, the more intense grows the "parochial spirit." The more obsessive becomes the defense of community prompted by that spirit, the freer is the flow of global powers.[5]

What Bauman identifies as a snowball effect of privatizing and individualizing logic that further undermines collective political action to alleviate the sources of insecurity is exemplified by such incidents as (1) the rise of domestic militarization in schools post-Columbine, (2) Sun Trust Equities publishing a report to investors with a title "At-Risk Youth—A Growth Industry," (3) the U.S. Surgeon General declaring that obesity in schoolchildren is a threat to national security because kids will be unfit to later become soldiers, (4) a company called My Rich Uncle that offers investors an opportunity to speculate on the future earnings of students by lending them money for university and then later collecting a percentage of their income, (5) the provision in No Child Left Behind that requires student information to be used for military recruitment purposes. In what follows, some of these events are used to elaborate on the different political uses of the discourse of security on students and in schools.

SECURITY I: THE POLITICAL USE OF SECURITY APPARATUS ON YOUTH

The individual student in U.S. public schools is increasingly being subject to an intensified security apparatus. In this first sense of the term, security refers to coercive measures that are justified on the grounds of protecting youth. These measures—such as zero tolerance policies, surveillance, uniforms, and police presence—redefine youth as simultaneously culpable for social problems while undermining the possibilities of youth agency. Such school reforms participate in the broader move to legislate and publicize youth as the cause of social problems through, for example, trying children as adults in criminal court and blaming kids for crime, poverty, sexual promiscuity, unwed pregnancy, and consumerism. At the same time, youth are discouraged from acting as political agents through institutional and discursive regulation that takes the form of infantalizing youth in mass media and school curricula—that is, they are discouraged from (1) understanding how their actions participate in larger social, political, cultural, and economic formations that have a bearing on their own lives and the lives of others, and (2) they are discouraged from having a sense of the possibility of acting on such knowledge to transform those conditions.

An important dimension to this aspect of security is the way that it links into the racialized discourse of discipline. Prior to Columbine, a politics of containment was largely reserved for predominantly nonwhite urban public schools while mostly white suburban schools have been viewed as worthy of investment in educational resources. Treated as containment centers, urban public schools in the United States do not receive the kinds of resources that suburban schools receive. They do receive, however, strict disciplinary measures for low performance after having been deprived of resources, such as books, adequate numbers of teachers and administrators, and physical sites. Such punitive measures include remedial teacher training in which teachers are forced to follow strict guidelines for curriculum content and instructional method. And of course U.S. public schools are subjected not only to scripted lessons but also to the growing calls for such discipline-oriented accountability schemes as high-stakes testing, remediation, and probation for schools and teachers who do not meet the scores, standardized curriculum, and so on. These discipline-oriented reforms and this discipline-based language, which are widely promoted across the political spectrum, shift the focus and blame for a radically unjust system of allocation onto students, teachers, and administrators who appear to lack the necessary discipline for success. They shift the focus and blame away from the conditions that produce a highly unequal system of public education. When market enthusiasts refer to the "failure" of the public schools, they are talking about urban, largely nonwhite public schools that are deprived of adequate resources and located in neighborhoods that have been subject to capital flight and systematic disinvestment and not about the suburban, largely white, professional class schools that are glaring successes with massive resources, small class sizes, and communities that have employment and infrastructure. Just as the highly racialized broader public discourse of discipline functions politically and pedagogically to explain social failings as racial and ethnic group pathologies that have infected individuals with sloth, mass media and educational reformers extend the discourse of discipline to explain away unequal allocations of resources to schools as the individual behavioral failings of students, teachers, and administrators. Moreover, the discourse of discipline shuts down any kind of discussion of whose knowledge and culture is taught in schools and valued in society.

SECURITY II: AT-RISK YOUTH—A GROWTH INDUSTRY

Students are not only being subjected to disciplinary security, they are also being transformed into securities. This sense of security refers to the ways that students are being viewed as investment opportunities by the financial sector. In 1998, SunTrust Equitable Services investment company issued a report to investors about the investment potential of for-profit services for "at risk" youth. The report was titled, "At-Risk Youth—A Growth Industry."

> As Betty Reid Mandell, among others, points out, millions of youth, who were the primary recipients of welfare, are the prime victims of its dismantling. Their increasingly at-risk status transforms youth into commodities in a $21 billion for-profit service market. . . . Who are these for-profits who have scored on the dismantling of social services for youth? One of the biggest poverty profiteers is big three military contractor Lockheed Martin, which is operating welfare-to-work schemes in four states. For-profit Youth Services International, purchased in 1998 by Correctional Services Corporation, makes over $100 million a year running juvenile detention "boot camps," subjecting youth to physically demanding military training. . . . What is particularly egregious about these examples is that after youth have been put "at risk" by the denial of public services, such as the late AFDC, they then become an investment for the same people who lobbied for the destruction of the same public services that were designed, when properly supported, to keep youth out of risk.[6]

These examples of how the military and prison industries are investing in the undermining of security for youth demonstrates that the disciplinary form of security is deeply interwoven with the financial form of security in which students are made into investments, in part through the undermining of caregiving forms of security.

SECURITY III: THE STUDENT AS WEAPON, THE STUDENT AS SOLDIER

Recently, critics of school commercialism, such as Alex Molnar and the Commercialism in Education Research Unit that he directs, as well as the U.S. Surgeon General, have taken note of just how fat U.S. students are getting. For Molnar, who is one of the nation's most prominent critics of school commercialism, and other authors on his site (www.schoolcommercialism.org), childhood obesity must be understood in relation to the deluge of junk food marketing aimed at children and infiltrating schools. The goal of these authors is to get the marketers and profiteers out of the schools. For the U.S. Surgeon General, the goal is somewhat different. Addressing the largest ever conference on childhood obesity, Surgeon General Dr. Richard Carmona was quoted in the *San Francisco Chronicle*, "Our preparedness as a nation depends on our health as individuals," he said, noting that he had spent some of his first months in office working with military leaders concerned about obesity and lack of fitness among America's youth. "The military needs healthy recruits," he said.[7] The article noted that Carmona was careful not to criticize the junk food industry for its part in threatening the national defense by flabbifying the nation's chubby little defenders.

We find a further example of how the language of security shapes educational policy issues in *The New York Times*'s discussion of the U.S. Supreme Court case over affirmative action at the University of Michigan. In April 2003, the *Times* described that case not on ethical grounds of racial equity, but on the pragmatic grounds of national security. Military officers, the *Times* reported, submitted briefs to the Court supporting educational affirmative action as serving the interests of military academies and troops in the field. This action, perhaps as much as anything, inspired the *Times* to portray the University of Michigan, and educational institutions more generally, as a military training ground.[8]

Most significant to our considerations of how the language of security shapes educational policy and practice, however, is the testimony of Paul Vallas to the U.S. Congressional Committee on Education and the Workforce. Chicago Mayor Richard Daly appointed Vallas, an accountant, to the position CEO of Chicago Public Schools. He currently serves as CEO of Philadelphia Public Schools, which has socioeconomic and racial demographics similar to Chicago. In his testimony before the Congressional Committee on Education and the Workforce, Vallas explained how:

> To assist teachers in teaching to the standards, we have developed curriculum frameworks, programs of study, and curriculum models with daily lessons. These materials are based on training models designed by the Military Command and General Staff Council. . . . Increasingly, we have built collaborative relationships with the private sector."[9]

While Vallas makes quite explicit that the model for his reforms are the military's training methods and his background is in accounting, he does not address the role of such rigid and authoritarian methods in a democratic nation. Is democracy about nothing more than individuals competing with each other for test scores? For prestigious degrees? For jobs? For consumer goods? Unfortunately, to a great extent, that's how neoliberal doctrine conditions us to define democracy—equate it with the market. We can develop and embrace alternative definitions of the term. Democracy can also be about collaboration, collective action, and a different kind of competition that fights for social justice rather than individual advancement—the well-being of all rather than the ascendancy of one.

Vallas's perspective is consistent with the reauthorized Elementary and Secondary Education Act (Bush's No Child Left Behind Act) that was widely supported across party lines. A central aspect of No Child Left Behind (aptly titled with a military metaphor referencing Vietnam-era troop recovery) is defining educational accountability through testing, which is a boon for the corporate testing and textbook publishing companies, such as big three McGraw-Hill, Houghton Mifflin, and Harcourt General. No Child Left Behind makes states create performance-based achievement measures that must be met within a specific time frame. When those goals are not met, states will be required to spend public money on remediation. Much of this will be a boon for private for-profit test companies, educational publishers, and for-profit consulting companies. In his article "Reading between the Lines" in *The Nation,* Stephen Metcalf shows how the "scientific" standards of No Child Left Behind were created by the same companies lined up to do remediation, such as McGraw-Hill.[10]

The Bush legislation has ardent supporters in the testing and textbook publishing industries. Only days after the 2000 election, an executive for publishing giant NCS Pearson addressed a Waldorf ballroom filled with Wall Street analysts. According to *Education Week,* the executive displayed a quote from President-elect Bush calling for state testing and school-by-school report cards, and announced, "This almost reads like our business plan."

Remediation by test companies and educational publishers means that this "accountability-based" reform was in large part set up as a way for these testing and publishing companies to profit by getting federally mandated and state-mandated business. The market ideal of "competition" driving testing-based reform could not be further from the lack of market competition in the state and corporate practice of setting up these reforms through the kind of crony capitalism Metcalf details.

These ever more frequent tests, which largely measure socially valued knowledge and cultural capital (most of which students learn at home and in their social class milieu), will be used to justify remediation by states and locales. The federal government will insist that test scores be improved by either (1) allowing students to go to other schools or (2) using public money for remediation efforts. The courts have already determined that the federal government will not enforce at the local level the freedom of students to go to better schools. So the remediation route is the one that is going to be the biggest result of No Child Left Behind. As a result, for-profit education companies are going to cash in on this with terribly unprogressive pedagogical methods that aim to deskill and deintellectualize teaching through tactics like scripted lessons in those places hardest hit by the results of corporate lobbying to evade taxes and where neoliberal reforms have allowed capital flight to leave communities with no employment.

The threat posed by neoliberal reforms exemplified by Vallas, No Child Left Behind, and McGraw-Hill should not be understood as primarily or exclusively a threat to progressive pedagogical methods. The fact is, there are in evidence many corporate-produced and corporate-administered curricula that are methodologically progressive, such as Disney's Celebration Schools that cater to professional class kids, as well as, for example, some of what the oil companies dump on schools. Here, the distinction between critical-thinking skills (called for by liberal critics of corporate school initiatives) and critical pedagogy really matters. Much of the corporate-produced curricula do emphasize knowledge that is "meaningful" to students, "collaborative," and "student-centered." These can all be part of a very conservative curriculum that does not address the sociopolitical realities informing the production of knowledge that involves relating knowledge to the interlocking systems of capitalism, white supremacy, and patriarchy, as well as to many other critical relationships, such as those between knowledge and pedagogical authority, ethics, and identity formation.

Metcalf makes fantastic criticism of crony capitalism between McGraw-Hill and three generations of Bushes.[11] However, he misses the chance to explore the implications of how John Negroponte, who left McGraw-Hill to become U.S. ambassador to the United Nations and a leading figure in the "War on Terrorism," participated in the 1980s in what are regarded in the international community as crimes against humanity and U.S.-backed terrorism in Honduras. It is imperative that future work on corporatization of schools consider the relationship between the disciplining of particular populations in the United States through the mechanisms of capitalist schooling and how this relates to the disciplining of populations in other nations through both direct coercion and the production of consent that is largely accomplished through cultural production. It is also time for the global dynamics of discipline to be understood in relation to how the discourse of discipline, drawn from the market-based metaphor of "fiscal discipline" and the military ideal of physical and behavioral discipline, is the basis for the most recent educational reforms.

Some of the more critical approaches to criticizing corporate involvement in schools link corporate initiatives and their aforementioned effects to much broader social issues and, most centrally, the concerted efforts by corporations in conjunction with states to expand their power locally, nationally, and internationally. This can be found in the work of scholars such as Michael Apple, Ramin Farahmandpur, David Gabbard, Henry Giroux, Robin Truth Goodman, Don Trent Jacobs, Pepi Leistyna, Pauline Lipman, Donaldo Macedo, Peter McLaren, and E. Wayne Ross, among others. This broader approach recognizes that corporations know just how much knowledge, schooling, and education more generally matter in the exercise of power. Knowledge, schooling, and education broadly conceived matter to corporations to frame events, construct meanings, and disseminate values in ways favorable to corporate financial and ideological interests. In this larger formulation, it becomes difficult not to make the links between, say, when a company such as Amoco (now BPAmoco) in conjunction with Scholastic, Waste Management, and public television freely distributes middle school science curriculum in Chicago Public Schools portraying the earth under benevolent corporate management when that curriculum fails to mention domestic pollution that has resulted in vast environmental devastation and cancer in entire neighborhoods in the Midwest, the spilling of millions of barrels of oil in pristine Alaskan artic land, the defiance of government orders to stop spilling, the involvement of the company in the murderous actions of right-wing paramilitaries in Colombia, or how BPAmoco and other oil companies will benefit from the United States waging war on states with great oil reserves. ChevronTexaco, involved in helicopter gunship attacks on protesters in Nigeria, is quite clear on what is at stake in the battle over who controls knowledge: "We are," they write, "a learning company."

Sadly, few of the critics of corporate involvement in schools have made such links. Critics of school commercialism, public school privatization, and all the varieties it takes should be concerned with the threats to the global public posed by the expansion of corporate power over meaning-making technologies that include not just schools but mass media as well. As the United States takes on an increasingly open imperial mission in defiance of the international community and intensifies domestic militarization, it becomes clear that George W. Bush's ultimatum following September 11 about other states being either "with us or against us" increasingly applies to the ethical and political positions that educators must take. The battle lines for educators, however, should not be drawn the way Bush would have it—between a jingoistic unquestioning nationalism versus a treasonous questioning of the motives of the state. Rather, ideally, the battle lines for educators are over, on the one hand, the expansion of public control over not just knowledge and foreign and domestic policy but also the meaning and future of work, leisure, consumption, and culture. On the other side of the battle lines is the state-backed intensification of corporate control over knowledge, foreign and domestic policy, work, leisure, consumption, and culture simultaneous with the continued diminishment of public control. The repressive elements of the state in the form of such phenomena as the suspension of civil liberties under the USA PATRIOT Act, militarized policing, the radical growth of the prison system, and intensified surveillance accompany the increasing corporate control of daily life. The corporatization of the everyday is characterized by the corporate domination of information production and distribution in the form of control over mass media and educational publishing, the corporate use of information technologies in the form of consumer identity profiling by marketing and credit card companies, and the increasing corporate involvement in public schooling and higher education at multiple levels.

By remaining focused on pedagogical methods, the threat of an abstract notion of "quality education," and pretending that if commercialism can be fended off, it will allow students the benefits of a neutral education, liberal critics of the corporate assault on public schooling miss the extent to which the entire school curriculum is wrapped up with both material and symbolic power struggles or cultural politics—that is, the struggle over values, meanings, identities, and signifying practices.

The deep structural ways that schools function in the interests of capital complicates the commonsense revulsion that most people feel about school commercialism—a common sense echoed in liberal educational policy circles that presumes that everyone knows what is wrong with business getting into schools. That is, it threatens some abstract notion of a "quality" education. Despite the limitations of the model,[12] the insights of Bowles and Gintis[13] from the 1970s remind us that corporate entry into schools is not brand new but, further, that it runs far deeper than the introduction of advertising and product placement in curriculum, which so many liberal critics of corporatization have focused on in the past few years.

One of the central and best aspects of the public nature of public schooling is that, in its best forms, it allows for the interrogation and questioning of values and beliefs. While historically and presently too much of public schooling has followed an authoritarian model that discourages intellectual curiosity, debate, and a culture of questioning, what makes public schools special is their capacity, by virtue of their public nature, to be places where such a culture of political and ethical questioning can flourish and be developed. The same cannot be said of private for-profit schools. Disney's Celebration School in its corporate community in Celebration, Florida, despite its progressive pedagogical methods, is not likely to encourage questioning about what part ABC Disney plays in the corporate media monopoly[14] or in U.S. imperialism[15] or about the intensifying corporate control over information production and meaning-making, more generally, that spans mass media and schooling. There are, of course, countless examples of public schools that do demonstrate democratic culture. However, most of the reforms tied to No Child Left Behind do not foster such a culture that makes questioning power central. Rather it deepens and expands authoritarian values, counters teaching as an intellectual endeavor and, by standardizing curriculum and employing discipline-based remediation, it simultaneously inhibits the critical engagement with knowledge and turns to the corporate sector to use tests, scripts, and prepackaged curriculum to drill knowledge into kids. The instrumentalism of the standards-based reform movement is inseparable from the corporate logic infecting education. The same neoliberal ideology that aims to privatize and commercialize schools to teach students to make an enterprise of themselves is the same neoliberal ideology that has dismantled welfare and gutted and privatized social services domestically, the same neoliberal ideology that uses state resources to invest in disciplinary tactics throughout civil society, and the same neoliberal ideology that the government exports through the threats of military and economic revenge.

Recently, the successor to Paul Vallas, Arne Duncan, the CEO of Chicago Public Schools, mentioned that roughly 90 percent of the students in Chicago come from families living below the poverty line and that 90 percent are also nonwhite. The structural analysis, typified by Bowles and Gintis, undermines the liberal and conservative fiction of the innocence of the school as a space outside of the relations of capital that only gets tainted with the most explicit entry of business. One of the important tasks for critics of the neoliberal assault on schooling to comprehend now is how the reproduction of the conditions of production is shifting from an industrial to a service model in some places and in others shifting from an industrial to a prison/military model. This means that privileged, largely white schools are being remade on the model of corporate culture with the goal of training future managers and consumers in a service economy while the public schools serving economically redundant working-class and poor segments of the population are being increasingly given discipline in schools. The meritocratic ideal structuring educational discourse and policy debate is both itself an example of capitalist ideology structuring schools and a gross distortion of the continuing realities of the oppressive function schools serve. Such educational reform efforts concerned with, for example, individual "resilience" are grounded on lies of equal opportunity and mobility, and they individualize the systemic nature of how schools further the interests of power. This should not be read as an attack on public schools (though it is a call for rejecting the plethora of garbage educational research that simultaneously affirms and effaces the oppressive function of schools) but rather a call for honesty about what schools really do, as the first step for planning remaking schools into places where democratic cultures flourish and students can learn to imagine human possibilities beyond the market. Some students are leading the way in resisting neoliberalism and imagining the school as a place for democratic culture to be built through struggles for collective security rather than individualized forms of security. And some students are taking great risks to do so.

HEROIC STUDENTS DEFYING RISK

Alissa Quart, in her book *Branded: The Buying and Selling of Teenagers*, extensively illustrates the teen marketing phenomenon of trend-spotters and insiders in privileged schools and milieus. Fashion, clothing, accessory, and cosmetic companies and the advertising and marketing companies that work for them hire teen girl spies to spot fashion trends and to offer advice on what products fashion companies should manufacture and promote. The teens are paid less in cash and more in inexpensive promotional gimmicks and through the idea that this is training for future work in these industries. Quart[16] estimates that there are about 10,000 teens working as fashion spies in schools. Quart paints a picture of a vicious culture of consumerism in schools that corporations promote through multiple strategies. Within the commercial culture of schools, students value themselves and others through their place on the consumption hierarchy, but as Quart points out, there are exceptions:

> Katie Sierra, a fifteen-year-old tenth grader at Sissonville High School in Charleston, West Virginia, was suspended for her antiwar sentiments in October 2001. Those sentiments were expressed in a sardonic handwritten message on her T-shirt: "When I saw the dead and dying Afghani children on TV, I felt a newly recovered sense of national security. God Bless America."[17]

Katie Sierra is not alone, as student political awareness and action has intensified with many young people identifying with the political struggles for global justice and foreign debt relief, and against sweatshops, the U.S. wars in Afghanistan and Iraq, and the new educational reforms, such as high-stakes testing. One global student protest, billed as "Books Not Bombs" on Wednesday March 5, 2003, drew students to the streets with slogans, signs, and chants, as well as discussion and information-sharing. *The Red Streak*, a new *Chicago Tribune* publication aiming for a younger demographic than the *Tribune* and modeled on British tabloid dailies, had a story with the following on its front page:

> Putting aside their books to protest the potential bombing of Iraq, thousands of students at high schools and colleges across the Chicago area walked out of class Wednesday to protest the war buildup in the Persian Gulf. The students here joined tens of thousands of students at more than 300 colleges and universities nationwide, according to the National Youth and Student Peace Coalition, which helped organize the day of action. "We're spending all this money on the war, and some schools don't have enough money for books," said Lucy Dale, 16, a junior at Francis Parker, who cut class to head downtown. "High schoolers will have to pay for this in the future."[18]

Students at College of Dupage carried a mock casket draped in an American flag with the field of stars replaced with the peace symbol.

The Redeye, *The Chicago Sun-Times*'s competitor to the Tribune's *Red Streak*, had a two-page spread that included chants: "We cut school because Bush is a fool"; "I called in sick of war"; "Books not bombs"; "Stop the U.S. war machine, from Palestine to the Philippines."[19]

The events covered above by corporate media were the result of grassroots organizing. There are a number of organizations exemplified by Monterrey Bay Educators against the War, Teachers for Social Justice in Chicago, or the Military Out of Our Schools campaign that bring together teachers, students, university faculty, and citizens to link efforts for global justice to local school policy. They are organizing walkouts, teach-ins, curriculum fairs, and sessions to discuss, debate, educate the public, and organize. They are challenging high-stakes testing, military recruiting in schools, and recognizing that authoritarian curriculum reforms are part of the threat to democratic and public forms of schooling that need to be understood as part of the movement for global democracy.

CONCLUSION

Neoliberalism as the doctrine behind global capitalism should be understood in relation to the practice of what Ellen Meiskins Wood, writing in response to the 1999 U.S.-led attack on former Yugoslavia, called the "new imperialism" that is "not just a matter of controlling particular territories. It is a matter of controlling a whole world economy and global markets, everywhere and all the time."[20] The project of globalization again made crystal clear by Thomas L. Friedman "is our overarching national interest" and it "requires a stable power structure, and no country is more essential for this than the United States" for "[i]t has a large standing army, equipped with more aircraft carriers, advanced fighter jets, transport aircraft and nuclear weapons than ever, so that it can project more power farther than any country in the world. . . . America excels in all the new measures of power in the era of globalization."[21] As Friedman explains, rallying for the "humanitarian" bombing of Kosovo, "The hidden hand of the market will never work without the hidden fist—McDonald's cannot flourish without McDonnell Douglas, the designer of the F-15. And the hidden fist that keeps the world safe for Silicon Valley's technologies is called the United States Army, Air Force, Navy, and Marine Corps." The Bush administration's new military policies of permanent war for the maintenance of U.S. military and economic hegemony confirm Wood's thesis. The return to Cold War levels of military spending, approaching $400 billion (not including the Iraq war) with only 10 to 15 percent tied to increased antiterrorism measures,[22] must be understood as part of a more overt strategy of U.S. imperial expansion facilitated by skillful media spin amid post-9/11 anxiety.

I have sought to show how new aspects of neoliberalism simultaneously strengthen the repressive arm of the state while continuing to weaken the caregiving role of the state. I have illustrated how public education is increasingly defined as an issue of national security, thereby justifying its continuation, but on repressive grounds. Why is this? One reason has to do with the way that the drive for privatization and liberalization of trade favored by the corporate sector threatens to undermine the repressive uses of state institutions. National security is one way of fending off the impositions of global trade agreements, such as the FTAA, without invoking a public role of schooling. In other words, the usefulness of national security as a defense of schools as public institutions evades embracing public schools for their citizen-building capacity as institutions that foster democratic participation. Instead, it affirms the dominant justification for public schooling that is consistent with neoliberal ideology—that is, upward individual economic mobility and global economic competition. Schooling for national security links to the broader discourse of security and the war on terrorism that makes schools and other public institutions into the basis for national and international community defined through personal safety, thereby individualizing the public possibilities for schools. By understanding how the discourse of security unites educational policy reform with other U.S. foreign and domestic policy, it becomes possible to challenge security as it is being used to justify repressive state policy and the amassing of corporate wealth and power. One step in such a challenge is to understand why the discourse of security succeeds as widely as it does and to understand the hopeful fact that with so many students it fails. In the course of critical pedagogical practice, teachers and other cultural workers should both develop pedagogies that translate individualized insecurities into matters of public security and redefine security through its public possibilities in the form of social protections, resources, and the redistribution of deliberative power for the future of labor, health care, and education.

Enforcing the Capitalist Agenda *For* and *In* Education: The Security State at Work in Britain and the United States

Dave Hill

Contemporary government and society serves to perpetuate the interests of capital at the expense of workers and serves to reproduce the existing economic system and power relations. At different historical periods, it does this in more or less hidden ways, with greater or lesser use of the repressive/controlling functions of the state.

In the current period, education has been increasingly—and increasingly nakedly— subordinated not just to the general requirements of capital, but to the specific demands made of governments by the capitalist class. The relative autonomy of education from the requirements of capital, from the government, and within education at various levels has been blowtorched. In the name of "accountability," the rhetorical and policy accretions of "professionalism" and of relative autonomy burned away, leaving the skeletal structure of command in its unadorned nakedness. This increasing subordination of education to the requirements of national and international capital runs through school education, through teacher education, and through university education. Education and humanity itself suffers increasing commodification, leading to the restructuring of education on an international scale under pressure from international capitalist organizations and compliant governments. This restructuring has two major aspects:

1. The capitalist agenda *for* education—what capital wants education to provide (i.e., how capital wants to make *indirect* profits from education) and
2. The capitalist agenda *in* education (how capital wants to make direct profits from education).

THE CAPITALIST AGENDA *FOR* EDUCATION

This agenda centers on socially producing labor-power (people's capacity to labor) for capitalist enterprises.

Within universities and other institutions of postsecondary education, the language of the market rapidly displaces the language of education. In this language, lecturers "deliver the product" "operationalize delivery,"and "facilitate clients" learning' within a regime of "quality management and enhancement.' Students function as "customers" selecting "modules" on a pick 'n' mix basis. "Skill development" at universities has surged in importance to the derogation of the development of critical thought.

The capitalist agenda *for* education entails controlling the curriculum, teachers, and educational institutions through common mechanisms. Pauline Lipman notes that

> George W. Bush's "blueprint" to "reform" education, released in February 2001 No Child Left Behind, crystallizes key neo-liberal, neo-conservative, and business-oriented education policies. The main components of Bush's plan are mandatory, high-stakes testing and vouchers and other supports for privatizing schools.[1]

These U.S. conditions mirror the situation in England and Wales.

David Hursh[2] details the interconnections and collaboration in the United States between corporations, government, and education and a series of educational summits. In sentiments startlingly reminiscent of critics of the test-driven agenda in England and Wales, Hursh notes how, in the United States, states have developed subject area standards and then aligned the standards with statewide, standardized tests. School districts increasingly rely on standardized test scores to determine whether they should promote students to the next grade or graduate them from high school. Further, some states, such as Florida and New York, use test scores to rank schools and districts with the purpose of "rewarding" those teachers and schools with high scores and "punishing" those with low.

These policies in the United States bear striking resemblance to the punitive rhetoric and policy of the Thatcher governments (1979–1991), the John Major governments (1991–1997) and the first New Labour government (1997–2001). New Labour has introduced and amplified policies of closing down "Failing Schools" (i.e., schools—nearly all of them to date in very poor areas—failing to reach national minimum SATS or exam passes), dismissing teachers, and restaffing the schools as "Fresh Start" schools. To date, all but one of the states in the United States have followed the route of developing standards and implemented standardized tests. In England and Wales, local education authorities (LEAs) and schools have no choice in the matter. "Noncompliant" head-teachers/school principals are dismissed and noncompliant schools are pilloried in the press.

Hursh suggests that "the effort to impose standards, assessments, and accountability has been devastating for teachers and students," citing Linda McNeil's conclusion that standardization reduces the quality and quantity of what is taught and learned in schools. "Over the long term," following McNeil's argument, "standardization creates inequities, widening the gap between the quality of education for poor and minority youth and that of more privileged students."[3] McNeil's research reveals the emergence of

> phoney curricula, reluctantly presented by teachers in class to conform to the forms of knowledge their students would encounter on centralized tests. The practice of teaching under these reforms shifted away from intellectual activity towards dispensing packaged fragments of information sent from an upper level of bureaucracy. And the role of students as contributors to classroom discourse, as thinkers, as people who brought their personal stories and life experiences into the classroom, was silenced or severely circumscribed by the need for the class to "cover" a generic curriculum at a pace established by the district and the state for all the schools.[4]

We also see this standardization of pedagogy rapidly advancing in England and Wales—with teachers teaching to the test, increasingly using closed instead of open questions, and mimicking the modeled pedagogy provided in the government-provided videos about how to teach the National Literacy Strategy.

The Businessification of Higher Education

Higher education is also becoming big business. The General Agreement on Trade in Services (GATS) views state education as being liberalized so that it generates internationally tradable commodities, students are viewed as paying customers, and the higher education formal curriculum and the informal curriculum in nonelite universities is viewed widely as skills training and worker training. Harvie points to studies of higher education indicating that it too falls increasingly under the truncheon of capitalist social relations. He suggests that a "research-bourgeois" revolution in United Kingdom higher education is seeing research use-values subordinated to research assessment exercise–value—what is validated and recompensed for by government. Research workers are becoming alienated from their work. With the enclosure of "intellectual commons," some research workers are being forced to alienate their own research-labor-power, as two new classes are emerging within academia, a "research proletariat" and a class of "research capitalists."[5]

THE CAPITALIST AGENDA *IN* EDUCATION

After the capitalist agenda *for* education, the capitalist agenda *in* education refers to the desire to make profits from education (as indeed from public or privatized services, such as water supply and health care).

The New Labour government has introduced into England and Wales a plethora of policy initiatives opening up state schooling and local education authorities to private ownership, private management, or private comanagement. These range from giving contracts to private education companies to run "failing" LEAs (school districts in the United States or parts of their services), running "failing schools," to the Private Finance Initiative, whereby private capital (major national or multinational companies) finances and profits from building, maintaining, and running schools and educational buildings and settings. This is big business indeed!

The Education Act for England and Wales of 2002 really does open up the school system in England and Wales to private sector involvement to an unprecedented degree, facilitating further business takeovers of schools and LEA services. The 2002 Education Act enables school governing bodies to constitute themselves as companies; once they have set themselves up as companies, these schools can invest in other companies, enter into deals with private sector operators, and join a "federation" or chain of schools. Private companies can lead these federations, and their leaders do not need teaching qualifications. Schools can also set up educational services and sell them to other schools, and the Secretary of State for Education has the power to form companies for involvement in any area of school life or LEA service.

With respect to schools in England and Wales, the Education Act of 2002 also gives the private sector the freedom to vary or change the curriculum and to change teachers' pay and conditions. This derives from the new "earned autonomy" status that top-performing schools can obtain.

Privatization forms a major component of the agenda of U.S. capital. Lipman discusses the Bush proposal to use federal funds for vouchers, which students in failing schools (again determined by test scores) could use to attend private schools or to receive educational services from private providers. Other Bush plans promoting privatization include funding for charter school start-ups, creating a fund to promote "school choice," and raising the ceiling on tax-free education savings accounts, which could be used for K–12 private schools and college tuition.

Mathison and Ross detail the many recommended interventions, both direct (the capitalist agenda *in* education) and indirect (the capitalist agenda *for* education) by capital in the U.S. environment of corporate take-over of schools and universities:

> In K–12 schools some examples are school choice plans (voucher systems, charter schools), comprehensive school designs based on business principles (such

as economies of scale, standardization, cost efficiency, production line strategies), back to basics curricula, teacher merit pay, and strong systems of accountability. In universities, some examples are the demand for common general
education and core curricula (often not developed or supported by faculty),
demands for common tests of student core knowledge, standardized tests of
knowledge and skill for professional areas, promotion of "classic" education,
and elimination of "new" content areas such as women's studies, post-mod-
ernism, and multiculturalism.[6]

PROLETARIANIZATION, CASUALIZATION, AND IN-TENSIFICATION OF LABOR IN THE EDUCATION STATE APPARATUSES

The enforcement of the agenda *for* education requires that teachers be
reduced to appendages to the great machine of capitalist-dominated
schooling. One means for affecting their compliance with their own
deprofessionalization entails heightening their sense of job insecurity.
McLaren et al. comment that

> the last decade witnessed a rising tide of part-time and "perma-temp" faculty
> and instructors who teach full-time at institutions of higher education but are
> nevertheless denied healthcare and pension benefits offered to tenure-track fac-
> ulty. Leslie Berger of the *New York Times* reports that 43% of professors and
> instructors who are teaching at higher education institutions are part-time
> employees . . . downsizing, outsourcing and flexible methods of labor practices
> on production lines in factories have now trickled down to encompass univer-
> sities and colleges across the United States.[7]

The same writers point out that "In California more than 47,000 uncertified
teachers are teaching in its public schools . . . in Baltimore . . . over one third
of the school district's teachers do not hold full teaching credentials."

In the United Kingdom, the government wishes to dramatically increase
the number of teaching assistants. This, taken together with the introduction of new sets of proposals that would allow schools and universities to
set their own pay levels, can be seen as a downgrading of education workers. In England and Wales, for example, where it was once the case in the
1980s that teachers were recruited from the top 20 percent of the attainment range, that figure is now from the top 40 percent of the attainment
range.

Current (winter/spring 2004) action by the National Union of Teachers
(NUT—the largest teachers' labor union in England and Wales) is to oppose the 2003 "Workload Agreement" whereby schoolteachers are giving up
various nonteaching administrative duties to be carried out by a dramatically
increased force of "teacher assistants." NUT opposes these plans in fear that
these "teaching assistants" will become "teachers on the cheap," reminiscent

of the "Mum's Army" proposed by John Major's Conservative government (to have nongraduate women trained mainly "on the job," for one year only, to become "infant teachers," referred to later). Government-leaked plans that schools may in the future be run by a handful of trained teachers overseeing a plentiful supply of teaching assistants have added fuel to the fire of teachers' anger.

THE IMPORTANCE OF EDUCATION STATE APPARATUSES: THE RECOMPOSITION AND COMMODIFICATION OF TEACHER AND STUDENT PERSONALITY

In *The Communist Manifesto*, Marx and Engels analyze the impact of global capital on the worker: "It has resolved personal worth into exchange value, and in place of the numberless indefeasible chartered freedoms, has set up that single unconscionable freedom—Free Trade."[8] They pointed out that capitalism "left remaining no other nexus between man and man than naked self-interest, than callous 'cash payment' and 'egotistical calculation.' All would be reduced to 'paid laborers.'"

Similarly, Polanyi noted that, in market societies, rather than embedding the economy within social relations, market societies embed their social relations within the economy. Individual gain motivates productive activity, rather than what productivity lends to the welfare of the group. Individuals derive status from how much they gain from market activity. In capitalist society, "well-being" is now equated with "well-having"—we are what we consume. As David Gabbard notes in his Introduction to this volume, Jimmy Carter's "Crisis of Confidence Speech" of 1979 bemoaned that "Human identity is no longer defined by what one does but by what one owns." In educational terms, our worth is how many years and credits we have accumulated. Indeed, being a student is now a serious game that requires people to play by the unstated rule of accumulating credit hours in order to get a better job. In the United States and England and Wales today, as in other advanced capitalist states, the economic goals of education have sidelined social/societal/community goals, the traditional social democratic goals of education, and have also replaced education and learning for its own sake, the traditional liberal and liberal-progressive goals of education.

As Tomlinson states, the project of constructing the post-welfare state entails giving an unprecedented salience to the role of education and relies heavily on shaping people's values and social identities.[9] Gabbard's work supports this view, emphasizing the centrality of compulsory schooling to the enforcement of a market society. Through the ritual of schooling, he contends, people learn to *need* school, with educational credentials being regarded as "testimonials to the degree to which a person's use-value has been developed."[10]

Examining how education fits into the neoliberal agenda, Glenn Rikowski develops a Marxist analysis based on an analysis of labor-power. He suggests that, from the perspective of capital, teachers are the most dangerous workers because they have a special role in shaping, developing, and managing *the single commodity on which the whole capitalist system rests: labor-power*. In the capitalist labor process, labor-power is transformed into value-creating *labor*, and, at a certain point, *surplus value*—value over and above that represented in the worker's wage—is created. Surplus-value is the first form of the existence of capital. It is the lifeblood of capital. As Rikowski notes, without it, capital could not be transformed into money, on sale of the commodities that incorporate value, and, hence, the capitalist could not purchase the necessary raw materials, means of production, and labor-power to set the whole cycle in motion once more. But most important for the capitalist is that part of the surplus-value forms his or her profit—and it is this that drives the capitalist on a personal basis. It is this that defines the personal agency of the capitalist![11]

Teachers are dangerous because they are intimately connected with the social production of labor-power, equipping students with skills, competences, abilities, knowledge, and the attitudes and personal qualities that can be expressed and expended in the capitalist labor process. Teachers are guardians of the quality of labor-power. This potential, latent power of teachers explains why representatives of the state might have sleepless nights worrying about their role in ensuring that the laborers of the future are delivered to workplaces throughout the national capital of the highest possible quality.

Rikowski suggests that the state needs to control the process for two reasons. First, it must make every effort to ensure that this occurs. Second, the state must try to ensure that modes of pedagogy that are antithetical to labor-power production do not and cannot exist. In particular, it becomes clear, on this analysis, that the capitalist state will seek to destroy any forms of pedagogy that attempt to educate students regarding their real predicament—to create an awareness of themselves as future labor-powers and to underpin this awareness with critical insight that seeks to undermine the smooth running of the social production of labor-power. This fear entails strict control, for example, of the curriculum for teacher education and training, of schooling, and of educational research.

Teacher education policy by both Conservative and New Labour governments in England and Wales share a number of characteristics. New teachers (1) are now "trained" rather than "educated," (2) are trained largely "on-the-job" in school, (3) learn mainly in an apprenticeship system, (4) do so without experiencing any *variety* of school ethos and style, (5) have minimal opportunity to collaboratively critique and evaluate what they have seen or done, and (6) are substantially denied theoretical and analytical perspectives other than those of their school mentor and class teacher. Very few come across critical pedagogy, or the radical egalitarian, antisexist and antiracist teacher education programs that emerged in a number of colleges in Britain during the 1970s and 1980s.

They would be "trained" but not "educated," trained to deliver but not educated to systematically question and evaluate.[12] They would also, in some cases, be nongraduate. This would have clear implications for both their pay and their status in the staff room. Once in the classroom, the work of teachers continues to be deprofessionalized—a process, ironically, facilitated through what Simon Boxley points out as the strict regulation and self-regulation by teachers of their own pedagogy. In the name of "improving standards," the certification and standards agenda of New Labour's education policy demand a reconceptualization of what it actually *is* to be such a teacher or learner.[13]

Jane Mulderrig, too, discusses the instrumental rationality underlying New Labour's education policy discourse, manifested in the pervasive rhetoric and values of the market in the representation of educational participants and practices. She theorizes this as an indicator of a general shift toward the commodification of education and the concomitant consumerization of social actors:

> Discourse plays an important role, not only in bringing about these reforms, but also in legitimizing and enacting the ongoing project of globalization and concomitant changes in the relationship between the State and the economy. Central to this work is creating a hegemonic consensus on the inevitability of it all; that our educational practices and relationships must necessarily be shaped to meet the "challenges" posed by this rapidly changing and competitive world . . . an important role for the government is to represent its policy reforms as being both necessary for Britain's economic survival, in the interests of everyone involved, and socially just.[14]

Considerable research attention has been given over the last two decades to the deprofessionalization of teachers. Ironically, the removal of their professional autonomy is legitimized and partly enacted through a discourse of professionalism, which constructs them as committed to self-improvement and skills-upgrading, ambitious, collaborative, and strategically oriented to the effectiveness of their work. This discourse institutes a mentality of self-regulation by which the teachers themselves become the mechanism for legitimizing the surveillance, marketization, and codification of their work practices.

REPRESSIVE AND IDEOLOGICAL STATE APPARATUSES AND THE REPRESSION OF CRITICAL THOUGHT

Currently, the capitalist class is ratcheting up the use of ideological state apparatuses in the media and education systems in particular to both "naturalize" and promote capitalist social and economic relations on the one hand and to marginalize and demonize resistant/anticapitalist hegemonic oppositional ideologies, actions, and activists. In the current period of capitalism, there is increasing and naked use of repressive economic, legal, and military force globally to ensure compliance and subordination to multinational capital and its state agents. These efforts involve repressive state apparatuses, such as the police, goal/jail, legal systems, and surveillance procedures.

Capital and neoliberal force and ideology seek to neutralize and destroy potential pockets of resistance to global corporate expansion and to its interests. Education and the media are the dominant ideological state apparatuses. Each of these ideological state apparatuses contains disciplinary repressive moments and effects. The most powerful restraint on capital (and the political parties funded and influenced by capitalists in their bountiful donations) is that capital needs to persuade the people that the bulwarks of neoliberalism—competition, privatization, poorer standards of public services, greater inequalities between rich and poor—are legitimate. If not, there is a delegitimation crisis; government and the existing system are seen through as grossly unfair and inhumane. It may also be seen as in the pocket of the international and/or national ruling classes and their weaponry.

To minimize this delegitimation, to ensure that the majority of the population considers the government and the economic system of private monopoly ownership to be legitimate, the state uses the ideological state apparatuses, such as schools and colleges and the media to "naturalize" capitalism—to make the existing status quo seem "only natural." (Of course, if and when this does not work, the repressive state apparatuses kick in—sometimes literally, with steel-capped military boots or incarceration programs consigning more and more of the poor in the United States to prison.)

The freedom of the press and the media belongs to those who own that press and media. Rupert Murdoch is more powerful than I am, although the ideas he represents, ultimately, may not be. The freedom of school choice, despite the "naturalization" of "choice" and "competition" in the mass media and schools and universities as "common sense," remains confined to those with the economic and cultural capital to be chosen. A car helps, too. Similar racialized and class-based hierarchical economic reproduction occurs in higher education also but is broadly "hidden from current history," unexposed by an education system and mass media that are overwhelmingly noncritical of capital and its effects.

The Naturalization of Capital and the Denaturalization of Dissent

As Peter McLaren notes, one of its greatest achievements is that capital presents itself as natural, free, and democratic, as if it has now replaced the natural environment. It announces itself through its business leaders and politicians as coterminous with freedom, and indispensable to democracy such that any attack on Capitalism as exploitative or hypocritical becomes an attack on world freedom and democracy itself.[15]

Or, in Bourdieu's phrase, "everywhere we hear it said, all day long—and this is what gives the dominant discourse its strength—that there is nothing to put forward in opposition to the neo-liberal view, that it has succeed in presenting itself as self-evident, that there is no alternative."[16]

When capitalism is *not* accepted as "natural," "god-given," "the way things are and the way things always will be," then the "delegitimization of the delegitimizers" sets in—sometimes brutally. James Petras, perhaps, says it best when he argues that the United States is a veritable police state, at the cusp of a totalitarian regime. He writes:

> One of the hallmarks of a totalitarian regime is the creation of a state of mutual suspicion in which civil society is turned into a network of secret police informers. The Federal Bureau of Investigation (FBI) soon after September 11 exhorted every U.S. citizen to report any suspicious behavior by friends, neighbors, relatives, acquaintances, and strangers. Between September and the end of November almost 700,000 denunciations were registered. Thousands of Middle Eastern neighbors, local shop owners, and employees were denounced, as were numerous other U.S. citizens. None of these denunciations led to any arrests or even information related to September 11. Yet hundreds and thousands of innocent personals were investigated and harassed by the federal police.[17]

McMurtry considers "America's New War" as the latest expression of a much deeper and wider terrorist campaign of an emergent totalitarian pattern of instituting world corporate rule with no limit of occupation or accountability beyond itself. He forcefully claims that the United States has effectively created a new form of totalitarianism. The old totalitarianism culture of the "Big Lie" is marked by "a pervasive overriding of the distinction between fact and fiction by saturating mass media falsehoods." This Big Lie is an omnipervasive lie that "is disseminated by round-the-clock, centrally controlled multi-media which are watched, read or heard by people across the globe day and night without break in the occupation of public consciousness instead of national territories." McMurtry writes, "in the old totalitarian culture of the Big Lie, the truth is hidden. In the new totalitarianism, there is no line between truth and falsehood. The truth is what people can be conditioned to believe"[18]

The Education Ideological State Apparatuses

Changes to schooling, teacher education, and university education in various advanced capitalist states have been effected through the *repressive* as well as *ideological* means available to the state. Gabbard's concept of "the Security State" embraces the ideological aspects and machinery (*listen you . . . it's common sense, buddy! . . . accept it!*) and the repressive aspects and machinery (*or else . . . or else we're on to ya, an' ya won't like it!*) of what Althusser termed "the state apparatuses." The term "state apparatus" does not refer solely to apparatuses such as ministries and various levels of government. It applies to those societal apparatuses, institutions and agencies, that operate on behalf of and maintain the existing economic and social relations of production—in other words, the apparatuses that sustain capital, capitalism, and capitalists. Althusser referred to the schools, family, churches, and the media as the primary ideological state apparatuses. This is strikingly echoed by the Jimmy Carter speech quoted at the beginning of this chapter, in his references to "churches . . . schools, the news media, and other institutions" not doing their ideological brainwashing procapitalist job well enough. Jimmy Carter unwittingly uses French Marxist philosopher Louis Althusser in describing the ideological state apparatuses.

Althusser argues that the ideological dominance of the ruling class is, like its political dominance, secured in and through definite institutional forms and practices: the ideological apparatuses of the state. As Althusser suggests, every ideological state apparatus is also in part a repressive state apparatus, punishing those who dissent: "There is no such thing as a purely ideological apparatus . . . Schools and Churches use suitable methods of punishment, expulsion, selection etc., to 'discipline' not only their shepherds, but also their flocks."[19]

Ideological state apparatuses have internal "coercive' practices" (for example, forms of punishment, nonpromotion, displacement, being "out of favor"). Similarly, repressive state apparatuses attempt to secure significant internal unity and wider social authority through ideology (for example, through their ideologies of patriotism and national integrity). Every repressive state apparatus, therefore, has an ideological moment, propagating a version of common sense and attempting to legitimate it under threat of sanction.

For example, in England and Wales, by means of the governmental regulatory organizations, higher education institutions (HEIs) and education departments/faculties can now have their resources reduced, their staff contracted, and their specializations (in "race," social class, gender, disability, sexuality) thereby altered. Oppositional teachers and teacher educators can lose heart and lose pay; schools and HEIs can lose pupils and students and, therefore, income and, therefore, teachers' and lecturers' jobs; their successors are likely to be appointed because they are "covered in chalk dust" and due to mandated National Curriculum expertise rather than equal opportunities policies or the lust for justice.

Governments, and the ruling classes in whose interests they act, prefer to use the second form of state apparatuses—the Ideological State Apparatuses

(ISAs). Changing the school and initial teacher education curriculum, abandoning "general studies" and liberal studies in the United Kingdom for working-class "trade" and skilled worker students/apprentices in "Further Education" (vocational) colleges is less messy than sending the troops onto the streets or visored, baton-wielding police into strike-bound mining villages. And it is deemed more legitimate by the population in general.

As Althusser and Bourdieu have also noted, schooling and the other sectors of education are generally regarded as politically neutral, not as agencies of cultural, ideological, and economic reproduction. The school, like other institutions in society such as the legal system and the police, is always presented in official discourse as neutral, nonpolitical, and nonideological. (Of course, those who have direct, negative experiences of any of these, such as being half-strangled in a police assault or a community whose children are frequently excluded from school and those who have a critical political consciousness, do not see it this way).

The Suppression and Compression of Critical Space in Education Today

Critical space for critical education studies and research is being compressed through curriculum control, through the remaking of human personality, and through a gamut of ideological and repressive state apparatuses. This is especially so for fundamental critique—"how the core processes and phenomena of capitalist society (value, capital, labor, labor-power, value-creation and capital accumulation, and so on) generate contradictions and tensions in everyday life—for individuals, groups, classes, societies, and on an international scale."[20]

The marginalization of resistant anticapitalist forces, individuals, and ideas takes place through the compression and suppression of critical space within the media and within education. Critical space consists of those social places and spaces where critique (especially fundamental critique) is possible. Effective critical space is those social places and spaces where such critique actually occurs. Critical space is about the potential and actuality for criticism of existing society and the search for and promulgation of alternatives. Critical space is being compressed in education today. There are fewer opportunities for engaging with critiques of society and education within formal education, within schools, further vocational education, and within higher and teacher education.

And for those who do protest, who do stick their heads above the parapet . . . sometimes it gets blown off—in dramatic or in undramatic but effective ways. In the period prior to and since the U.S.-led invasion of Iraq, oppositional school students, college students, and faculty have suffered something of a witch hunt. McLaren et al. detail what they term "witch-hunting" by teachers against students who participated in antiwar protests, such as organizing teach-ins in both K–12 (Kindergarten to Grade 12 schooling) and higher education, witch hunts against students who express opinions critical of U.S. policy. They give examples of disciplinary actions taken by school managements and by the police.[21]

At a less dramatic, but more pervasive, level Gabbard describes the drip, drip, repression and sidelining of "those who have challenged the viability of the market as a mode of social organization." They receive no (positive) attention. "Neither does the school afford the vast majority of children the opportunity to study the lives of people like themselves, much less the opportunity to study their *own* lives."[22]

The Teacher Education Curriculum in England and Wales— Detheorized, Sanitized, Technicist Skills Training

Prior to the 1997 general election, the message from the New Labour leadership was that they intended to launch a back-to-basics drive in the classroom, with more emphasis on basic skills, classroom discipline, and whole-class teaching as part of a drastic overhaul of teacher training. These changes resulted from the New Labour leadership's dissatisfaction with the quality and the attitudes of newly qualified teachers.

The British government has, in effect, expelled most potentially critical aspects of education, such as critical, sociological, and political examination of education and society from the national curriculum for schooling in England and Wales and from what is now termed "teacher training." This was formerly called "teacher education." The change in nomenclature is important both symbolically and in terms of actual accurate analysis of the new, "safe," sanitized and detheorized education and training of new teachers.

There was, and is now, an emphasis on school-based learning and practical skill development, and the abjuring of theory per se, as well as of critical reflection, with its attendant social justice underpinnings. The content of undergraduate and postgraduate "teacher training" courses became more rigidly circumscribed than at any other time in living memory. The teacher training curriculum is locked into the schools' National Curriculum, ensuring that student teachers learn how to teach the relevant (school) National Curriculum subject(s). In itself, this was not a contentious requirement, but the criteria have effectively *excluded* other forms of learning from the initial teacher education (ITE) curriculum, or at least, considerably marginalized them.

Emphasis on and time for education issues such as race, gender, sexuality, special needs, and social class factors in schooling have declined. So, too, have policy responses to counter stereotyping and educational underachievement, the ideological and political analysis of classroom and school pedagogy, and of national policy and legislation. Progressively, the "squeeze" on time for education courses affected issues such as bullying, styles of classroom management, child abuse, and the study of cross-curricular issues. This resulted in courses described by a *Times Educational Supplement* editorial of 20 September 1996 as "Basics Training."[23] This Basics Training has become even more basic in working-class schools, now dominated by the National Literacy Strategy and the National Numeracy Strategy.

The current teacher-training curriculum, under New Labour, comprises:

- a neoconservative, utilitarian national curriculum with increased focus on "the basics" in the school curriculum and preparing student teachers for teaching, particularly Language and Numeracy
- a neoconservative, utilitarian national curriculum in ITE that prepares student teachers to uncritically "deliver" the existing school national curriculum;
- an emphasis within the ITE curriculum on classroom management skills and technical reflection as opposed to, and leaving little space and less demand for, critical reflection;
- an emphasis within the ITE curriculum on managerialist solutions to problems in schooling, as opposed to solutions targeted at schools' financial, pupil intake, and curriculum solutions and policies
- an acceptance that student teachers may need only two school-based experiences, thereby limiting students' comparative critical appreciation of school ethoses and procedures
- the "naming and shaming" and closures of "failing" teacher training courses
- overall (if not universal) denigration of the education research community, and an insistence on its focusing on applied technicist research.

Anti-Intellectual Thuggery

The combined forces of captial and the state have worked to detheorize, technicize, and deintellectualize teacher education, and teaching more generally, in England and Wales and other states. Deintellectualize the school teacher and you deintellectualize a large part of the citizenry. This anti-intellectual thuggery reflects the ideological and repressive aspects of the education state apparatus in action. Designer dissent is managed. Deep dissent here is damned. As McLaren et al. put it, what "Capital has enforced is intellectual thuggery that pervades teacher education programs, particularly the kind that rejects 'theory'" (the knowledge of totality).[24]

Currently, the banks (finance capital, together with other capitals) control the books, the curricula, and the pedagogy. Where the books do not work, or reach, then bullets and bombs —"shock and awe" bullets in the noncompliant ghettoes, bombs against the governments of noncompliant states—are used. The ideological and the repressive state apparatuses—school books, banks and bullets—combine in permanent "Culture Wars" to control our minds in support of the global project of imperialistic and militaristic neoliberal capital. Education policy is subordinated to and is part of the project of contemporary capital.

But there is resistance, there are spaces, disarticulations, and contradictions. And there are always sometimes minor, sometimes major, awakenings—that the material conditions of existence, for teacher educators, teachers, students, and workers and families more widely—simply do not match or recognize the validity of neoliberal (or other capitalist) discourse and policy. It is then and there that coherent understanding and action, in pursuit of economic justice and social justice can potentially triumph. And in a general socialist redistributive and egalitarian reorganization of the economy and society, develop schools, vocational education, teacher education, and universities to suit nobler purposes than being the ideological and repressive state apparatuses of capital.

— 14 —

Privatization and Enforcement: The Security State Transforms Higher Education

John F. Welsh

You are either with us or with the terrorists.
—President George W. Bush, September, 2001

To those who scare peace-loving people with phantoms of lost liberty, my message is this: your tactics only aid terrorists—for they erode our national unity and diminish our resolve.
—Attorney General John Ashcroft, September 2001

HIGHER EDUCATION, THE WAR ON TERROR, AND THE SECURITY STATE

In many respects, these two quotes from President Bush and Attorney General Ashcroft capture the *Zeitgeist* of social thought as the United States pursues the War on Terror. According to the administration, the totality of human thought and action must be aligned with the efforts of the U.S. government as it prosecutes the war against Islamic-based terrorism. Those thoughts and actions that depart from, or are critical of, the government's strategy are suspected of providing aid and comfort to the enemy.

But the Bush-Ashcroft *Zeitgeist* can be challenged on logical, empirical, and political grounds. It is possible, as we are discovering in the later part of 2003, to be critical of, or opposed to, the War on Terror and the political regime pursuing it, *while at the same time* opposing the terrorism promulgated by

Islamic-based fascist groups. In fact, there are a plethora of perspectives about the War on Terror and how it can be fought, even among those who are adamantly opposed to Islamic terrorism. A wide array of political actors, ranging from the American Civil Liberties Union to the conservative Eagle Forum, are concerned about the role of the state in society and the erosion of civil liberties as the government pursues the War on Terror. Yet they are not supporters of terrorism, nor does their concern adumbrate a capitulation to Islamic fundamentalism.

An alternative hypothesis to the Bush-Ashcroft formula for political correctness is that, if national unity and resolve is eroding, it may be more a consequence of the policies and practices of the Bush administration as it pursues the War on Terror than it is any type of sympathy with al-Qaeda, Saddam Hussein, or Hamas. Perhaps national unity and resolve are more weakened by efforts that undermine civil liberty and political freedom than they are by acts of external terrorism. The quotes from Bush and Ashcroft are primarily rhetorical efforts to mobilize political support, intimidate potential political opposition, and ensure submission to those wielding political power. They are not infallible observations about what is necessary to defeat Islamic fascism. They are legitimations of efforts by the Bush administration to pursue its strategy on the War on Terror, even if it entails the unnecessary loss of freedoms and protections historically available in democratic societies.

The effort by Bush and Ashcroft to mobilize support by promoting compliance and submission in a time of national crisis is hardly unique to the current administration. Randolph Bourne observed early in the twentieth century that "war is the health of the state" because it provides governments with a rationale and the leverage to align behaviors, values, and social knowledge with the survival and agenda of the state. Historically, war enabled political elites in the United States to limit or neutralize political opposition by insisting on either/or thinking about the homeland and its enemies.[1] Furthermore, critical analyses of capitalism and the social institutions that support it emphasize that the statist insistence on political conformity during times of crisis is layered on top of the inherent instability of the capitalist social system in the United States. The base of political support for the social system in the United States tends to shrink as a result of exacerbated class antagonisms generated by the tendency toward increased capital accumulation. The societal consensus that supports capitalism tends to disintegrate as the material and cultural benefits of the system become privatized and inaccessible to large segments of the population. Those who are excluded from enjoying the *desiderata* of the system tend to withdraw loyalty from it as social divides widen.[2]

In order to manage internal conflict and social disorganization in times of crisis, the capitalist state must often resort to forms of both ideological and direct social control to pacify, constrain, and repress restive and potentially disruptive populations. When capitalist states are threatened externally as well as internally, the historical tendency is for the state to expand its power and focus priority, attention, and resources on its security needs.[3] The security state is a more recent form of political organization under advanced capitalism in which state power expands dramatically while public policy and social institutions are transformed and redirected toward the primary goals of protection and preservation of the state. The evolution of the security state in the United States was given significant impetus by the events occurring on and subsequent to September 11, 2001, including the mysterious anthrax attacks of October 2001. The institutionalization of the War on Terror in American society is the full historical realization of the security state.

Higher education is one of the social institutions being transformed by the security state as a component of the War on Terror. Historically, higher education in North America, and the United States in particular, enjoyed a somewhat unique status among social institutions in that its relative autonomy from the vicissitudes of capitalism and intrusion by federal and state governments was valued and protected by both its internal and external constituents. Among other things, higher education never acquired the same compulsory character that P–12 education acquired. In addition, federal and state governments rarely intervened into the instructional, curricular, and institutional operations of higher education in quite the same way they did with P–12 education. Until recently, higher education never had quite the same penetration by either private capital or the state into its structure and operations that characterizes the relationship between the state and P–12 education.[4]

There are important reasons why higher education enjoyed a measure of intellectual distance from the demands of the state and the economy. Most significant among these is the need to promote free inquiry. Higher education is an enterprise that is devoted to the discovery, application, and dissemination of knowledge about humanity, society, and nature. It is difficult to understand how higher education can fulfill its research, teaching, and service missions if its participants cannot freely explore and communicate about the world around them, which includes the right to question and criticize government policies and practices in times of national crisis. Certainly, the nature of the knowledge that is generated, disseminated, and applied varies to the degree that free inquiry is permitted. Today, arguably, the most significant challenge confronting higher education is how to preserve its free and ordered space at a time of increasing intrusion by capital and a government that has elevated national security above all other possible societal interests.

It is tempting to overestimate the historical autonomy and exceptionality of higher education in regard to its relationship with the government. The incipient role of colleges and universities as instruments of public policy, or as tools of the state, did not emerge in the post–September 11 world.[5]

In fact, colleges and universities in the United States have been subject to considerable control by both the federal and state governments and, in many respects, have historically been instruments of state policy.[6] What is different today are the specific ways in which the security state has transformed higher education as an instrument of public policy and the scope and intensity of the academy's role in the expansion of capitalist exchange relations and the enforcement of state policy. The modern state has considerable authority over other social institutions, except perhaps where the scope of its power and authority has been constitutionally or statutorily limited. In the United States, while the role of government has been limited historically, the state wields considerable power and authority over public and private colleges and universities.

Federal and state governments regulate the organizations that can operate legitimately as colleges and universities. Postsecondary institutions must be authorized by state governments through charter, statute, or license to offer their services and to confer degrees. State governments also regulate or delineate the scope of programming that institutions can offer. In the United States, institutional legitimacy and authority to operate is determined through a system of regional and program-specific accrediting bodies that are responsible for determining whether institutions meet a set of standards regulating their structure and functioning. While accrediting bodies are not specifically state agencies, they are approved by the United States Department of Education. Much of the federal government's policy toward higher education and control over higher education is founded on the accreditation system. For instance, institutional eligibility to receive federal funds is dependent upon accreditation status and approval by the United States Department of Education.

In addition, the U.S. Department of Education promulgates and enforces rules for institutional behavior as directed by federal law. Much of the role of the U.S. Department of Education is focused on surveillance and monitoring of institutional behavior. Postsecondary institutions have considerable reporting requirements through the Integrated Postsecondary Education Data System (IPEDS) and the Student Right-to-Know and Campus Security Act of 1990. IPEDS is an enormous database managed by the National Center for Educational Statistics that includes data elements on many aspects of institutional characteristics and operations, such as enrollments, graduations, programs, human resources, finances, and facilities. The Student Right-to-Know and Campus Security Act of 1990, as an example, requires institutions to report data on student enrollments and campus crimes to the U. S. Department of Education.

At the level of state government, institutions are regulated through not only state statute, but through a system of governing and coordinating boards, each of which has an agency composed of a professional staff who oversee the day-to-day operations of state policy in higher education.[7]

About half of the states in the United States control their public institutions through a statewide governing board that has direct control over colleges and universities. Governing boards hire and compensate institutional executive officers, promote and tenure faculty, establish tuition and fee rates, and approve personnel, student, and academic policy. The other half of states control their public institutions through a system of local governing boards that are themselves subordinate to a statewide coordinating board. Despite the softer terminology, coordinating boards have broad powers to regulate the behaviors of both public and private institutions. State-level boards in all states have responsibilities to license the operation of private institutions; most have authority approve, review, and discontinue degree programs; and all have authority to review and recommend institutional budgets to the executive and legislative branches of state government. Beyond the state higher education board, other state agencies have authority over the operation of academic units and programs. Professional programs such as medicine, dentistry, law, social work, counseling psychology, and teacher education are all regulated at the state level by professional boards that accredit their operations, and certify and license the ability of program graduates to practice their profession within the borders of the state.

Thus, colleges and universities are subject to a complicated but clear pattern of control by federal and state authorities. Historically, the basic policy question for higher education has been to what extent and in what ways should the federal and state governments regulate and direct the behaviors and priorities of institutions? As McGuinness demonstrates, the degree of state control over institutions has persistently increased since the 1970s.[8] The autonomy and exceptionality of higher education have eroded incrementally over the course of the past three decades as federal and state officials demand increased accountability and responsiveness, and as they implement financing and assessment schemes designed to subordinate academic and institutional goals to state policy. The security state has accelerated the level of both federal and state control over higher education as it refocuses many of the responsibilities of higher education toward the extension of capitalist exchange relations, as it converts academic research into an ally in the military and technological dimensions of the War on Terror, and as it enlists institutional administrations and information systems as vehicles designed to monitor and control individual behavior.

The trend toward increased governmental control of higher education prompts questions about the impact of this transformation on the major responsibilities of higher education and the democratic and public character of the higher learning in North America. This chapter explores *privatization* and *enforcement* as the two macro-level dynamics that define the security state's transformation of higher education in North America. Through privatization and enforcement, the security state is altering the fundamental structure and operations of colleges and universities, largely by elevating their corporate responsibilities at the expense of their collegial relations and sense of community. The chapter argues that the transformation of higher education engendered by privatization and enforcement has seriously weakened higher education as a platform for public discourse and social self-knowledge in a democratic society.

PRIVATIZATION AS PROCESS AND IDEOLOGY IN HIGHER EDUCATION

Privatization is propelling significant changes within many colleges and universities, as well as their relationships with the state and their many constituents. Privatization is also an ideology, or a body of ideas, that explains, justifies, and promotes the process of integrating the logic of capitalist exchange relations into the operations of the academy, and subordinating academic goals and values to the goals and values of private capital. As an ideology, privatization legitimates increased intervention by private capital and the state into the operations of higher education. It also undermines the role of higher education as a vehicle for enhancing public discourse, defining public initiatives, and pursuing the collective good.[9]

In the higher education policy community privatization refers to the increased cooperation and integration among private capital, the state, and postsecondary institutions to realign the goals and operations of higher education toward the needs of economic development.[10] This is accomplished in four ways. First, privatization implies that the mix of funding for higher education has changed, with the public or governmental share of financing in decline and the various private forms of financing, including tuition and philanthropy, on the rise. An increasingly popular financing strategy in higher education is to increase the proportion of educational costs financed by students and to stimulate competition by putting public funds into the hands of students, not institutions, through tuition grant or financial aid programs financed by state governments.

Second, for the state and its agencies, privatization also means assigning to private contractors responsibilities or tasks that were once undertaken by public employees and units of public agencies. This dimension of privatization reflects a conscious decision on the part of government to transfer to private management, including for-profit entities, responsibility for operations that had previously been fulfilled by institutional offices. Examples include the initiatives taken by state boards and institutions to reduce costs by outsourcing functions and to increase revenues by raising the prices for the services they deliver. In this sense, privatization refers to the government's inability or unwillingness to funds its agencies at previous levels, often transferring a greater degree of authority and initiative to individual agencies or institutions, while continuing to work under nominal public control.

Third, privatization entails the idea that institutions of higher learning can reorient their missions and statutes toward the increased acquisition of wealth through participation in the marketplace. Dubbed the "entrepreneurial university" or "academic capitalism," this dimension of privatization refers to the efforts of institutions to commercialize their many "products."[11] The expansion of distance learning and continuing education courses, programs, and units that are aimed at corporate training, or that have been reinvented as for-profit entities, are examples of institutional entrepreneurship. Efforts by institutions to create for-profit "spin-off" companies or to transfer technologies to the marketplace, capitalizing on faculty research or service activities, are other examples.

Fourth, privatization refers to the increased alignment of academic programs with the workforce needs of private capital. Control over the scope of academic programs offered by institutions has been modified since the mid-1980s by pressure from state higher education boards and by state and regional economic development offices to ensure that colleges and universities produce workers in occupations where there is the greatest need.[12] It is common for institutions to assess programs based on occupational outcomes or to discontinue programs based on low enrollments and marginal relationship to workforce needs. Still other programs are initiated or expanded based on needs identified by state economic planners and by private firms.

Privatization suggests that institutions are being cut off, against their will, from assured support from the state to the vagaries of market forces. This is a misunderstanding. Privatization is not particularly market-driven. In postsecondary education, privatization has as much to do with the desires of policymakers and administrative leadership to increase their managerial flexibility and to maximize internal organizational control as it does with the reduced ability or willingness of the state to fund public agencies. Institutional chief executives and academic officers generally welcome privatization as a new relationship with private capital, as well as a new relationship with the state and its agencies. Privatization forges new relationships that enable administrators to better achieve their managerial objectives within institutions and to better control the environment their organizations must operate in. Privatization is a type of interaction between the state, private capital, and institutional leadership that enables those who control organizational power and resources to pursue their agendas using the resources and technologies of higher education, state power, and private capital. Privatization is not a new concept, but it has been cast in a new form that empowers the state, higher education, and private capital to reinforce each other's needs and control. It blurs the distinction between the public and the private. It is a form of state capitalism that is based on the collusion and cooperation of academic administrators, governmental officials, and private capital.

Historically, postsecondary education in North America was characterized by a mixed and pluralistic economy of public and private colleges and universities. Recently, the two types of institutions have come into direct, increasingly undifferentiated competition for corporate, philanthropic, individual, and state resources. Public funds are sufficiently pervasive that institutions once described as private are now commonly but inappropriately described as "independent." Student financial aid is one example of the blurring between the public and private. While school vouchers are a divisive issue for P–12 education, in postsecondary education Pell grants, federally guaranteed loans, and state-level scholarship and grant programs are commonly accepted as equitable programs for funding student access to a broad range of both public and independent colleges and universities. Public funds are increasingly used by states to finance the education of students at private institutions. Similarly, public institutions have been quick to learn the benefits of the historical funding strategies of independent institutions. Public colleges and universities today expect their private constituents to contribute as much or more than the state toward operations, facilities, and academic programs.[13]

Privatization is a pervasive phenomenon in higher education today, but the important issues are why it has occurred and what impacts it will have. For most of the 1980s, the cuts in postsecondary education budgets that occurred at the state and federal levels were presented as practical, financial necessities. Shortfalls in state funding were coupled with increased spending on mandated, but unfunded, federal programs. One impact was that all public agencies would have to provide services with less revenue. Another impact was that postsecondary education's share of public revenue dwindled. Postsecondary institutions were told that, at least in the short run, they would have to rely more on their own revenues and less on public revenues.[14] As the fiscal crisis continued through most of the 1990s and into the twenty-first century, the new form of allocating public funds required a rationale that became the basis for public policy toward higher education, thus ensuring that privatization received official sanction as an explanation for the changing trends. The result is a social system and ideology that legitimates less governmental fiscal support, dismantled programs, diminished aspirations for improved lives, and less inclination to design a collective future, in favor of a government that focuses on its security and the economic base that supports it. Privatization reflects a reallocation of public funds and purposes toward the military, law enforcement, and other agencies of direct social control that are seen as more central to the needs of the economy and the security state.

An important component of privatization as an ideological tool of the security state attacks the public purposes of higher education, including both public and private institutions. The attack on higher education's commitment to public purposes, accompanied by reduced public funding, erodes higher education's credibility as an agent of public improvement and the collective good. It makes the collusion of the state and private capital the dominant force shaping the nation's postsecondary institutions, a concept that has become the guiding principle behind the privatization of post-secondary education.

According to this facet of the ideology of privatization, the academy reflects the individual choices of its customers more than the collective decisions made by faculty and students. The public consensus that both the individual and society benefit from the public investment in higher education has been subverted. It was once possible to argue that the ways in which colleges and universities defined their own futures overlapped with public goals to a greater degree than is the case today. Today, the goals and needs of the security state dominate the behavior of institutions and have eclipsed the aspirations of faculty, students, and communities in policy discourse about the future of higher education.

Privatization has become the prevailing ideology for the coordination and control of higher education because those responsible for the governance of higher education lack the insight to reform colleges and universities. They also lack the inclination and the will to challenge the state. They have not offered any viable alternative to meeting the new demands for postsecondary education in an era of budget constraints and growing uncertainty as to what kinds of education best prepare an educated citizenry. Public officials, such as legislators, governors, institutional administrators, trustees, and privileged firms, celebrate privatization as the most viable approach for focusing and organizing institutional services in an era in which the state's primary concern is the War on Terror.

ENFORCEMENT AS PROCESS AND IDEOLOGY IN HIGHER EDUCATION

Enforcement is the process through which the teaching, research, and service missions of higher education are increasingly subordinated to the interests, needs, and directives of the state and private capital. The War on Terror has greatly enhanced the ability of the government to enforce its will and mitigate threats to its power primarily through the PATRIOT Act, which was signed into law by President Bush on October 26, 2001. The USA PATRIOT Act is an acronym for the "Uniting and Strengthening America by Providing Appropriate Tools Required to Intercept and Obstruct Terrorism" Act. The purpose of the PATRIOT Act is to preempt, frustrate, and punish terrorist acts in the United States and elsewhere by enhancing intelligence and law enforcement tools. The PATRIOT Act is the most invasive and profound legislation in the United States impacting individual rights since the Espionage Act of 1917 and the Sedition Act of 1918.[15] The PATRIOT Act greatly expands the surveillance powers of the government and reduces the privacy rights many Americans enjoyed before September 11, 2001.

The PATRIOT Act provides federal intelligence and law enforcement officials great latitude in obtaining orders for tapping phones that a suspect might use; it allows officials to conduct searches and delay notifying the suspect if they believe notification would jeopardize the investigation; it enables the Attorney General to detain foreigners suspected of terrorism; it permits nationwide search warrants in terrorism investigations, including Internet use, e-mail records, and computer billing records. It also allows for greater sharing of information between criminal investigations and intelligence officials in foreign intelligence and counterterrorism cases. While some of the provisions of the PATRIOT Act were intended to amend existing legislation, much of it is new and raises new concerns about individual freedom and the power of the state.

Although it was intended to assist the government in the War on Terror, the PATRIOT Act is not limited to terrorism. Instead, it empowers the government to invoke most of its new powers even when the government seeks only to investigate routine criminal offenses. It allows for the surveillance of any number of domestic organizations and advocacy groups. It allows governmental agencies to collect vast amounts of information on individuals and requires businesses, private organizations, and other governmental entities to participate in the data collection. Several of its provisions directly affect higher education and, thereby, help transform the relationship between the state and higher education, and between higher education and its many constituents. The same is true for other statutes that have been implemented, revised, or funded as part of the War on Terror. The primary impacts of the legislation enabling the War on Terror in higher education have been in the areas of scholarly communications, life sciences research, and student access to higher education.

As an example of the impact on scholarly communications, the PATRIOT Act expanded provisions in the Foreign Intelligence Surveillance Act (FISA) that now empower FBI agents to obtain business and educational records without any legal constraint requiring demonstration that the student is considered a foreign agent or a terror suspect in any way. A key feature of FISA is that it permits wiretaps and electronic surveillance more readily than the federal law that governs criminal investigations. The transformation of FISA by the PATRIOT Act has a profound impact on scholarship in higher education, including both teaching and research, because of the expanded authority of the federal government to intercept and track the communications and scholarship of faculty, students, and academic support personnel.

Operationally, the PATRIOT Act alters FISA by lowering the barrier between the domains of criminal law and foreign counterintelligence. It provides greater governmental access to e-mail and Internet routing information and consumer behavior information, including library and bookstore records. Arguably one of the most important innovations of the PATRIOT Act is the extension of the technology of telephone surveillance to e-mail communications in both criminal and FISA investigations. The federal government may now obtain "to" and "from" information in electronic communications in order to track the communicative behavior of suspicious individuals. This includes tracking e-mail addresses, Internet Service Provider addresses, port numbers, dialing, routing, addressing, and signaling information. In order to collect this information from organizations about the behavior of individuals, the federal government now needs only to satisfy the relatively low standard of "relevant to an ongoing investigation," rather than the more difficult standard of "probable cause." The concepts of "free inquiry" and "academic freedom" cannot retain their original meanings in an environment in which the government intimidates and constrains inquiry and discourse through unrestricted access to the communications of individuals.

After the 1993 bombing of the World Trade Center, investigators discovered that one of the Islamic terrorists entered the United States on a student visa and overstayed after he dropped out of school. Congress reacted quickly to this discovery by passing laws that regulate which students should be allowed into the United States, what they will be allowed to study, and how they will be monitored while they are here. Surveillance of international students in this country and the denial of visas to potential international students are now seen as important tools for excluding potential spies and terrorists from other countries.

Congress and President Clinton responded in 1994 by signing into law an amendment to the Immigration and Naturalization Act that created the "Technology Alert List" of sixteen disciplines in engineering and the sciences that are off-limits to students from countries that have been designated as state sponsors of terrorism. Applicants to U.S. colleges and universities from countries that have been identified as state sponsors of terrorism are automatically refused visas, while applicants from nuclear powers who want to study in these fields are evaluated on a case-by-case basis.[16]

More significantly, perhaps, in 1996, Congress and President Clinton created the Student Exchange Visa Information System (SEVIS), which is a national database that is "populated" by data provided by college and university information systems about international students. Institutional information systems feed current addresses and educational activities of international students into SEVIS. The data is used by the Immigration and Naturalization Service to monitor student compliance with their visa restrictions. Initially, institutions resisted becoming unpaid accountants for the INS and opposed the implementation of SEVIS as a costly effort to track students. However, higher education dropped its opposition after September 11 because the PATRIOT Act authorized $36 million to implement SEVIS and directed the country's postsecondary educational institutions to begin inputting data for nearly 600,000 international students by the end of January 2003.

The anxiety generated by the terrorism, the statutory response, and the impending assessment helps to shape the disposition of visa applications filed by students, researchers, and professors. Data collected by the Association of International Educators indicates that, while international student enrollments did not decline at the undergraduate level from September 2001 to October 2002, international graduate enrollments declined 8 percent in the same period. In addition, approximately 200 international scholars had either their visas delayed or denied as they sought to enter the country for the 2002–2003 academic year.[17] The changes in FISA and SEVIS prompted by the PATRIOT Act are having an impact on revenue and enrollments in graduate programs, particularly in engineering, mathematics and the natural sciences, where international student enrollments and contributions to research programs are particularly strong. However, a more principled concern is with the threat that these restrictions pose for academic freedom, since unclassified research cannot be conducted on an open campus if students are excluded for reasons of race, sex, or national origin.

The PATRIOT Act does not limit governmental controls to foreign-born students and faculty. In fact, it includes controls on higher education researchers who work with certain nuclear, chemical, and biological agents. The law excludes people convicted of any crime carrying a sentence of a year or more, unlawful users of controlled substances, and anyone with a dishonorable discharge from the U.S. military. Because many of the senior faculty in colleges and universities today were undergraduates during the turbulent 1960s, postsecondary institutions could be forced to disqualify researchers who were once convicted of drug use, arrested during a civil rights or anti-war demonstration, or discharged from the military for reasons of conscience or sexual orientation.

In addition, new statutes assisting the government in the War on Terror are impacting the research mission of higher education through surveillance and control of research laboratories. The Public Health Security and Bioterrorism Preparedness and Response Act of 2002 put the Department of Health and Human Services and the Department of Agriculture in charge of formulating and enforcing regulations on institutional laboratories that work with select agents. One provision of this statute requires researchers and university administrators to provide an inventory of select agents they use in their laboratories and justify their use by March 2003. Higher education laboratories were also given until April 2004 to complete background checks on everyone with access to these materials, and they were given until September 2003 to make their laboratories physically secure to prohibit unauthorized people from gaining access. Institutions were given until November 2003 to become fully compliant with all rules and regulations pertaining to the Public Health Security and Bioterrorism Preparedness and Response Act. It is ironic that institutions are required to interrogate laboratory workers about their personal backgrounds at a time when they cannot even casually ask job applicants about their age or marital status.

Other surveillance innovations in the War on Terror have specific implications for academic support in higher education. Specifically, agents of federal law enforcement agencies now have access to what faculty, staff, and students communicate to each other through e-mail and to what they borrow and read from their institutional libraries if they are suspected of terrorist or criminal activities. The Federal Bureau of Investigation created an e-mail wiretapping system originally and appropriately called "Carnivore." The system was authorized and renamed in the PATRIOT Act as Digital Collection System 1000 or DCS 1000. DCS 1000 is attached to the operating systems of all Internet Service Providers and may collect the e-mails of targeted individuals or the e-mails of all of the users of a system.[18] DCS 1000 is capable of scanning millions of e-mails per second. Thousands of faculty in the United States now use e-mail or discussion boards made available in course management systems as integral components of their course delivery in both fully online or face-to-face courses. DCS 1000 provides a technological solution for the federal government to monitor what students and faculty say to each other electronically in college classrooms. It is ironic that higher education institutions go to great lengths to ensure that course websites are secure in that they exclude those who do not pay tuition, but faculty and students are now expected to teach and learn in environments that are not secure from the snooping of the federal government.

Another disturbing feature of the intrusion of the War on Terror into the academic support systems of higher education is the authority the Federal Bureau of Investigation now has to collect information on what people read. The PATRIOT Act compels libraries and bookstores to provide the FBI with lists of what people have borrowed or bought if a secret court established by the Foreign Intelligence Surveillance Act concurs with a request from federal agents to investigate individuals suspected of terrorist or criminal activities. In effect, the PATRIOT Act nullifies federal, state, and local laws, as well as institutional or corporate policies, protecting the privacy of library users and bookstore customers from federal agents. Further, the PATRIOT Act prohibits librarians and bookstore employees from disclosing to targeted individuals that the FBI is scrutinizing their reading habits. If agents of the federal government obtain a search warrant or a court order to acquire information on an individual, librarians must provide the information. They cannot appeal the demand to a judge nor can they tell anyone about it, including their supervisors. Once the principle of governmental spying into individual behavior in libraries and bookstores becomes accepted practice, there is nothing to stop the expansion of governmental snooping into topics or disciplines that today are perfectly legitimate areas of inquiry, including pharmaceuticals, chemicals, as well as philosophies or methodologies that are critical of existing social relations and forms of knowledge.[19]

The important policy question is, to what extent is free inquiry or academic freedom compromised when academic discourse is subject to governmental oversight? As the PATRIOT Act and other laws that place national security above civil liberties are implemented, more academics are likely to be arrested or banned from the classroom and laboratories. If there is a second September 11–style terrorist attack or a second bioterrorist attack, the dossiers that universities have built on their students and faculty, which are now centralized in a Justice Department database, will likely be the first place the FBI looks for suspects. Higher education is no longer a sheltered haven for free inquiry into humanity, society, and nature.

THE STRUGGLE FOR THE FUTURE

How is the security state likely to affect the structure and operation of colleges and universities as the processes of privatization and enforcement are pursued on a broad scale? In his study of the organizational components of colleges and universities, James Downey[20] argues that postsecondary institutions are a curious and simultaneous blend of three incarnations. First, colleges and universities are a *corporation* in the sense that they are legal entities created by official acts of state or federal governments, whether that occurs through a charter, a statute, or a constitution. As corporations, they can own property, make contracts, and appoint officers who have a delineated scope of authority. As corporations, they have a hierarchical structure with authority vested in a corporate board that can be delegated to officers with a delineated scope of responsibility. Because legal compliance is required of corporations across a range of responsibilities, the postsecondary institution cannot operate as a consensual community in every facet of its operation. In their corporate functions, colleges and universities are creatures of the state.

However, a postsecondary institution is not only a corporation, it is also what Downey calls a *collegium* and a *community*. As a collegium, postsecondary institutions possess an amalgam of assumptions, traditions, protocols, rituals, relationships, and structures that permit the professorate to conduct and control the academic affairs of the institution. The collegium is not hierarchical nor is it particularly responsive to external pressures. It is the practical realization of free inquiry and academic freedom. As a community, the college or university is not just a physical space but an inclusive, ambiguous, amorphous, and complex network of equals, who interact and pursue a variety of agenda based on a diversity of values and beliefs about the academy, its role in society, and in their personal lives.

From a historical standpoint, there is a need to protect basic societal thresholds pertaining to the role and power of social institutions. For higher education, this means that there must be a balance among corporations, collegia and communities within colleges and universities. While the relative parity of corporation, collegium, and community has been destroyed in some sociohistorical circumstances, such as in Nazi Germany, Soviet Russia, and Islamic Iran, the relative parity of corporation, collegium, and community in colleges and universities has proved to be fairly effective for nearly a thousand years in ensuring that the societal need to generate, disseminate, and apply new knowledge is met. However, the rise of the security state poses an important challenge to the structure of higher education by upending the balance of corporation, collegium, and community.

The elevation of national security above all other societal values and the extension of the logic of the market into the operation of all social institutions, including higher education, ensures that the *corporation* will become the predominant incarnation of the college and university. The *collegium* and the *community* are not structurally nor culturally capable of supporting the expansion of privatization and enforcement. Instead, they tend to militate against the expansion of state power and capitalist exchange relations precisely because of their inclusiveness, ambiguity, and unfettered inquiry.

The frustration that national and state policymakers often express about the responsiveness of higher education to accountability demands can be understood as a normal and fairly predictable outcome of the difficulty that collegia and communities can pose for authority. The behavior of institutions and the participants within collegia and communities are rarely linear, uncritical responses to the dictates of external actors and organizations. We appear to be entering a new historical period in the relationship between the academy and the state in which the corporation is elevated above the collegium and the community because it is the only one of the three that can respond to the economic, political, and technological demands of the security state. The specter of this transformation of higher education should be generally alarming since it adumbrates a profound change in the process by which knowledge is generated, applied, and disseminated. Free inquiry and academic freedom are central to the preservation of the type of self-knowledge and the sense of a collective future that has historically characterized democratic societies. The elevation of security above free inquiry, and the elevation of corporation above collegium and community in colleges and universities, will likely have much broader societal implications, including the subversion of democratic and participatory processes of generating and disseminating knowledge about humanity, society, and nature. The security state emerged in the absence of a broad and serious societal discussion about the role of the state in a time of crisis. An inclusive and participatory discussion about the relationship among the state, private capital, and higher education would provide an excellent point of departure for a societal conversation about the future of democracy and democratic institutions.

— 15 —

Schooling and the Security State

Julie Webber

> Yet, although one might have expected the notion of immortality to perish completely, to become a casualty of the Enlightenment's secularization of reason and its dissolution to the links of its past, the truth turns out to be more complex. For while officially we moderns are committed to the notion of our own mortality, we nevertheless harbor the secret, inarticulable conviction that we are *not* mortal.
>
> —Joan Copjec, *Imagine There's No Woman*[1]

We hear a lot of discussion about school "choice" and democratic freedom and expression in the United States. We also hear, at the same time, a lot of discussion about security especially in the wake of the September 11 attacks on the World Trade Center and the Pentagon. The two conversations take place simultaneously in the news media and in educational settings. Middle-class parents who are concerned for the safety of their children will take them out of public schools and opt for affordable private ones or charters that cater to their political or spiritual preferences (another fear is evoked here: fear that children will be assaulted with bad ideas). Or, conversely, working-class parents of color might work extra hard to move their families to middle- and upper-class districts to give their kids a better opportunity structure and chance at life, only to find that discrimination follows them there, too.[2] After the highly publicized school attacks in the United States and elsewhere, parents are even more concerned about school security and safety, despite the fact that school violence has actually declined and has been slowly declining since the early 1990s. Every presidential administration since Truman has made national influence on educational standards a rhetorical centerpiece of campaigns, but none has actually passed coherent legislation with a solid policy backed by a national educational philosophy or standard to which citizens might direct their concerns about school safety and purpose. In studies of ideology, we call this the "absent presence" after deconstructionist Jacques Derrida's formulation, by which the lack of a unifying ideology (or "common ideal" as was the goal of the "common school") comes to be what determines national unity through misrecognition: People believe they are unified as "Americans" or as "humans" but in reality hold opposing and contradictory views about the nature of life, the process of politics, and everyday living—we misrecognize other people's ideas as similar to our own. If I look at the flag, I may see something totally different, or be inspired in a much different way, from my neighbor by its physical presence. To me, it may be a revolting example of hypocrisy—a debased physical incarnation meant to cover over the history of injustice committed in the name of "the United States," but to my neighbor it may mean a symbol of freedom, the guarantor of living wages, or at least the opportunity for them at some point in the future. My neighbor may even concede that the United States has this checkered past of imperialist activity and destruction of indigenous peoples, slavery, oppression of women, and so on, but will say, if provoked, it's better than what he or she had elsewhere on this earth. Touché. I must agree, since my neighbor has been willing to concede my point as well, however, there is a loss embedded in this recognition of difference and that is the loss of dependence that we are together embarking on the same path, a project for protection and security. Instead, my neighbor is going his way, doing his thing, based on his past, and I am doing mine for separate reasons. Both are based on a kind of fear and separation, an individualism, if you will, that forever locks us apart from a common project. What binds my neighbor and me is the security state.

The security state is the political incarnation of protection. We are protected by the state so that we can pursue our individual ideals and projects. The security state is also the outcome of my neighbors and my mutually exclusive desires and fears. My neighbor may fear more terrorists, while I may fear too many guns in circulation in the United States. However, the government forms our national interest and defends it by making policies designed to protect us from others who may interfere with our ability to do our own thing or live our "way of life." We are not protected to act collectively against that state should we choose to do so (as Locke promised us) or even against corporations who might exploit our labor for the purposes of gaining more power and money by paying us lower wages and restricting our social benefits. We are protected as individuals, not groups. We can never question the role of the security state in providing protection to us because it is written into our social contract that the state protects us and we follow its laws, because they are better than the alternative: a war between my neighbor and me.

The democratic school has always been an instrument of the security state. This is by no means a new idea, *pace* 9/11. The school, as historians of education know well, was conceived as a warehouse for immigrant children at the turn of the nineteenth century. As any good liberal knows, when given lemons, make lemonade. So, we choose, as a country, to conceptualize the democratic public school as a place that would help immigrants, not warehouse them from the rich, propertied, white Americans who settled before waves of immigration and emancipation. The school was no longer conceived of as a space of security but of social progress and has been ever since. But the idea of school as a space of security has always been lying there under the surface, and at times such as these—growing inequality between people economically, increasing joblessness, growing hatred and fear—the security state comes to the surface as the primary objective of the democratic school. There are several reasons for this: (1) the United States has been the most avid promoter of democratic schooling throughout the world for the last sixty years, if not before then, as the means through which people can achieve social ascription under capitalism and through which poor countries can "develop"; (2) the United States is the preponderant power in the world; this means it is not only the most powerful country in the world but also that its power so far surpasses that of any other country that could challenge it that it doesn't even have to go to war to defend its title or get its way on any international matter (this is also called "hegemony"); (3) since the Cold War, the United States has been the number one developer and promoter of military supplies and technology, and it sells this military technology throughout the world; and (4) as inequality has risen throughout the world—both between countries of the developed North and the underdeveloped South and between the rich and poor within all nearly 200 of these countries—violence and hate has become the primary enemy of states' governments through their adoption of the "security state" policy and their purchase of U.S.-based surveillance technologies. The United States can sell the military and security technology necessary to alleviate the fears of governments and their wealthy constituencies to "contain" the violence and hatred that comes when the majority of people realize that they have been left out of the financial progress, and that the democratic school has failed to help them develop. There are several reasons the school has failed in these countries, among them the widespread knowledge by the majority of people that the states are redirecting money from education to buying military and security technology to contain them.

Schools have always been a hegemonic tool of the security state as "schooling" by which Ivan Illich understood it to be a process of training people to believe in the legitimacy of the state's orders. At school, students learn to become "citizens," and they learn to fear one another through the school's unwritten policy of allowing the strongest to dominate, the so-called "bully," and they learn hierarchy through "tracking" in differential learning spaces: special education, reading groups, math groups, sports teams. They learn that they are individuals when they are rated through grades and set against one another in competition through tables of assessment, and they really learn that they are individuals when they are notified of school status through their social security numbers. They learn not to question authority, even when its demands clearly go against their interests through "zero tolerance" policies. They learn to expect deviant behavior from the young and to question any altruistic or community-oriented ideas they may have, even if they are in the interest of repairing their own reputation in the eyes of teachers and authority figures or of making the school a better place. Consider this insight from renowned child psychotherapist Adam Phillips, as recounted from his experience with schoolteachers in England:

> One of the issues that continually exercised and divided people was whether the classrooms should be left unlocked when the children were outside during playtime. It was more or less generally agreed that an unlocked classroom was an invitation, at least for some of those children, to vandalize the place. These children, it was said, needed to be protected from themselves. If anything else, they were likely to steal anything that was left lying around. In one of these always slightly uneasy discussions the deputy head said she could see them "walking off with the lot." "But what if one of the kids wants to put something good in the classroom?" one of the teachers asked. "Like what?" somebody asked. And there was an immense relief when no one could think of anything.[3]

Most Americans view the public school as an instrument for social and economic ascription; this is an instrumental and pragmatic view of school. They do not see it as a citizen-building institution, as democratic theorists have viewed it historically or as comparative political scientists have used it in arguments concerning the formation of "rule of law" in developing societies. They suppose that if it is a citizen-building institution, then that's okay too, but the primary purpose of education in the United States has been its promise as a means to get out of poverty or move up the social ladder one more notch. Thus, most Americans do not view the public school as a space where their children might learn to think critically, that is, to call into crisis, in petite ways, the order of things. They more often than not wish that their children would conform at school and learn to conform if it makes life easier for them in the long run. There is already in this attitude toward schools and conformity a willingness to bind oneself to concepts of security based on fear: fear of retaliation, harassment, alienation, and poverty. This is always called a Hobbesian fear, named for the base political philosopher Thomas Hobbes, who said that life was "poor, nasty, brutish and short," and, therefore, we should take cover from others and bind ourselves to the law in order to gain protection from them, these others that threaten our existence, livelihood and happiness. I have a friend, a fellow political theorist, who smartly says we can't get over Hobbes because we secretly need to believe him: It's too hard to make life pleasant; thus, it is much easier to consign it to the status of difficult and resign ourselves to competition.

Even the most liberal of educational theorists, John Dewey, had to hide his radicalism. While hiding it may have worked to protect his authority and perceptions of his expertise from the public, it did not exceed the boundaries of educational expectations and begin to question or call into crisis this ideology that the public school is an instrument for social ascription. It may have even reinforced it. Since Immanuel Kant and other thinkers of the Enlightenment gave the "Western" world the notion of enlightenment and autonomy, they also put into the minds of educational radicals and liberals the idea that one can have independent thought and that independent thought can inspire independent action.[4] This is the notion that a person can be autonomous, that is, not determined by the general structure of conformist ideals, expectations, and politics. This would presume that students would learn at school to question the ideal of social ascription and economic determinism. Sadly, it has not meant that in the United States or elsewhere as far as policy analysts can tell. Instead, the notion of autonomy of thought has reinforced the idea that students should treat themselves and others as individuals and ends. As many theorists of social movements have pointed out when referencing the United States, there is no such thing as class consciousness[5] nor is the concept of group rights appealing, since it violates the principle of individualism that is the cornerstone of American democracy.[6] So, even though women, African-Americans, Latina/Latinos, Arab Americans, and gays and lesbians may be presently discriminated against because of their perceived membership in a group that has historically been marked for degraded social, political, and economic treatment, they cannot be enabled or capacitated as a group but only as individuals under the standards of equal opportunity. Because there is clearly nothing that binds these groups or individuals together as a "nation," the state's policies and the underlying fears that motivate them come into place to structure social relations between people with diverse interests in school and society. The security state is the last thread holding together democratic citizenship in the United States and elsewhere, and unless we can reconceive of the mission of the public school, as educators, we will lose it to the security state completely.

SCHOOLING AS THE REINFORCEMENT OF THE SECURITY STATE

The remainder of this chapter will explore the new role of the public school in the *reinforcement* of the security state. The security state is not a

national security state, as has traditionally been held, but rather a security
state that binds democratic students in allegiance (as subjects) to the shifting rhetorical concept of state forged by what James Der Derian has called
the "media-infotainment network" of militarized authority structures.[7] These
are structures that work to discipline and control students without a physical body present to take responsibility for discipline or to interact with students in a face-to-face environment. These may include remote surveillance
technologies, such as video cameras, or even random searches. They may
further include the enlistment of the cohort of students to police each other
by notifying school authorities of suspicious or deviant behavior, a policy that
exactly mimics the citizen duties set forth in the USA PATRIOT Act of 2001.

As I have argued elsewhere,[8] television is the social. What is meant by this
is that the media determines for the society what counts as the elements of
an enlightened conversation about politics and community in the absence
of face-to-face discussion. This means, for example, if there are no women
discussing the war in Iraq on television as experts, people come to believe
that women can't discuss war and have no place in the conversation. Or it
means that if a high-profile black man is arrested for child molestation, he
has committed the crime that white men are actually four times as likely to
commit, and this absolves the public of discussing the actual demographic
that is responsible for the majority of child molestation cases. This is exactly
what Der Derian means by the military infotainment network; the media
works to make war seem like a necessary aim, and it implants the notion in
people's minds that school security is necessary, even though school violence
is, in actuality, a very rare occurrence. While bullying and cliques are among
the vast experiences of the majority of children in the state's nearly 100,000
schools, the real problem, it seems, is that one boy who *might* bring a gun
to school. The media will run this story over and over again for days until
something more terrorizing captures widespread interest. It makes it seem
as if this boy is everywhere, and the schools respond to the concerns of parents about this possible boy by installing remote security measures and encouraging peer suspicion and reporting, even when no threat is present in a
particular community. We can see the power of the media to determine
society's priorities, which are based on fear of a possible school attack. People
are led to imagine virtually any possible terrorizing scenario, and they have
little encouragement to speak to one another to determine whether the media
presentation is accurate or distorted. What is actually happening in this mediated process is that people are becoming less inclined to respond to one
another in a civil manner and more inclined to view each other with suspicion, especially young people in school. This is how the media confirms the
objectives of the security state, one of which is to make many people feel
very insecure and in need of these military and surveillance technologies. This
is, in turn, how the school becomes a space where people become uncivi-
lized through a process of security that is designed to protect them. It makes

perfect sense if the outcome is increased state legitimacy and control, but little sense if the objective of public schooling is to develop "citizens" that are civilized and respectful of one another, and possibly critical of the government's financial management.

At stake in the debate surrounding "schooling" as a decivilizing process (versus education or critical literacy, pedagogy) is the notion of "autonomy." Is the security state encouraging students to become autonomous citizens capable of making critically democratic judgments, or is the notion of "autonomy" precisely the problem in that it encourages students to think of themselves as whole and distinct rational entities (automatons) that must ward off potential assaults from objects circulating in their environments to the exclusion of other forms of *being* and *having* in democratic spaces? To examine this goal of the security state in relation to schooling, it is important to understand how "schooling" has been understood as a process by which students are evacuated of critical and desiring capacities in schools by the architecture of the security state.[9] The remainder of the chapter will detail how the imperatives of the security state relate to student conformity and "boredom"[10] and are an effort to squash the citizens' and students' capacity to view and exploit democratic spaces (such as public schools) as exemplars of "little pieces of being."[11]

Let's return to the problem with individualism and its relationship to security. Schools teach students to see themselves as independent, self-reliant individuals with little or no responsibility owed to others; in other words, they are possessive individuals; they are taught to mind their own business and pay attention to their own success. John Taylor Gatto recently published a provocative essay in *Harper's* magazine charging that "schooling," by which he means compulsory education, not education, does a great disservice to the nation's children by training them to be conformist and also by encouraging boredom.[12] I happen to agree with Gatto, although I suspect that his claims were designed to provoke a critical public discussion that should be taking place about schools, not to really dismiss the idea of public schooling itself. If Gatto's claims, which echo Illich's from the seventies, that we "dis-establish" school are sincere, then he is missing two very large pieces of the puzzle: (1) the majority of Americans need public education because it acts as a very important substitute for the lack of affordable daycare in the this country; they could not work if their kids did not go to school, and (2) the school can be used as a citizen-building institution, it is simply that as a country we have chosen not to let it perform that function by the policies we impose on it and the way, as discussed already, it has been used to inculcate the values of the security state to the exclusion of other public virtues.

On this latter point, Gatto would seemingly agree with me as he outlines the origins of the American public school system in the Prussian state of the mid- to late-eighteenth century, under the tutelage of Enlightenment thinkers, such as Kant, with the support of enlightened rulers such as Frederick the I and II. These rulers benefited from Enlightenment political ideas while simultaneously developing a potent military force capable of running over North Germany, the implication is that the origin of the later "peaceful" school is that it is itself proto-fascist in orientation while combining ideas about "Enlightenment education" with militarism and imperialism. If we recall that the Prussian state was indeed gesturing toward a "Second Reich" only to be perfected by the "Third" in the 1930s, then we have grounds to fear it and the basis upon which it schools students in allegiance to the security state. Further, the Prussian state of the nineteenth century also experienced a pronounced military and technological superiority that enabled it to incorporate larger masses of surrounding territory (and, importantly, populations) through the use of the train to deploy soldiers and surround enemies. One of the major advances in military technologies was made by the Prussians in what is now known as the ongoing "RMA" or Revolution in Military Affairs. The RMA sets out this thesis: Revolutionary advances in technology applied to military strategy change the entire nature of warfare in a given historical period that is politically decisive to world order (i.e., the state hailed as innovator can either challenge a stronger state using this new technological advantage or an already preponderant power [like the U.S.] can use it to further secure power and benefits from others). Further, these changes are always introduced into the general population through management techniques, (for example, Taylorism) schooling, and pedestrian forms of technology (usually consumed as entertainment, such as video games) that help to pay for the research necessary to develop and market the technology in the first place through "economies of scale." Thus, the proliferation of the technology for commercial profit, plus the increasing benefits of social control provided by it as a selling point, help to pay for the research that was experimental, expensive, and "necessary" to increase one country's military power over others.

Gatto intimates in his article that the logic of the Enlightenment, with its notions of autonomy, has actually worked to produce the conformity and boredom necessary in school populations to render them helpless against the security state that may become, or is, a bellicose world power. We know where this ends: the camps. I am less inclined to make such summary judgments about the function of schools, though I agree with Chomsky that theirs is a "subtler" form of control than that of, say, a tank rolling down my street. Autonomy works well with capitalist competition because it *needs* me and my neighbor to see ourselves as set against each other in competition that is regulated by the state, instead of as allies against a growing security state that may be turning us into conformists who will not question its international designs against others or its rapid accumulation of wealth that we are not ourselves experiencing. Gatto would like to see students take more responsibility for their own boredom and argues that the schools not only leave them bereft of ideas for entertaining themselves on a boring Sunday afternoon, but also leaves them with little imagination for creative political thinking. Phillips's teachers might be seen as a product of this compulsory system when they are "relieved" that no one can imagine a good thing a student might want to put in a classroom! As Gatto writes, "Of course, teachers are themselves the products of the same twelve-year compulsory school programs that so thoroughly bore their students, and, as school personnel, they are trapped inside the structures even more rigid than those interposed upon the children. Who, then, is to blame?"[13] Gatto has an answer: the "crippling" effect of the decline in maturity in the United States. Again, I can't help but agree with him, but do not support his conclusions to wipe out compulsory education. There are creative options out of this situation, and the major thrust of Gatto's argument is that schools leave citizens handicapped to entertain themselves with creative pursuits that might be innovative and help other people, but his conclusions are less than creative; they are nihilistic.

A recent foray into political philosophy demonstrates the same growing concern with the security state over questions of population control. The school is a form of population containment. This new politics has been labeled "biopolitics" by its discoverer Michel Foucault in the last chapter of an unlikely source, *The History of Sexuality*, Volume One.[14] Foucault's argument is that biopolitics is the means by which the security state (he would not use such a brisk term) gains control over populations by using these management techniques developed by the social sciences and medicine (we could definitely add education) to control them for their own good, in the interest of making populations "healthier" and more "normal." The state gains access to a previously foreclosed space of human existence: "bare life," or the private sphere. More recently, political philosopher Giorgio Agamben has applied Foucault's insights about biopolitics, with Hannah Arendt's sober warnings of imperialism, to contemporary issues surrounding the management of populations.[15] Agamben locates a historical figure, *Homo sacer*, who is the life that can be killed but not sacrificed; that is, it is not prohibited by the state for *Homo sacer* to be killed, but the act of murder cannot be considered homicide or a sacrifice to the sake of the community. It's just a "bare life" that can be killed. Agamben further speculates that the model of this form of sovereign power over bare life is the concentration camp, where people were stripped of their citizenship rights in both religious and civil contexts, and then summarily executed by technologies that took responsibility for the act of killing out of the direct hands of the executioners; the gas chamber did not rely upon face-to-face interaction between the executioners and the victims, just as the trains that carried the victims to the camps had been developed by a Prussian RMA innovation seventy years before.

Homo sacer is able to be killed through processes that are the outcome of enlightenment-inspired technologies and forms of managing populations to the benefit of the security state. Those who process the security state are not inclined to ask questions about the purpose of the technology or of its effects on general populations. If this technology and techniques of management encourage people to mind their own business and cultivate their own gardens, while ignoring the negative impact that it may have on others, including bringing about their deaths, it is because enlightenment notions of autonomy have encouraged this kind of conformism and quietism. As Agamben explains it, the camp is the "paradigm" of our biopolitical time period. Against those who would argue that the paradigm is the city or urban space, he argues that the camp represents the opening up of a space in modernity (the time period in which we are said to live) where the powers that be, the "sovereigns," suspend the rule of law in certain circumstances and call it the "state of exception" or "state of emergency." In this space, seemingly necessary security measures may be taken, and the life of the people subject to this space is deemed a "bare life"; that is, without constitutional, legal or religious protections and subject to any and all machinations, the security state can conjure up to exploit their humanity in the name of everyone else's security. From Guantanamo Bay (where no law, neither martial nor international, holds sway) to the refugee camps in Australia that house the increasing number of refugees displaced by the two wars in the Middle East and back to school where students increasingly have no rights or constitutional protections, the logic of the camp, not the crowded city of the late nineteenth century, holds sway.[16] As he writes, "The camp is the space that is opened up when the state of exception begins to become the rule. In the camp, the state of exception, which was essentially a temporary suspension of the rule of law on the basis of a factual state of danger, is now given a permanent spatial arrangement, which as such nevertheless remains outside the normal order."[17]

Did the majority of the U.S. population complain to their government that it was bombing unarmed populations in Afghanistan and Iraq using advanced aerotechnologies and satellite information to increase the distance and reality of the killing by bombing from 4,500 feet (not hand-to-hand combat) and by broadcasting a seemingly bloodless proxy war through embedded journalists, all in their name? No. However, many people did protest, especially if they did not live in the United States! Furthermore, it is not clear that this lack of protest is the fault of the schools but only of the security state that has overrun them with standards and security policies that enforce conformity. So, the question is not why are Americans conformists if they subscribe to the Enlightenment philosophy of autonomy, which Kant very precisely argued meant *maturity* (to give Gatto his due, and he explicitly states that it was his grandfather who taught him this lesson), but more precisely, why do they use technology to make decisions for themselves and avoid the entire Enlightenment debate over independent thought and action altogether? Perhaps it is the noted obsession that all great powers have had historically with immortality, as the quote from Joan Copjec rightly pointed out at the start of this essay. In their struggle to live forever, to be immortal and to avoid the reality of death and confront mortality, the powerful, drunk with their superiority, forget that they are only "human all too human."

Indeed, they may use their technology to act is if they are immortal and extend their existence beyond the physical realm of decision making and maturity that comes with age, which is a sign of progress toward the end of life. Wisdom comes with age, they say, but what do you say to people who refuse to age and yet think they are wise? Who are united in only one respect: their mutual adherence to the will to power?

Copjec has an answer, and it's as simple and downright wise as we're going to get: Resist the urge to view life as the sum total of experiences that hurtle one toward death, and view it as a process that is mediated by ideas about sex, or more precisely, by pleasure and desire. All of our educational sacred cows—progress, development, freedom, prosperity, security, unity, and respect—have been killed but not sacrificed by the security state. However, we do not have to accept the logic that Enlightenment ideals are dependent and entirely congruent with another influential mode of thought that dominated the early part of the twentieth century, existentialism.[18] Gatto's reading of American education as the sum total product of Prussian influence, and Agamben's reading of biopolitics, leave us with a future that truly looks "empty and intense," to quote Peter McLaren[19] on predatory culture, but we can resist the idea that what is guiding this movement is a fear of death by locating our most profound anxieties and pleasures in the smaller moments and experiences in the life of "bodies that matter," to recast Judith Butler's treatise on the "discursive limits of sex."[20] Unlike Butler, Copjec has found an answer in psychoanalysis, and its profound attention is not to the end of life (a space it rightly ascertains we cannot access or avoid) but to "little pieces of being" we encounter along the way that are scattered along the path of existence that has no ultimate end state.

In *Imagine There's No Woman*, Copjec undertakes a revision of the commonplace notion that the "body is the seat of death" (as in biopolitics or existentialism) and replaces it with the notion that "the body is the seat of sex"; and that the "sexualization of the body" (the ideas and affects we project onto the body about sex that confuse us, the body that confounds our expectations of it, pleasantly surprises us, and demonstrates difference and perhaps "life" to us) is what drives us. To do this, Copjec dispels another common illusion: the death drive is what motivates us in life (we are back to biopolitics); instead she argues that the death drive is only interesting in its failure to achieve its aims. What Copjec argues that is so radical is that the problem is not that we are mortal (to return to the quote at the start of this essay) but that we have persistently thought ourselves, the human race and especially Americans, as capable of reaching beyond a past simple existence or bare life. In our quest to "cheat death" or "die with the most toys and win," we are not confronting the ultimate human obstacle, death (more precisely the death drive), but are avoiding the banal conclusion that we could substitute virtually any other aim for the object of the drive: The notion that "everyone is confronting death" and using upward mobility, especially through education, as a means to cheat death, is absurd from Copjec's point of view. We are choosing to make the cheating of death the aim or idealized quest of human existence, and when we choose death and the finitude of the body, our technologies and forms of security will necessarily reflect that *legislative* decision. People chose it; it was not fated for them. For example, philosophical realism posits that the ultimate goal of life is to avoid death, to the point where most people would agree to let a power-hungry, bellicose leader legislate every aspect of their lives in exchange for protection from an uncertain world, other people (like neighbors), terrorists, or teenage boys. This concession (which is really the ultimate form of hostage-taking, that of citizens by legislators) is exacted through an unrelenting campaign of scaring people into believing two things: They can cheat death by becoming successful through the vehicle of education that will lead to wealth and power, and they can look forward to a beyond of life and the body, provided by technology. Finally, it urges them to believe that they are forever in jeopardy of becoming "bare life," that is, subject to the harsh realities of the natural world without the protection and security of the state.

Copjec argues that to dispel this one idea of transcendence that has come to dominate an entire historical pattern of metaphysics and education (in the life sciences), we should see the split from which the drive emerges (the drive to do better, be successful, die, be complacent); it could emerge, as she says, and have it be that "Virtually any object will serve as well as any other to satisfy the drive, which aims not at the object but at the satisfaction it can derive from it."[21] This is reminiscent of the early John Dewey, who argued that the child is not looking for the object but for his aim and the ability to repeat the quest for attaining it over and over again,[22] and D. W. Winnicott, who argued that the child is not looking for an object (when she or he steals) but for the capacity to find.[23] What can the body and a new look at an underused notion of it bring to education and social life in the form of a sobering realization? We are not the sum total of our life's experiences, and we are not determined by the beyond of death, but are situated within life here on earth as people who make discriminating judgments that bar some from success and enable others, despite the relative talents of each of them as individuals. The school does not have to be a laboratory for *Homo sacer*; it can be an experimental space for encouraging tolerance, diversity, and a space for teaching students to view the small moments of being, the obstacles poised in front of them, and the objectives they set for themselves as challenges of both body and mind, a lifelong quest to enjoy and improve themselves, not a burden to shoulder while competing for first prize in the endgame, one that no one and everyone already wins.[24]

It seems I agree with Gatto (and he with Copjec), for the school can become a space where people can have the time and gather the energy to find these "little pieces of being" and relate to them in a way that will have lasting effects on the quality of life later in the "real world," where they will be challenged with obstacles too numerous to name in the space of this writing. Perhaps they will find love in the actual practice of photography and the image as Cindy Sherman has, or they will find a way around the narcissism inherent in wanting to sell their knowledge for profit, and decide they love it for its own sake and the pleasure it brings them. Or maybe they'll just find a good job and live a decent life.

Notes

GENERAL EDITOR'S INTRODUCTION

1. Portions of this section draw upon E. Wayne Ross, "Remaking the Social Studies Curriculum," in *The Social Studies Curriculum: Purposes, Problems, and Possibilities*, rev. ed., ed. E. Wayne Ross (Albany: State University of New York Press, 2001).

2. John Dewey, *Democracy and Education* (New York: Free Press, 1966), p. 87.

3. Robert W. McChesney, Introduction to *Profits over People: Neoliberalism and Global Order*, by Noam Chomsky (New York: Seven Stories Press, 1988).

4. Madison quoted in Chomsky, *Profits over People*, p. 47.

5. For an explication of these issues see Edward S. Herman and Noam Chomsky, *Manufacturing Consent: The Political Economy of the Mass Media* (New York: Pantheon, 1988).

6. Noam Chomsky, *Media Control: The Spectacular Achievements of Propaganda* (New York: Seven Stories Press, 1997).

7. A. A. Lispcom and A. Ellery, eds., *The Writings of Thomas Jefferson*, vol. 16 (Washington, DC: The Thomas Jefferson Memorial Association, 1903), p. 96.

8. Dewey quoted in Noam Chomsky, *Class Warfare* (Vancouver: New Star Books, 1997).

FOREWORD

1. Naomi Klein, "The Year of the Fake," *The Nation* 278, no. 3 (January 2004), p. 10.

2. See Arjun Makhijani, "U.S. Monetary Imperialism and the War on Iraq," *The Black Commentator* no. 73 (2002).

3. See John Alan, *Dialectics of Black Freedom Struggles: Race, Philosophy, and the Needed American Revolution* (Chicago: News and Letters Publications, 2003).

INTRODUCTION

1. Jimmy Carter, *The "Crisis of Confidence Speech,"* July 15, 1979, http://www.pbs.org/wgbh/amex/carter/filmmore/ps_crisis.html.

2. Ibid.

3. Ibid.

4. President's Commission for a National Agenda for the Eighties, *A National Agenda for the Eighties* (Washington, DC: U.S. Government Printing Office, 1980), p. 84.

5. Ibid., p. ii.

6. Ibid., p. 1.

7. Ibid., p. 84.

8. Jimmy Carter, *The "Crisis of Confidence Speech."*

9. Noam Chomsky, *Chronicles of Dissent: Interviews with David Barsamian*, (Monroe, ME: Common Courage Press, 1992), p. 105.

10. President's Commission for a National Agenda for the Eighties, p. iv.

11. Walter Lippmann, *The Essential Lippmann: A Political Philosophy for Liberal Democracy*, ed. Clinton Rossiter and James Lare (Cambridge, MA: Harvard University Press, (1982). Quoted in *Chomsky on Democracy and Education,* ed. Carlos Otero (New York: Routledge, 2002), pp. 33, 34, 199, 211, 250, 396–97.

12. Ibid.

13. President's Commission for a National Agenda for the Eighties, p. 84.

14. Milton Goldberg and James Harvey, *A Nation at Risk: The Report of the National Commission on Excellence in Education*, ed. Fred Schultz (Guilford, CT: Dushkin Publishing Group, 1985), p. 73. Reprinted from *Phi Delta Kappan*, September 1983 in *Education 85/86*, pp. 72–76.

15. Ibid.

16. Dean Acheson, *Present at the Creation: My Years in the State Department* (New York: W.W. Norton, 1969), p. 375.

17. Stephen Ball, *Education Reform: A Critical and Post-structural Approach* (Buckingham, England: Open University Press, 1994), p. 54.

18. See David A. Gabbard, "Education IS Enforcement: The Centrality of Compulsory Schooling in Market Societies," in *Education Is Enforcement: The Militarization and Corporatization of Schools* (New York: Routledge, 2003), pp. 61–78.

CHAPTER 1

1. All unidentified quotes are from *The Matrix* (Warner Bros. release, 1999).

2. Everett Reimer, "Freeing Educational Resources," in *After Deschooling, What?*, ed. Ivan Illich, Alan Gartner, Frank Riessman, and Colin Greer (New York: HarperCollins, 1976), p. 49.

3. Ibid.

4. A recent Google search for the phrase "The Matrix" generated nearly 5 million results.

5. Ivan Illich, *Tools for Conviviality* (San Francisco:, Heyday Books, 1973), p. 1.

6. Ibid.

7. Richard Schaull, foreword to *Pedagogy of the Oppressed,* by Paulo Freire, 30th anniversary ed. (New York: Continuum Books, 1970, 2000), p. 32.

8. Paulo Freire, *Pedagogy of the Oppressed,* 30th anniversary ed. (New York: Continuum Books, 1970, 2000), p. 43.

9. Jean Baudrillard, "The Violence of the Global," http://www.ctheory.net/text_file.asp?pick=385.

10. Karl Polanyi, *The Great Transformation* (New York: Farrar & Rinehart, Inc., 1944), p. 46.

11. R. H. Tawney, *Religion and the Rise of Capitalism* (New York: Penguin Books, 1938/1984), p. 153.

12. L. Rothking, *Opposition to Louis XIV: The Political and Social Origins of the French Enlightenment* (Princeton: Princeton University Press, 1965), pp. 301–2, quoted in Gérald Berthoud, "Market," in *The Development Dictionary* (Atlantic Highlands, NJ: Zed Books, 1992), p. 78.

13. Gérald Berthoud, "Market," in *The Development Dictionary* (Atlantic Highlands, NJ: Zed Books, 1992), p. 78.

14. J. L. Sadie, "The Social Anthropology of Economic Underdevelopment," in *The Economic Journal* (June 1960), p. 295.

15. Ibid., p. 302.

16. Polanyi, p. 34.

17. Ibid.

18. See David Gabbard, *Knowledge and Power in the Global Economy: Politics and the Rhetoric of School Reform* (Mahwah, NJ: Laurence Erlbaum, 2000), pp. xix–xx.

19. William Townsend, *Dissertation on the Poor Laws 1786 by A Well-Wisher of Mankind,* cited in Polanyi, p. 113.

20. Polanyi, p. 117.

21. Adam Smith, *An Inquiry into the Nature and Causes of the Wealth of Nations* (Chicago: Encyclopedia Britannica, 1952), p. 288.

22. Ibid., p. 277.

23. James Madison, quoted by Sean Gonsolves, "The Crisis in Democracy," *The Common Dreams Newscenter,* http://www.commondreams.org/views01/0619-01.htm.

24. Michel Foucault, *Discipline and Punish: The Birth of the Prison* (New York: Vintage Books, 1979), p. 136.

25. Ibid., p. 137.

26. Ibid., p. 138.

27. Michel Foucault, "Governmentality," in *The Foucault Effect: Studies in Governmentality,* ed. Graham Burchell, Colin Gordon, and Peter Miller (Chicago: University of Chicago Press, 1991), p. 93.

28. Michel Foucault, "Truth and Power," in *Power/Knowledge: Selected Interviews and Other Writings 1972–1977,* ed. Colin Gordon (New York: Pantheon, 1981), p. 125.

29. Peter McLaren, *Life in Schools: An Introduction to Critical Pedagogy in the Foundations of Education,* 4th ed. (New York: Allyn and Bacon, 2003), p. 254.

CHAPTER 2

1. *Culture* is frequently defined as the integrated pattern of human knowledge, belief, and behavior. This is a definition broad enough to include all major aspects of culture: language, ideas, beliefs, customs, taboos, codes, institutions, tools, techniques, works of art, rituals, ceremonies, and so on.

2. By this I mean the system of beliefs, ideas, and the corresponding values that are dominant (or tend to become dominant) in a particular society at a particular moment of its history as most consistent with the existing political, economic, and social institutions. The term "most consistent" does not imply, of course, any kind of structure/superstructure relationship à la Marx. Both culture and the social paradigm are time- and space-dependent, that is, they refer to a specific type of society at a specific time. Therefore, they both change from place to place and from one historical period to another, and this makes any "general theory" of history, which could determine the relationship between the cultural and the political or economic elements in society, impossible.

3. For the differences between culture and dominant social paradigm, see Takis Fotopoulos, "Mass Media, Culture and Democracy," *Democracy & Nature* 5, no. 1 (March 1999), pp. 33–64.

4. See Takis Fotopoulos, *Towards an Inclusive Democracy* (London/NY: Cassell/Continuum, 1997).

5. See Takis Fotopoulos, "Towards a Democratic Liberatory Ethics," *Democracy & Nature* 8, no. 3 (November 2002), pp. 361–96.

6. Cornelius Castoriadis, *Philosophy, Politics, Autonomy* (Oxford: Oxford University Press, 1991), p. 162.

7. Technical knowledge here means the absorption of some general skills (reading, writing) as well as the introduction, at the early stages of schooling, to some general scientific and technological ideas to be supplemented, at later stages, by a higher degree of specialization.

8. C. Castoriadis, *World in Fragments* (Stanford: Stanford University Press, 1997), p. 132. Following Castoriadis, we may call autonomous "a society that not only knows explicitly that it has created its own laws but has instituted itself so as to free its radical image and enable itself to alter its institutions through collective, self-reflective, and deliberate activity." On the basis of this definition, Castoriadis then defines politics as "the lucid activity whose object is the institution of an autonomous society and the decisions about collective endeavors"—something that implies, as he points out, that the project of an autonomous society becomes meaningless if it is not, at the same time, the project of bringing forth autonomous individuals, and vice versa. In the same sense, he defines democracy as the regime of collective reflectiveness.

9. Ibid., p. 131.

10. See Takis Fotopoulos, "Transitional Strategies and the Inclusive Democracy Project," *Democracy & Nature* 8, no. 1 (March 2002), pp. 17–62.

11. See Takis Fotopoulos, "The Myth of Postmodernity," *Democracy & Nature* 7, no. 1 (March 2001), pp. 27–76.

12. See Fotopoulos, *Towards an Inclusive Democracy*, ch. 1.

13. Will Hutton, *The State We're In* (London: Jonathan Cape, 1995), p. 174.

14. See Nicholas Barr, *The Economics of the Welfare State* (London: Weidenfeld & Nicolson, 1987), ch. 2.

15. See Fotopoulos, *Towards an Inclusive Democracy*, pp. 75–79.

16. Ibid., pp. 21–33.

17. Ibid., ch. 2.

18. Ibid., pp. 73–85 and 100–4. See also, Takis Fotopoulos, "The Catastrophe of Marketization," *Democracy & Nature* 5, no. 2 (July 1999), pp. 275–310.

19. A. H. Halsey and Anthony F. Heath. *Origins and Destinations, Family, Class, and Education in Modern Britain* (Oxford: Clarendon Press, 1980).

20. J. H. Goldthorpe, *Social Mobility and Class Structure in Modern Britain* (Oxford: Clarendon Press, 1980), p. 252.

21. Takis Fotopoulos, "Globalization, the Reformist Left and the Anti-Globalization Movement," *Democracy & Nature* 7, no. 2 (July 2001), pp. 233–80.

22. See Fotopoulos, *Towards an Inclusive Democracy*, pp. 33–46.

23. See Stephanie Pain, "When the Price Is Wrong," *The Guardian*, February 27, 1997.

24. See *The Castoriadis Reader*, ed. David Ames Curtis (Oxford: Blackwell, 1997), p. 260.

25. Tracy McVeigh, "Level of Illiteracy among Young Is Above That of 1912," *The Observer*, August 19, 2001.

26. Ian Murray, "Class and Sex Still Decide Who Goes to University," *The Times*, 29 April 1993.

27. Will Woodward, "Students Are the New Poor," *The Guardian*, June 27, 2001.

28. David Walker, "Snakes and Ladders," *The Guardian*, March 28, 2002.

29. Ibid.

30. See Will Hutton, "The Class War Destroying Our Schools," *The Observer*, May 26, 2002.

31. Charlotte Denny, Paul Brown, and Tim Radford, "The Shackles of Poverty," *The Guardian*, August 22, 2002.

CHAPTER 3

1. John Milton, quoted in *Manufacturing Consent: Noam Chomsky and the Media*, ed. Mark Achbar (Montréal: Black Rose Books, 1994), p. 14.

2. Max Weber, *From Max Weber*, trans. and ed. H. H. Gerth and C. Wright Mills (New York: Galaxy, 1958), p. 78.

3. Plato, *The Republic*, trans. R. W. Sterling and W. C. Scott (New York: W. W. Norton, 1985), p. 85.

4. Ibid., pp. 112–13.

5. Ibid., p. 151.

6. Ibid., p. 113.

7. Margaret Judson, cited by Leonard W. Levy, *Emergence of a Free Press* (Oxford

University Press, 1985), p. 91; cited by Noam Chomsky in *Deterring Democracy* (New York: Hill and Wang, 1992), p. 357.

8. Noam Chomsky, *Deterring Democracy* (New York: Hill and Wang, 1992), p. 358.

9. Ibid.

10. James Madison, quoted by Sean Gonsolves, "The Crisis in Democracy," *The Common Dreams Newscenter*, http://www.commondreams.org/views01/0619-01.htm.

11. All unidentified quotes are from *The Matrix* (Warner Bros. release 1999).

12. Benjamin Rush, "Thoughts upon the Mode of Education Proper in a Republic, 1786," http://www.schoolchoices.org/roo/rush.htm.

13. Thomas Jefferson, Letter to Colonel Charles Yancey (January 6, 1816), Wikiquote, the free encyclopedia, http://quote.wikipedia.org/wiki/Thomas_Jefferson.

14. Thomas Jefferson, "A Bill for the More General Diffusion of Knowledge," in *Crusade against Ignorance: Thomas Jefferson on Education,* ed. Gordon C. Lee (New York: Teachers College Press, 1961), pp. 83–97.

15. Alex Carey, *Taking the Risk Out of Democracy: Corporate Propaganda versus Freedom and Liberty* (Urbana and Chicago: University of Illinois Press, 1997), p. 19.

16. Ibid., p. 21.

17. Chomsky, *Deterring Democracy*, p. 366.

18. Ibid.

19. Ibid., p. 367.

20. Ibid., pp. 367–68.

21. John Dewey, quoted by Noam Chomsky in prologue to *Chomsky on Democracy and Education,* ed. Carlos Otero (New York: Routledge, 2002), p. 35.

22. Ibid., p. 25.

23. Richard A. Brosio, *A Radical Democratic Critique of Capitalist Education* (New York: Peter Lang, 1994), p. 385.

24. See David A. Gabbard, "A Nation at Risk—Reloaded, Part I," in *The Journal for Critical Educational Policy Studies* 1, no. 2 (October 2003), http://www.jceps.com/index.php?pageID=article&articleID=15.

CHAPTER 4

1. Samuel Huntington, "The United States," in *The Crisis of Democracy: Report on the Governability of Democracies to the Trilateral Commission,* ed. Michel Crozier, Samuel Huntington, and Joji Watanuki (New York: New York University Press, 1975). This essay is a must for those who wish to understand how the U.S. ruling class responded to the progressive movements of the 1960s and 1970s. As Pentagon adviser, Huntington urged the genocidal bombing that killed hundreds of thousands of rural peasants in South Vietnam and drove millions of others to the cities and strategic hamlets—essentially concentration camps—in an effort to undercut their support for the resistance to U.S. aggression. See his "The Bases of Accommodation," *Foreign Affairs* 46, no. 4 (1968).

2. For an analysis of this process with reference to the Vietnam War and the Persian Gulf War of 1991, see my *Civic Illiteracy and Education: The Battle for the Hearts and Minds of American Youth* (New York: Peter Lang, 1997). For an analysis of the treatment of the Vietnam War in secondary school history texts, see William L. Griffen and John Marciano, *Teaching the Vietnam War: A Critical Examination of School Tests and an Interpretive Comparative History Utilizing the Pentagon Papers and Other Documents* (Montclair, NJ: Allanheld, Osmun and Co., 1979).

3. Herbert Marcuse, *An Essay on Liberation* (Boston: Beacon Press, 1969), p. 62.

4. Paul Shannon, "The ABCs of the Vietnam War," *Indochina Newsletter* (spring–summer 2000), pp. 21–22. For a discussion of the Vietnam War that supports the view of this chapter, see Noam Chomsky, *American Power and the New Mandarins, For Reasons of State, Towards a New Cold War*, and *Rethinking Camelot: JFK, the Vietnam War, and US Political Culture*; Marvin Gettleman, Jane Franklin, Marilyn Young, and H. Bruce Franklin, *Vietnam and America: A Documented History*; Gabriel Kolko, *Anatomy of a War: Vietnam, the United States, and the Modern Historical Experience*; Carl Oglesby and Richard Schaull, *Containment and Change: Two Dissenting Views of American Foreign Policy*; Marilyn Young, *The Vietnam Wars: 1945–1990*; and Howard Zinn, *Vietnam: The Logic of Withdrawal*.

5. Arthur Westing, *Herbicides in War: The Long-Term Ecological and Human Consequences* (London: Taylor and Francis, 1984), p. 22.

6. For an analysis of SDS and the New Left, see Bill Ayers, *Fugitive Days: A Memoir*; Wini Breines, *Community and Organization in the New Left, 1962–1968*; Greg Calvert and Carol Neiman, *A Disrupted History: The New Left and the New Capitalism*; Alice Echols, *Shaky Ground: The Sixties and Its Aftershocks*; Tom Hayden, *Reunion: A Memoir*; Todd Gitlin, *SDS: Years of Hope, Days of Rage*; Maurice Isserman, *If I Had a Hammer: The Death of the Old Left and the Birth of the New Left*; Maurice Isserman and Michael Kazin, *America Divided: The Civil War of the 1960s*; Kirkpatrick Sale, *SDS*.

7. Michael Harrington, long-time socialist activist, quoted in Kirkpatrick Sale, *SDS* (New York: Random House, 1973), p. 691.

8. For a history of SNCC, see Howard Zinn, *The New Abolitionists*.

9. James O'Brien, "The New Left's Early Years," *Radical America* 2 (May–June 1968), p. 10.

10. Tom Hayden, *Reunion: A Memoir* (New York: Random House, 1988), p. 99.

11. Sale, p. 50.

12. Ibid., p. 89.

13. Hayden, p. 205.

14. Jack Newfield, *A Prophetic Minority* (New York: New American Library, 1966), p. 29.

15. Sale, p. 231.

16. Renata Adler, "Reporter at Large," *The New Yorker*, XLI (December 11, 1965), p. 99. Oglesby's essay on Vietnam and imperialism in *Containment and Change* is a brilliant and devastating critique of the liberal position on the war.

17. Max Elbaum, *Revolution in the Air: Sixties Radicals Turn to Lenin, Mao and Che* (London: Verso, 2002), p. 23.

18. Maurice Isserman and Michael Kazin, *America Divided: The Civil War of the 1960s* (New York: Oxford University Press, 2000), p. 72.

19. The resistance against the war by the Vietnamese and within the U.S. military ultimately defeated the U.S assault on that country. See Colonel Robert D. Heinl Jr., "The Collapse of the Armed Forces," *Armed Forces Journal* (June 7, 1971), pp. 30–37. He concluded that the "morale, discipline, and battle-worthiness of the U.S. armed forces are . . . lower and worse than at any time in this century and possibly the history of the U.S." For the early anti-Vietnam war efforts of U.S. merchant marines and later GI actions, see H. Bruce Franklin, *Vietnam and Other American Fantasies* (Amherst, MA: University of Massachusetts Press, 2000), pp. 51–52, 60–69.

20. Elbaum, p. 16.

21. Ibid., p. 24.

22. Ibid., p. 25.

23. Sale, pp. 427–28.

24. Marcuse, p. 77.

25. Sale, p. 514.

26. Ibid., p. 544.

27. Elbaum, pp. 2–3.

28. Hayden, p. 417.

29. Ibid.

30. Sale, pp. 637–38.

31. Ibid., p. 639.

32. Elbaum, p. 3.

33. Hayden, p. 439. In 1967, Robert McNamara, Secretary of Defense, commissioned a massive top-secret history of the U.S. role in Indochina, including Vietnam, to cover the period from WW II to May 1968. The study, known as *The Pentagon Papers*, was motivated by a rising frustration with the Vietnam War by McNamara and his Pentagon colleagues. TPP constitute a huge archive of government decision making on the war over three decades. While the analysts generally agree that U.S. involvement was a costly mistake, they uncritically accept the government's official ideology. See the Gravel Edition of TPP, especially volume 5 of critical essays edited by Noam Chomsky and Howard Zinn.

34. Noam Chomsky, "Some Thoughts on Intellectuals and the Schools," *Harvard Educational Review* 36 (fall 1966), p. 484. "Arguably the most important intellectual alive today," in the words of a *New York Times* book reviewer, Chomsky personifies the grand tradition of critical dissent by admirable and courageous individuals—the recently deceased Edward Said is another—to extend the ideals and democracy and freedom to all. Chomsky's works on U.S. domestic and foreign policies are outstanding and accurate.

35. Isserman and Kazin, p. 178.

36. Ibid., p. 183.

37. Elbaum, p. 2.

38. Ibid., p. 39.

39. See William Blum, *Rogue State: A Guide to the World's Only Superpower*, Michael Parenti, *The Terrorism Trap, The Sword and the Dollar*, and *Against Empire*; and Howard Zinn, *War and Terrorism* for an extensive documentation of U.S. violence abroad.

40. Chomsky, *Rethinking Camelot: JFK, the Vietnam War, the U.S. Political Culture* (Boston: South End Press, 1993), pp. 1–3.

41. Andrew Kopkind, "The Warrior State: Imposing the New Order at Home," *The Nation*, April 8, 1991, p. 433.

42. Hayden, pp. 501–2.

43. Sale, pp. 636–37.

44. Ibid., pp. 5–6.

CHAPTER 5

1. Charles Taylor, *Multiculturalism: Examining the Politics of Recognition* (Princeton: Princeton University Press, 1994), p. 159.

2. Joel Spring, *Deculturalization and the Struggle for Equality*, 4th ed. (Boston: McGraw-Hill, 2003), p. 124.

3. Eric Foner, *The Story of American Freedom* (New York: W. W. Norton, 1998), p. 327.

4. Geoffrey Nunberg, "The Lost Vocabulary of Disinterested Politics," *New York Times*, September 14, 2003, Week in Review section, p. 3.

5. Patrick Slatterly, *Curriculum Development in the Post Modern Era* (New York: Garland Publishing, 1995), p. 192.

6. Michael Engle, *The Struggle for Control of Public Education: Market Ideology vs. Democratic Values* (Philadelphia: Temple University Press, 2000), p. 18.

7. Ibid., p. 20.

8. Wilfred Carr and Anthony Hartnett, *Education and the Struggle for Democracy: The Politics of Educational Ideas* (Buckingham: Open University Press, 1966), p. 11.

9. Herbert Kliebard, *Forging the American Curriculum* (New York: Routledge, 1992), p. xiii.

10. William Pinar, William M. Reynolds, Patrick Slattery, Peter M. Taubman, *Understanding Curriculum* (New York: Peter Lang, 1995), p. 325.

11. Ibid., p. 364.

12. W. B. Carnochan, *The Battle of the Curriculum: Liberal Education and American Experience* (Stanford, CA: Stanford University Press, 1993), pp. 89–90.

13. Sandra Stotsky, *Losing Our Language: How Multicultural Classroom Instruction Is Undermining Our Children's Ability to Read, Write and Reason* (New York: Free Press, 1999).

14. Carr and Hartnett, *Education and the Struggle for Democracy*, p. 18.

15. Ibid., p. 192.

16. Taylor, p. xii.

17. Carnochan, p. 99.

18. Carr and Hartnett, p. 4.

19. Ibid., p. 24.

20. Joe L. Kincheloe and Shirley R. Steinberg, *Changing Multiculturalism* (Buckingham: Open University, 1997), p. 2.

21. Taylor, p. 8.

22. Engle, p. 1.

23. Lawrence A. Cremin, *American Education: The Metropolitan Experience 1876–1980* (New York: Vintage, 1988), p. 270.

24. Taylor, p. 78.

25. Kincheloe and Steinberg, p. 63.

26. Pinar et al., p. 357.

27. Taylor, p. 36.

28. Ibid., p. 37.

29. Elizabeth Minnich, Jean F. O'Barr, Rachel Rosenfeld et al., *Reconstructing the Academy* (Chicago: University of Chicago Press, 1988), p. 38.

30. Kliebard, p. xiii–xiv.

31. Jeannie Oaks, *Keeping Track: How Schools Structure Inequality* (New Haven: Yale University Press, 1986).

32. James W. Lowen, *Lies My Teacher Told Me* (New York: New Press, 1995), p. 2.

33. Christine E. Sleeter and Carl A. Grant, "Race, Gender, Class and Disability in Current Textbooks," in *The Politics of the Textbook*, ed. Michael W. Apple and Linda K. Christina-Smith (New York: Routledge, 1991).

34. Louis A. Castenell and William F. Pinar, *Understanding Curriculum as Racial Text: Representations of Identity and Difference in Education* (New York: State University Press, 1993), p. 6.

35. Lowen, p. 296.

36. Devona Futch, "The Case for Regulation of Hate Speech and Pornography: Are They the Same or Different," in *The Price We Pay: The Case Against Racist Speech, Hate Propaganda, and Pornography*, ed. Laura Lederer and Richard Delgado (New York: Hill and Wang, 1995), p. 329.

37. Christine Sleeter, "Multicultural Education as a Form of Resistance to Oppression," *Journal of Education* 171, no. 3 (1989), p. 55.

38. Kincheloe and Steinberg, pp. 24–26.

39. Minnich et al., pp. 48–50.

40. Richard Otheguy, "Thinking about Bilingual Education: A Critical Appraisal," in *Language Issues in Literacy and Bilingual/Multicultural Education*, ed. Masahiko Minami and Bruce P. Kennedy (Cambridge, MA: Harvard Educational Review Reprint Series, no. 22, 1991), p. 419.

41. David Spener, "Transitional Bilingual Education and the Socialization of Immigrants," in *Language Issues in Literacy and Bilingual/Multicultural Education*, p. 434.

42. Tove Skutnabb-Kangas, *Linguistic Genocide in Education or Worldwide Diversity and Human Rights?* (Mahwah, NJ: Lawrence Erlbaum Associates, 2000), p. xxi.

43. David Spener, p. 424–43.

44. Skutnabb-Kangas, p. 654.

45. Ibid., p. 569.

46. Kincheloe and Steinberg, p. 39.

47. Michael Engle, p. 8.

CHAPTER 6

1. Max Weber, *From Max Weber,* trans. and ed. H. H. Gerth and C. Wright Mills (New York: Galaxy, 1958), p. 78.

2. Plato, *The Republic,* trans. R. W. Sterling and W. C. Scott (New York: W. W. Norton, 1985), p. 85.

3. David A. Gabbard, *Knowledge and Power in the Global Economy: Politics and the Rhetoric of School Reform* (Mahwah, NJ: Laurence Erlbaum, 2000).

4. Milton Goldberg and James Harvey, *A Nation at Risk: The Report of the National Commission on Excellence in Education,* reprinted from *Phi Delta Kappan,* September 1983, in *Education 85/86,* ed. Fred Schultz (Guilford, CT: The Dushkin Publishing Group, 1985), p. 73.

5. Dean Acheson, *Present at the Creation: My Years in the State Department* (New York: W. W. Norton, 1969), p. 375.

6. Goldberg and Harvey, p. 73.

7. Ibid., pp. 72–73.

8. Ibid., p. 73.

9. Memorandum E-A10, 19 October 1940, CFR, *War-Peace Studies,* Baldwin Papers, Box 117, Yale University Library, cited in Laurence H. Shoup and William Minter, "Shaping a New World Order: The Council on Foreign Relations' Blueprint for World Hegemony," in *Trilateralism: The Trilateral Commission and Elite Planning for World Management,* ed. Holly Sklar (Boston, MA: South End Press, 1980), p. 139.

10. Laurence H. Shoup and William Minter, "Shaping a New World Order: The Council on Foreign Relations' Blueprint for World Hegemony," in *Trilateralism: The Trilateral Commission and Elite Planning for World Management,* ed. Holly Sklar (Boston, MA: South End Press, 1980), p. 141.

11. Ibid., p. 142.

12. Ibid., p. 142.

13. Bowman to Hamilton Fish Armstrong, 15 December 1941, Bowman Papers, Armstrong File, Johns Hopkins University Library, cited in Shoup and Minter, p. 146.

14. Memorandum E-B32, 17 April 1941, CFR, War-Peace Studies, Northwestern University Library, cited in Shoup and Minter, p. 146.

15. Memorandum E-A18, 19 July 1941, CFR War-Peace Studies, Baldwin Papers, Yale University Library, cited in Shoup and Minter, p. 145.

16. Minutes S-3 of the Security Subcommittee, Advisory Committee on Postwar Foreign Policy, 6 May 1942, Notter File, Box 77, R.G. 59, cited in Shoup and Minter, p. 146–47.

17. George Kennan, "The Kennan 'Long Telegram,'" in *Origins of the Cold War: The Novikov, Kennan, and Roberts 'Long Telegrams' of 1946* (Washington DC: United State Institute for Peace, 1991), p. 30.

18. John Lewis Gaddis, *The Long Peace* (Oxford, UK: Oxford University Press,

1982) pp. 356–57, cited in Noam Chomsky, *World Orders Old and New* (New York: Columbia University Press, 1994), p. 34.

19. U.S. National Security Council, "NSC-68: A Report to the National Security Council, April 14, 1950," *Naval War College Review* (May–June, 1975), p. 99.

20. Jerry W. Sanders, *Peddlers of Crisis: The Committee on the Present Danger and the Politics of Containment* (Boston: South End Press, 1983), p. 78.

21. Acheson, p. 374.

22. Record of the Meeting of the State-Defense Policy Review Group, March 10, 1950, U.S. Department of State, *Foreign Relations* 1: 191 (1950), cited in Sanders, p. 45.

23. Ibid., p. 51.

24. Ibid., p. 45.

25. *Washington Times-Herald*, February 8, 1951, cited in Sanders., p. 59.

26. *New York Times*, January 6, 1951, p. 1, cited in Sanders, p. 57.

27. Noam Chomsky, *Necessary Illusions: Thought Control in Democratic Societies* (Boston: South End Press, 1989), p. 183.

28. National Commission on Excellence in Education, *A Nation at Risk* (Washington DC: U.S. Government Printing Office, 1983), p. 5.

29. Kim Moody and Mary McGinn, *Unions and Free Trade: Solidarity vs. Competition* (Detroit: Labor Notes, 1992), p. 11.

30. Goldberg and Harvey, p. 73.

31. Ibid., p. 72.

32. Holly Sklar, *Washington's War on Nicaragua* (Boston: South End Press, 1988), p. 245.

33. Ibid., p. 246.

34. Edward S. Herman and Noam Chomsky, *Manufacturing Consent: The Political Economy of the Mass Media* (New York: Pantheon, 1988), p. xi.

35. Noam Chomsky, *Deterring Democracy* (New York: Hill and Wang, 1992), pp. 366, 367.

36. Robert Reich, *The Work of Nations: Preparing Ourselves for 21st Century Capitalism* (New York: Vintage Books, 1991), p. 226.

37. Robert Reich, "Education for Meaning," *Tikkun* 9, no. 5 (September/October 1994), p. 2.

38. Reich, "Education for Meaning," p. 2, and *The Work of Nations*, p. 226.

39. H. Svi Shapiro, "Clinton and Education: Policies without Meaning" in *Tikkun* 9, no. 3 (May/June 1994), pp. 18, 91.

40. Ibid., p. 90.

41. Ibid., p. 18.

42. Reich, "Education for Meaning," p. 2.

43. Noam Chomsky, *Year 501: The Conquest Continues* (Cambridge, MA: South End Press, 1993), p. 34.

44. Cited in Noam Chomsky, *World Orders Old and New* (New York: Columbia University Press, 1994), p. 178.

45. Noam Chomsky, "'Mandate for Change,' or Business as Usual," in *Z Magazine* 6, no. 2 (February 1993), p. 41.

46. Tim Lang and Colin Hines, *The New Protectionism: Protecting the Future against Free Trade* (New York: New Press, 1993), p. 71.

47. Chomsky, *World Orders Old and New*, p. 187.

CHAPTER 7

1. Michael Apple, *The State and the Politics of Knowledge* (New York: Routledge, 2003).

2. David Gabbard, *Knowledge and Power in the Global Economy: Politics and the Rhetoric of School Reform* (Mahwah, NJ: Laurence Erlbaum, 2000), p. 53.

3. See Kevin Vinson and E. Wayne Ross, *Image and Education* (New York: Peter Lang Publishers, 2003) for a discussion of the notions of surveillance and spectacle in education; and Guy Debord's *The Society of the Spectacle* (New York: Free Press, 1995) for a discussion of the exercise of power through image and information.

4. Antonio Gramsci, *Selections from the Prison Notes* (New York: International Publishers, 1971).

5. For discussions of these issues see Apple Raymond E. Callahan, *Education and the Cult of Efficiency* (Chicago: University of Chicago Press, 1964); and Joel Spring, *American Schools, 1642–2000.* (New York: McGraw-Hill, 2001).

6. C. Bolon, Significance of Test-Based Ratings for Metropolitan Boston Schools. *Education Policy Analysis Archives*, 9, no. 42 (October 16, 2001), http://epaa.asu.edu/epaa/v9n42/.

7. Randy L. Hoover, *Forces and Factors Affecting Ohio Proficiency Test Performance: A Study of 593 Ohio School Districts*, http://cc.ysu.edu/~rlhoover/OPT/index.html

CHAPTER 8

1. Stephen Ball, *Education Reform: A Critical and Post-structural Approach* (Buckingham, UK: Open University Press, 1994), p. 54.

2. Susan Robertson, *A Class Act: Changing Teachers' Work, the State, and Globalization* (New York: Falmer Press, 2000), p. 187.

3. Jill Blackmore, "Globalization: A Useful Concept for Feminists Rethinking Theory and Strategies in Education," in *Globalization and Education: Critical Perspectives,* ed. Carlos A. Torres and Nicolas Burbules (New York: Routledge, 2000), p. 134.

4. In the United States, a community school board governs schools within a village or city. Depending on the fiscal arrangements within each state, almost all the funding for schools comes from taxes collected within the school district and from state allocations. A very small percentage comes from the federal government. Unless there is special cross-district agreement, students can attend schools only within their district. As we will show, in order to increase competition between schools, new federal legislation promotes students transferring from "failing" to "passing" schools within and across school districts.

5. See Audrey Amrein and David Berliner, "High-Stakes Testing, Uncertainty and Student Learning," *Education Policy Analysis Archives* (March 28, 2002).

6. Standardized tests are given in the fourth grade for English Language Arts, science, and math; fifth grade for social studies; and eighth grade for English Language Arts, science, social studies, and math.

7. The five exams are English in grade eleven, mathematics in grade ten, social studies (global studies) in grade ten, and United States history in grade eleven, and any one of earth science, living environments, physics, or chemistry.

8. See Walter Haney, "The Myth of the Texas Miracle in Education," *Education Policy Analysis Archives*, http://epaa.asu.edu/v8n1 (August 19, 2000); Michael Winerip, "The 'Zero Dropout' Miracle: Alas! Alack! A Texas Tall Tale," *New York Times*, August 13, 2003, p. B7; Tamar Lewin and Jennifer Medina, "To Cut Failure Rate, Schools Shed Students," *New York Times*, July 31, 2003, p. A1; Jennifer Medina and Tamar Lewin, "High School under Scrutiny for Giving Up on Students," *New York Times*, August 1, 2003, pp. A1, A21.

9. David Monk, John Sipple, and Kieren Killeen, *Adoption and Adaptation, New York States School Districts' Responses to State Imposed High School Graduation Requirements: An Eight-Year Retrospective*, Education Finance Research Consortium (September 10, 2001), www.albany.edu/edfin/CR01_MskReport.pdf.

10. See Abby Goodnough, "Strain of Fourth-Grade Tests Drives Off Veteran Teachers," *New York Times*, June 14, 2000, p. A1; and Monk, Sipple, and Killeen.

11. The state exams have also undermined thirty successful innovative public schools that previously were not required to give the exams.

12. See Michael Winerip, "2 English Tests Speak Different Tongues," *New York Times*, September 17, 2003, p. A23.

13. Roger Dale, "Globalization and Education: Demonstrating a 'Common World Educational Culture' or Locating a 'Globally Structured Educational Agenda'?" *Educational Theory* 50, no. 4 (Fall 2000), p. 427–48.

14. See *The Nation*, September 18, 2003.

15. Other analyses of the affect of neoliberalism are in David W. Hursh and E. Wayne Ross, *Democratic Social Education: Social Studies for Social Change* (New York: Routledge/Falmer, 2000); David Hursh, "Discourse, Power and Resistance in New York: The Rise of Testing and Accountability and the Decline of Teacher Professionalism and Local Control," in *Discourse, Power, Resistance: Challenging the Rhetoric of Contemporary Education*, ed. Jerome Satterwaite, Elizabeth Atkinson, and Ken Gale (Stoke on Trent, UK: Trentham Books, 2003); and David Hursh, "Social Studies within the Neo-Liberal State: The Commodification of Knowledge and the End of Imagination," *Theory and Research in Social Education* 29, no. 2 (Spring 2001), 349–56.

16. Margaret Thatcher, *The Downing Street Years* (London: HarperCollins, 1993), pp. 626–27, cited in David Gillborn and Deborah Youdell, *Rationing Education: Policy, Practice, Reform and Equity* (Philadelphia, PA: Open University Press, 2000).

17. David Gillborn and Deborah Youdell, *Rationing Education: Policy, Practice, Reform and Equity* (Philadelphia, PA: Open University Press, 2000), p. 39.

18. Ibid., p. 26.

19. Xavier Bonal, "The Neoliberal Educational Agenda and the Legitimation

Crisis: Old and New State Strategies," *British Journal of Sociology of Education* 24, no. 2 (2003), p. 160.

20. Ball, p. 54.

21. Ibid.

22. U.S. Department of Education, Office of the Secretary, *What to Know and Where to Go: April 2002 Guide to No Child Left Behind*, Washington, DC (April 2002), p. 12.

23. Samuel Bowles and Herbert Gintis, *Democracy and Capitalism: Property, Community, and the Contradictions of Modern Thought* (New York: Basic Books, 1986), pp. 57–59.

24. Christian Parenti, "Atlas Finally Shrugged: Us against Them in the Me Decade, *The Baffler* 13, (1999), pp. 108–20.

25. Ibid., p. 60.

26. Stephen Gill, *Power and Resistance in the New World Order* (New York: Palgrave Macmillan, 2003), p. 7.

27. Parenti, p. 119.

28. See Carlos Vilas, "Neoliberal Social Policy: Managing Poverty (Somehow)," *NACLA Report on the Americas* 29, no. 2, (1996), pp. 16–21.

29. William Tabb, *Unequal Partners: A Primer on Globalization* (New York: The New Press, 2002), p. 7.

30. See Joseph Collins and John Lear, *Chile's Free-Market Miracle: A Second Look* (Oakland, CA: Institute for Food and Development Policy, 1995).

31. Gill, p. 9.

32. Dale, p. 437.

33. See Michael Apple, *Education and Power* (New York: Routledge and Kegan Paul, 1982).

34. Michael Apple, *Educating the "Right Way": Markets, Standards, God, and Inequality* (New York: Routledge, 2001).

35. U.S. Office of Education, *Education Review International Report* (September 26, 2003), http://www.ed.gov.nclb.

36. U.S. Department of Education, Office of Elementary and Secondary Education, *No Child Left Behind: A September 2002 Reference* (Washington, DC: September 2002), p. 3.

37. New York State Education Department History of the University of the State of New York and the State Education Department 1884–1996: Jame Folts, 2002, http:// www.nysl.nysed.gov:80/eocs/education/sedhist/htm.

38. Carl Hayden, letter to the Hon. Richard Brodsky and Hon. Richard Green, N.Y. State Assembly, May 7, 2001, p. 1.

39. U.S. Department of Education, press release, August 26, 2003, Education Department *ABC Radio Network Launch Education Campaign to Help Close Achievement Gap*, http://www.ed.gov/PressReleases/08-2003/08262003.html (accessed on August 29, 2003).

40. Carl Hayden letter, p. 2.

41. U.S. Department of Education, Office of the Secretary, *What to Know and Where to Go: April 2002 Guide to No Child Left Behind* (Washington, DC: April 2002), p. 12.

42. Ibid.

43. Ibid., p. 9.
44. Ibid.
45. Ibid., p. 19.
46. Hayden letter, p. 1.
47. See Karen Arenson, "New York Math Exam Trials Showed Most Students Failing," *New York Times*, August 27, 2003, p. C12.
48. See Monk, Sipple, and Killeen.
49. See Winerip.
50. Jonathan Kozol, "Malign Neglect," in *The Nation*, June 10, 2002, pp. 22–23.
51. Campaign for Fiscal Equity, *Summary of the Decision by the Court of Appeals in Campaign for Fiscal Equity, Inc. v. State of New York*, June 26, 2003, http://www.cfe.org, p. 2.
52. Court of Appeals, cited in ibid.
53. Associated Press, *Number of People Living in Poverty in U.S. Increases Again,* http:// www.nytimes.com.
54. Lynnley Browning, U.S. Income Gap Widening, Study Says, *New York Times*, September 26, 2003, p. C3.
55. Michael Winerip, "Passing Grade Defies Laws of Physics," *New York Times*, March 12, 2003, secs. A22 & B7.
56. Arenson, p. C12.
57. U.S. Department of Education, *What to Know and Where to Go*, p. 9.
58. Ibid., p. 12.
59. Ibid., p. 29.
60. Matthew Pinzur, "State Schools Fail to Meet New Federal Test Standards: Federal, State Results Differ," *Miami Herald*, August 8, 2003.
61. Ball, p. 54.

CHAPTER 9

1. Jeffrey B. Henig, Richard C. Hula, Marion Orr, and Desiree S. Pedescleaux, *The Color of School Reform: Race, Politics, and the Challenge of Urban Education* (Princeton: Princeton University Press, 1999), pp. 30–62; Jeffrey Mirel, "After the Fall: Continuity and Change in Detroit," *History of Education Quarterly* 38, no. 3 (1998): pp. 237–67; John L. Rury, "The Changing Social Context of Urban Education: A National Perspective," in *Seeds of Crisis: Public Schooling in Milwaukee since 1920*, ed. John L. Rury and Frank A. Cassell (Madison: University of Wisconsin Press, 1993), pp. 10–41.
2. Barry M. Franklin, Marianne N. Bloch, and Thomas S. Popkewitz, "Educational Partnerships: An Introductory Framework," in *Educational Partnerships and the State: The Paradoxes of Governing Schools, Children, and Families*, ed. Barry M. Franklin, Marianne N. Bloch, and Thomas S. Popkewitz (New York: Palgrave Macmillan, 2003), pp.1–23.
3. Barry Bluestone and Bennett Harrison, *The Deindustrialization of America: Plant Closings, Community Abandonment, and the Dismantling of Basic Industry* (New York: Basic Books, 1982), pp. 25–48; Stephen Dandaneau, *A Town Abandoned: Flint, Michigan Confronts Deindustrialization* (Albany: State University of

New York Press, 1996), pp. xix–xxviii; Barry M. Franklin, "Community, Race, and Curriculum in Detroit: The Northern High School Walkout," *History of Education* 33, no. 2 (2004), pp. 137–156.

4. Jean Anyon, *Ghetto Schools: A Political Economy of Urban Educational Reform* (New York: Teachers College Press, 1997), pp. 3–13; Harvey Kantor and Barbara Brenzel, "Urban Education and the 'Truly Disadvantaged': The Historical Roots of the Contemporary Crisis, 1945–1990," in *The Underclass Debate: Views from History*, ed. Michael B. Katz (Princeton: Princeton University Press, 1993), pp. 366–402; Jeffrey Mirel, "Urban Public Schools in the Twentieth Century: The View from Detroit," in *Brookings Papers on Education Policy 1999*, ed. Diane Ravitch (Washington, DC: Brookings Institution Press, 1999), pp. 9–66.

5. Theda Skocpol, "Bringing the State Back In: Strategies of Analysis in Current Research," in *Bringing the State Back In*, ed. Peter B. Evans, Dietrich Rueschemeyer, and Theda Skocpol (Cambridge, UK: Cambridge University Press, 1985), pp. 3–37; Theda Skocpol and Dietrich Rueschemeyer, "Introduction," in *States, Social Knowledge, and the Origins of Modern Social Policies*, ed., Dietrich Rueschemeyer and Theda Skocpol (Princeton: Princeton University Press, 1996), pp. 3–7.

6. Samuel Bowles and Herbert Gintis, *Schooling in Capitalist America: Educational Reform and the Contradictions of Economic Life* (New York: Basic Books, 1976), pp. 125–48; Michael Katz, *The Irony of Early School Reform: Educational Innovation in Mid-Nineteenth Century Massachusetts* (Boston: Beacon Press), pp. 19–112.

7. Michael W. Apple, *Ideology and Curriculum* (Boston: Routledge and Kegan Paul, 1979), pp. 1–60; Paul Willis, *Learning to Labour: How Working Class Kids Get Working Class Jobs* (Westmead: Saxon House, 1977), pp. 171–84; Michael F. D. Young, "An Approach to the Study of Curriculum as Socially Organized Knowledge," in *Knowledge and Control: New Directions for the Sociology of Education*, ed. Michael F. D. Young (London: Collier-Macmillan Publishing, 1971), pp. 19–46.

8. Dietrich Rueschemeyer and Peter B. Evans, "The State and Economic Transformation: Toward an Analysis of the Conditions Underlying Effective Intervention," in *Bringing the State Back In*, pp. 56–47.

9. Kenneth Finegold and Theda Skocpol, *State and Party in America's New Deal* (Madison: University of Wisconsin Press, 1995), pp. 31–63; Theda Skocpol, *Protecting Soldiers and Mothers: The Political Origins of Social Policy in the United States* (Cambridge, MA: Harvard University Press, 1992), pp. 57–60.

10. Stephen Skowronek, *Building a New American State: The Expansion of National Administrative Capacities, 1877–1920* (New York: Cambridge University Press, 1982), pp. vii–viii, 3–18, 210.

11. Ibid., pp. 248–84.

12. Skocpol, *Protecting Soldiers and Mothers*, pp. 2–99, 301.

13. Ibid., pp. 494–512.

14. Finegold and Skocpol, pp. 3–4.

15. Ibid., pp. 52–53, 91.

16. Ibid., pp. 53–65, 81–86.

17. Ibid., pp. 92–102.

18. Ibid., pp. 4–20, 38–41, 64–73.

19. Raymond E. Callahan, *Education and the Cult of Efficiency: A Study of the*

Social Forces That Have Shaped the Administration of Public Schools (Chicago: University of Chicago Press, 1962), pp. 71–75; Barry M. Franklin, *Building the American Community: The School Curriculum and the Search for Social Control* (London: Falmer Press, 1986), pp. 104–7; Herbert M. Kliebard, *The Struggle for the American Curriculum*, 2nd ed. (New York: Routledge, 1995), pp. 102–13; Edward A. Krug, *The Shaping of the American High School, 1880–1920* (Madison: University of Wisconsin Press, 1969), pp. 318–22.

20. Martin Carnoy and Henry M. Levin, *Schooling and Work in the Democratic State* (Stanford: Stanford University Press, 1985), pp. 80–97; David John Hogan, *Class and Reform: School and Society in Chicago, 1880–1930* (Philadelphia: University of Pennsylvania Press), pp. 138–39, 228–35.

21. Herbert M. Kliebard, "Curriculum Policy as Symbolic Action: Connecting Education with the Workplace," in *Case Studies in Curriculum Administration History*, ed. Henning Haft and Stephen Hopmann (London: Falmer Press, 1990), pp. 143–58; David Tyack, *The One Best System: A History of American Urban Education* (Cambridge, MA: Harvard University Press, 1974); David Tyack and Elisabeth Hansot, *Managers of Virtue: Public School Leadership in America, 1820–1980* (New York: Basic Books, 1982), pp. 106–14.

22. Barry M. Franklin, "Race, Restructuring, and Educational Reform: The Mayoral Takeover of the Detroit Public Schools," in *Reinterpreting Urban School Reform: Have Urban Schools Failed, or Has the Reform Movement Failed Urban Schools*, ed. Louis F. Mirón and Edward P. St. John (Albany: State University of New York Press, 2003), pp. 95–106.

23. Ibid., 109–11.

24. Stephen Driver and Luke Martell, "Left, Right and the Third Way," in *The Global Third Way Debate*, ed. Anthony Giddings (Cambridge: Polity Press, 2001), pp. 36–49; Colin Leys, *Market Driven Politics: Neoliberal Democracy and the Public Interest* (London: Verso, 2001), pp. 1–80; Leo Panitch and Colin Leys, *The End of Parliamentary Socialism: From New Left to New Labour*, 2nd ed. (London: Verso, 2001), pp. 1–15, 237–61.

25. John Clarke and Janet Newman, *The Managerial State: Power, Politics and Ideology in the Remaking of Social Welfare* (London: Sage, 1997), pp. 28–30; Michael Foucault, "Govern Mentality," in *The Foucault Effect: Studies in Governmentality*, ed. Graham Burchell, Colin Gordon, and Peter Miller (Chicago: University of Chicago Press, 1991), pp. 87–104.

26. Barry M. Franklin, "Discourse, Rationality, and Educational Research: A Historical Perspective of RER, *Review of Educational Research* 69, no. 4 (1999), pp. 347–63.

27. Nikolas Rose, *Powers of Freedom: Reframing Political Thought* (Cambridge, UK: Cambridge University Press, 1999), pp. 174–75.

28. Robert Booth Fowler, *The Dance with Community: The Contemporary Debate in American Political Thought* (Lawrence: University Press of Kansas, 1991), pp. 1–4; Robert Booth Fowler, "Community: Reflections on Definition," in *New Communitarian Thinking: Persons, Virtues, Institutions, and Communities*, ed. Amitai Etzioni (Charlottesville: University Press of Virginia, 1995), pp. 8–95.

29. Franklin, Bloch, and Popkewitz, pp. 10–12.

30. Eva Gamarnikow and Anthony G. Green, "The Third Way and Social Capital:

Education Action Zones and a New Agenda for Education, Parents, and Community," *International Studies in Sociology of Education* 9, no. 1 (1999), pp. 3–22; Sharon Gewirtz, *The Managerial School: Post-Welfarism and Social Justice in Education* (London: Routledge, 2002), pp. 171–73.

CHAPTER 10

1. Milwaukee Public Schools, *Neighborhood Schools Plan—Final Report,* 2000, http://www.milwaukee.k12.wi.us/supt/ NIS/Final%20Plan/NSIFinalMAIN.PDF.

2. Milwaukee Public Schools, *Parent/Student Handbook on Rights, Responsibilities, and Discipline,* 2000, http://www.milwaukee.k12.wi.us/pub_aff/handbk_00.pdf.

3. Wisconsin Department of Public Instruction, *Wisconsin Model Academic Standards, Fourth Grade, Performance Standard,* 1997, http://www.dpi.state.wi.us/dpi/standards/elac4.htm; Wisconsin Department of Public Instruction, *Wisconsin Model Academic Standards, Eighth Grade, Performance Standards,* 1997, http://www.dpi.state.wi.us/dpi/standards/elac8.htm; Wisconsin Department of Public Instruction, *Wisconsin Model Academic Standards, Twelfth Grade, Performance Standards* 1997, http://www.dpi.state.wi.us/dpi/standards/elac12.htm.

4. Thomas S. Popkewitz and Sverker Lindblad, "Educational Governance and Social Inclusion and Exclusion: Some Conceptual Difficulties and Problematics in Policy and Research," *Discourse* 21, no. 1 (2000), p. 33.

5. Thomas S. Popkewitz and Marianne N. Bloch, "Administering Freedom: A History of the Present. Rescuing the Parent to Rescue the Child for Society," in *Governing the Child in the New Millennium,* eds. Kenneth Hultqvist and Gunilla (New York: Routledge Falmer, 2001), pp. 85–118.

6. Ibid.

7. Ibid., pp. 86–96.

8. Ibid., p. 85, and Nikolas Rose, *Powers of Freedom: Reframing Political Thought* (Cambridge, UK: Cambridge University Press, 1999).

9. Popkewitz and Bloch, p. 91.

10. Helene Silverberg, *Gender and American Social Science: The Formative Years* (Princeton, NJ: Princeton University Press, 1998); Popkewitz and Bloch.

11. Popkewitz and Bloch.

12. Ibid., pp. 106–7.

13. Thomas Pedroni, "Strange Bedfellows in the Milwaukee 'Parental Choice' Debate: Participation among the Dispossessed in Conservative Educational Reform" (Ph.D. diss., University of Wisconsin–Madison, 2003).

14. Wisconsin Department of Public Instruction, *Wisconsin Model Academic Standards, Fourth Grade;* Wisconsin Department of Public Instruction, *Wisconsin Model Academic Standards;* Wisconsin Department of Public Instruction, *Wisconsin Model Academic Standards.*

15. Wisconsin Department of Public Instruction, *Wisconsin Model Academic Standards, Fourth Grade.*

16. Wisconsin Department of Public Instruction, *Wisconsin Model Academic Standards, Eighth Grade.*

17. Ibid.

18. Ibid.

19. Ibid.

20. Ibid.

21. See James Paul Gee, Glynda Hull, and Colin Lankshear, *The New Work Order* (Sydney: Allen and Unwin, 1996).

22. Ibid.

23. Ibid.

24. Wisconsin Department of Public Instruction, *Wisconsin Model Academic Standards, Twelfth Grade.*

25. Ibid.

26. Popkewitz and Bloch, pp. 87–88.

27. Ibid., p. 108.

28. Milwaukee Public Schools, *Parent/Student Handbook*, p. 3.

29. Ibid., p. 11.

30. Ibid.

31. John Clarke and Janet Newman, *The Managerial State: Power, Politics and Ideology in the Remaking of Social Welfare* (London: Sage Publishers, 1997), p. 28.

32. Wisconsin Department of Workforce Development, Wisconsin Works (W-2): Learnfare, 2003, http://www.dwd.state.wi.us/dws/w2/learnfare.htm.

33. Milwaukee Public Schools, *Neighborhood Schools Plan—Final Report, 2000*, p. 5, http://www.milwaukee.k12.wi.us/supt/ NIS/Final%20Plan/NSIFinalMAIN.PDF.

34. Popkewitz and Bloch.

35 Milwaukee Public Schools, *Neighborhood Schools Plan*, p. 5.

36. Milwaukee Public Schools, *Parent/Student Handbook*, p. 3.

37. Ibid.

38. Milwaukee Public Schools, *Neighborhood Schools Plan*, p. 1.

39. Ibid., pp. 2–3.

40. Ibid., p. 85.

41. Ibid., p. 86.

42. Ibid., p. 87.

43. Ibid.

44. Ibid., p. 89.

CHAPTER 11

1. John A. Boehner, "Hold the Line on 'No Child Left Behind,'" *USA Today* Urges," press release, Committee on Education and the Workforce, U.S. House of Representatives, http://edworkforce.house.gov/issues/108th/education/nclb/dc121103.htm.

2. Jamie McKenzie, "The NCLB Wrecking Ball," No Child Left 1., no. 11 (November 2003), http://nochildleft.com/2003/nov03wrecking.html.

3. Gerald Coles, *Reading the Naked Truth: Literacy, Legislation and Lies* (New York: Heinemann, 2003), p. 117.

4. CBS News, The Texas Miracle (January 29, 2004), http://www.cbsnews.com/stories/2004/01/06/60II/main591676.shtml.

5. CBS News, In the Mail (January 29, 2004), http://www.cbsnews.com/stories/2003/06/30/60II/printable561029.shtml.

6. Ibid.

7. Ibid.

8. Coles, p. 1.

9. Joanne Yatvin, "Babes in the Woods: The Wanderings of the National Reading Panel," in *Big Brother and the National Reading Curriculum: How Ideology Trumped Evidence*, ed. Richard. L. Allington (Portsmouth NH: Heinemann, 2002), p. 365.

10. Jamie McKenzie, "Engineering Educational 'Miracles,'" (2003), http://nochildleft.com/2003/sept03miracles.html.

11. Monty Neill, "Leaving Children Behind: How No Child Left Behind Will Fail Our Children," *Phi Delta Kappan* 85, no. 3 (November 2003), pp. 225–28.

12. Boehner, p. 367.

13. George Ritzer, *Sociological Beginnings: On the Origins of Key Ideas in Sociology* (New York: McGraw-Hill, 1994), p. 79.

14. Ibid., p. 10.

15. Henry Giroux, *Teachers as Intellectuals: Toward a Critical Pedagogy of Learning* (New York: Bergin & Garvey, 1988), p. 30.

16. Ibid., p. 134.

17. Ibid., p. 120.

18. Ibid., p. 111.

19. Ibid., p. 121.

20. David Goodman, "Stealth Recruiting," *Rethinking Schools* 18, no. 2 (winter 2002), p.1, http://www.rethinkingschools.org/archive/18_02/stea182.shtml.

21. See David Berliner and Bruce Biddle, *The Manufactured Crisis: Myths, Fraud and the Attack on America's Public Schools* (New York: Perseus Publishing, 1996).

22. Jonathan Kozol, *Savage Inequalities: Children in America's Schools* (New York: Harper Collins, 1992), p. 10.

23. David M. Herszenhorn, "For U.S. Aid, City Switches Reading Plan in 49 Schools," *New York Times*, January 7, 2004, p. B1.

24. Ibid.

25. Rod Paige, "Letter Released from U.S. Education Secretary Paige to State School Chiefs on Implementing No Child Left Behind Act," U.S Department of Education (October 23, 2002), http://www.ed.gov/news/pressreleases/2002/10/10232002a.html.

26. Erik W. Robelen, "Paige: Some U.S. Students Face a Form of 'Apartheid,'" *Education Week* 23, no. 5 (October 1, 2003), p. 22, http://www.edweek.org/ew/ewstory.cfm?slug=05Paige.h23.

27. John Homans,"Lesson Plans: Public or Private Schools?" New York Metro.com (fall 2003), http://www.newyorkmetro.com/urban/guides/family/schools/features/feature_publicorprivate.htm.

28. Coles, p. 124.

29. Ibid., p. 129.

30. Ibid., 124.

31. Alfie Kohn, *The Case against Standardized Testing: Raising the Scores, Ruining the Schools* (Portsmouth, NH: Heinemann, 2000), p. 25.

32. Eleanor Chute, "School District Fights State over No Child Left Behind Sanctions," *Pittsburgh Post-Gazette*, December 17, 2003, p. 3, http://www.postgazette.com/localnews/20031217nclb1217p3.asp.

33. Stanley Aronowitz and Henry Giroux, *Education Still Under Siege* (Westport, CT: Greenwood Publishing Group, 1993), p. 38.

34. Jamie McKenzie, "Engineering Educational 'Miracles,'" No Child Left 1, no. 9 (September 2003), http://nochildleft.com/2003/sept03miracles.html.

35. Les Levidow, "Marketizing Higher Education: Neoliberal Strategies and Counter-Strategies," *Cultural Logic* 4, no. 1 (Fall 2000), p.1.

36. Dave Hill, *New Labour and Education: Policy, Ideology and the Third Way* (London: Tufnell Press, 1999), p. 5.

37. Coles, p. 124.

CHAPTER 12

1. Noam Chomsky, *Profits over People* (New York: Seven Stories Press, 1999).

2. See Sandra Mathison and E. Wayne Ross, "The Hegemony of Accountability in Schools and Universities," Workplace (2003), www.louisville.edu/journal/workplace/issue5p1/mathison.html.

3. Zygmunt Bauman, *The Individualized Society* (Malden, MA: Polity, 2001).

4. See Zygmunt Bauman, *In Search of Politics* (Malden, MA: Polity, 1999).

5. Ibid., pp. 195–96.

6. Kenneth J. Saltman, *Collateral Damage: Corporatizing Public School—A Threat to Democracy* (Lanham, MD: Rowman & Littlefield, 2000).

7. Kim Severson, "Obesity 'a Threat' to U.S. Security," *San Francisco Chronicle*, January 7, 2003, p. A1, http://sfgate.com/cgi-bin/article.cgi?file=/chronicle/archive/2003/01/07/MN166871.DTL.

8. Linda Greenhouse, "Supreme Court Hears Arguments in Affirmative Action Case," *New York Times*, April 1, 2003, Politics section.

9. See Paul Vallas, "Improving Academic Achievement with Freedom and Accountability." *Testimony to the U. S. Congressional Committee on Education and the Workforce* (March 2, 2001).

10. Stephen Metcalf, "Reading between the Lines," *The Nation*, January 28, 2002.

11. Ibid.

12. See Henry A Giroux, *Theory and Resistance in Education: A Pedagogy for the Opposition* (Westport, CT: Bergin and Garvey, 1983); and Stanley Aronowitz and Henry A. Giroux, *Education Still under Siege* (Westport, CT: Greenwood, 1994).

13. Samuel Bowles and Herbert Gintis, *Schooling in Capitalist America* (New York: Basic, 1976).

14. See Don Hazen and Julie Winokur, *We the Media* (New York: New Press, 1996); and Henry A, Giroux, *The Mouse That Roared: Disney and the End of Innocence* (Lanham, MD: Rowman & Littlefield, 2001).

15. Ariel Dorfman and Armand Mattelart, *How to Read Donald Duck: Imperialist Ideology in the Disney Comic* (New York: International General, 1991).

16. Alissa Quart, *Branded: The Buying and Selling of Teenagers* (New York: Perseus, 2003).

17. Ibid., p. 33.

18. Dave Newbart, Dan Rozek, and Ana Mendieta, "Peace Assignment," *Red Streak* 6 (March 2003), p. 1.

19. Crystal Yednak, "Prep Rallies," *Redeye* (March 6, 2003), pp. 10–11.

20. Ellen Meiskins Wood, "Kosovo and the New Imperialism," in *Masters of the Universe?: NATO's Balkan Crusade*, ed. Tariq Ali (New York: Verso, 2000), pp. 196–97.

21. Thomas L. Friedman, *The Lexus and the Olive Tree: Understanding Globalization* (New York: Random House, 2000), p. 373.

22. David Welna, "Defense Budget," National Public Radio (April 8, 2002).

CHAPTER 13

1. Pauline Lipman, "Bush's Education Plan, Globalization and the Politics of Race," *Cultural Logic* 4, no. 1. (fall 2000), http://eserver.org/clogic/4-1/lipman.html.

2. David W. Hursh, "Discourse, Power and Resistance in New York: The Rise of Testing and Accountability and the Decline of Teacher Professionalism and Local Control," in *Discourse, Power, Resistance: Challenging the Rhetoric of Contemporary Education*, ed. Jerome Satterthwaite, Elizabeth Atkinson, and Ken Gale (Stoke on Trent, UK: Trentham Books, 2003).

3. Linda McNeil, *Contradictions of School Reform: Educational Costs of Standardized Testing* (New York: Routledge, 2000), p. 3.

4. Ibid., p. 4.

5. David Harvie, "Alienation, Class and Enclosure in UK Universities," *Capital and Class* 71 (summer 2000), http://lists.village.virginia.edu/listservs/spoons/aut-op-sy.archive/papers/harvie.alienation.

6. Sandra Mathison and E. Wayne Ross, "The Hegemony of Accountability in Schools and Universities," in *Workplace* 5, no. 1 (2002), http://www.pipeline.com/~rgibson/hegemony.htm.

7. Peter McLaren, Gregory Martin, Ramin Farahmandpur, and Nathalia Jaramillo, *Teaching in and against Empire: Critical Pedagogy as Revolutionary Praxis* (Lanham, MD: Rowman & Littlefield, in press).

8. Karl Marx and Friedrich Engels, *The Communist Manifesto* (London: Phoenix, 1848/1996), p. 7.

9. Sally Tomlinson, *Education in a Post-Welfare Society* (Buckingham: Open University Press, 2001).

10. David A. Gabbard, "Education *Is* Enforcement: The Centrality of Schooling in Market Societies," in *Education as Enforcement: The Militarization and Corporatization of Schools*, ed. Kenneth J. Saltman and David A. Gabbard (New York: Routledge, 2003), pp. 69.

11. Glenn Rikowski, *The Battle in Seattle: Its Significance for Education* (London: Tufnell Press, 2001).

12. See Dave Hill, *Charge of the Right Brigade: The Radical Right's Attack on Teacher Education* (Brighton, UK: Institute for Education Policy Studies, 1989), http://www.ieps.org.uk.cwc.net/hill1989.pdf; Dave Hill, *Something Old, Something New, Something Borrowed, Something Blue: Teacher Education, Schooling and the Radical Right in Britain and the USA,* (London: Tufnell Press, 1990); Dave Hill, "Equality in Primary Schooling: The Policy Context, Intentions and Effects of the Conservative 'Reforms,'" in *Promoting Equality in Primary Schools*, ed. Mike Cole,

Dave Hill, and Sharanjeet Shan (London: Cassell, 1997); and Dave Hill, "State Theory and the Neo-Liberal Reconstruction of Schooling and Teacher Education: A Structuralist Neo-Marxist Critique of Postmodernist, Quasi-Postmodernist, and Culturalist Neo-Marxist Theory," *The British Journal of Sociology of Education,* 22, no. 1 (2001), pp. 137–57.

13. Simon Boxley, "Performativity and Capital in Schools," *Journal for Critical Education Policy Studies* 1, no. 1. (March 2003), http://www.jceps.com/index.php?pageID=article&articleID=3.

14. Jane Mulderrig, "Learning to Labour: The Discursive Construction of Social Actors in New Labour's Education Policy," *Journal for Critical Education Policy Studies* 1, no. 1 (March 2003), http://www.jceps.com/index.php?pageID=article&articleID=2.

15. Peter McLaren, *Che Guevara, Paolo Freire and the Pedagogy of Revolution* (Boulder, CO: Rowman & Littlefield, 2000), p. 32.

16. Pierre Bourdieu, *Acts of Resistance: Against the Tyranny of the Market* (New York: The New Press, 1999), p. 29.

17. James Petras, "Signs of a Police State Are Everywhere," *Z Magazine* 15, no. 1, (January 2002), http://www.zmag.org/ZMag/Articles/jan02petras.htm.

18. John McMurtry, "Why Is There a War in Afghanistan?" Speech at Science for Peace Forum and Teach-In, How Should Canada Respond to Terrorism and War? (2001), http://scienceforpeace.sa.utoronto.ca/Special_ActivitiesMcMurtry_Page.html.

19. Louis Althusser, "Ideology and State Apparatuses," in *Lenin and Philosophy and Other Essays* (London: New Left Books, 1971), p. 138.

20. Glenn Rikowski, *Critical Space,* unpublished manuscript.

21. McLaren et al., *Teaching in and against Empire.*

22. Gabbard, p. 71.

23. *Times Educational Supplement* (September 20, 1996), p. 30.

24. McLaren et al.

CHAPTER 14

1. Alan Brinkley, "A Familiar Story: Lessons from Past Assaults on Freedoms," in *The War on Our Freedoms: Civil Liberties in an Age of Terrorism,* ed. Richard C. Leone and Greg Anrig (New York: Public Affairs, 2003), pp. 23–46.

2. Janice K. Currie and Janice Newson, *Universities and Globalization: Critical Perspectives* (Thousand Oaks, CA: Sage Publications, 1998).

3. See Clyde W. Barrow, *Universities and the Capitalist State: Corporate Liberalism and the Reconstruction of American Higher Education* (Madison: University of Wisconsin Press, 1990); and Brinkley.

4. See David D. Dill, "The Changing Context of Coordination in Higher Education: The Federal-State Experience in the United States," in *Higher Education and the Nation-State: The International Dimension of Higher Education,* ed. Jeroen Huisman, Peter Maassen, and Guy Neave (Oxford, UK: Pergammon Press, 2001), pp. 75–106.

5. See Barrow.

6. See Aims C. McGuinness, *State Postsecondary Structures Sourcebook* (Denver: Education Commission of the States, 1997).

7. See Donald E. Heller, *The States and Public Higher Education Policy: Affordability, Access and Accountability* (Baltimore: The Johns Hopkins University Press, 2001); McGuinness; and Richard C. Richardson, Kathy Bracco, Patrick M. Callan, and Joni E. Finney, *Designing State Higher Education Systems for a New Century* (Phoenix: Oryx Press, 1999).

8. See McGuinness.

9. See Currie and Newson.

10. See Robert Zemsky, Gregory R. Wegner, and Maria Iannozzi, "Afterward to Part One: A Perspective on Privatization," in *Public and Private Financing of Higher Education: Shaping Public Policy for the Future*, ed. Patrick M. Callan and Joni E. Finney (Phoenix: Oryx Press, 1997), pp. 74–78.

11. See Currie and Newson; and Sheila Slaughter and Larry L. Leslie, *Academic Capitalism: Politics, Policies, and the Entrepreneurial University* (Albany: State University of New York Press, 1997).

12. McGuinness.

13. Zemsky et al.

14. See Heller; and Zemsky et al.

15. See Brinkley; and James Bovard, *Terrorism and Tyranny: Trampling Freedom, Justice and Peace to Rid the World of Evil* (New York: Palgrave Macmillan, 2003).

16. See Patricia Thomas, "From Saviors to Suspects: New Threats to Infectious Disease Research," in *The War on Our Freedoms: Civil Liberties in an Age of Terrorism*, ed. Richard C. Leone and Greg Anrig (New York: Public Affairs, 2003), pp. 23–46.

17. Ibid., p. 204.

18. Bovard, pp. 133–36.

19. Ibid., pp. 141–43.

20. See James Downey, "Balancing Corporation, Collegium, and Community," in *Organization and Governance in Higher Education*, 4th ed., ed. M. Christopher Brown II (Boston: Pearson Custom Publishing, 2000), pp. 305–12.

CHAPTER 15

1. Joan Copjec, *Imagine There's No Woman: Ethics and Sublimation* (Cambridge, MA: MIT Press, 2003), p. 20.

2. This is what Isaiah Shoel's parents attempted when they moved to the wealthy district in Littleton, Colorado, a few years before their son died in the Columbine High School shootings.

3. Adam Phillips, *Houdini's Box: The Art of Escape* (New York: Vintage, 2001), p. 133.

4. As Amartya Sen continues to point out, the concept of "freedom" and "autonomy" is not exclusively "Western," whatever that may mean. (I myself am curious about the concept of the West, especially when patterns of migration throughout the world have permanently disrupted any ideologies that may reinforce the notion of a monolithic culture ascribed to peoples living in the Western Hemisphere.) See Amartya Sen, "Democracy's Many Fathers: Why Freedom Isn't a Western Invention," *The New Republic*, October 6, 2003, pp. 28–35.

5. Louis B. Hartz, *The Liberal Tradition in America*, 2nd ed. (New York: Harvest, 1991).

6. Estelle B. Freedman, *No Turning Back: The History of Feminism and the Future of Women* (New York: Pallatine, 2002).

7. James Der Derian. *Virtuous War: Mapping the Military-Industrial Media Entertainment Network* (Boulder, CO: Westview Press, 2000).

8. Julie A. Webber, *Failure to Hold: The Politics of School Violence* (Lanham, MD: Rowman & Littlefield, 2003).

9. Paul Virilio, *Strategy of Deception*, trans. Chris Turner (London: Verso, 1999).

10. See John Taylor Gatto, "Against School: How Public Education Cripples Our Kids, and Why," *Harper's*, September 2003, pp. 33–38.

11. See Copjec.

12. Gatto.

13. Ibid., p. 33.

14. Michel Foucault, *The History of Sexuality,* vol. 1, trans. Robert Hurley (New York: Pantheon, 1977).

15. Giorgio Agamben, *Homo Sacer: Sovereign Power and Bare Life*, trans. Daniel Heller-Roazen (New York: Verso, 1998).

16. Many have argued that the city constitutes the paradigmatic form of organization of power and life in our time. There is much merit to this thesis: As the world economy has plummeted, people have been increasing their already existing trek toward urban centers; witness Mexico City, Buenos Aires, New York, and so forth.

17. Agamben, p. 169.

18. One of the major tenets of existentialism is that philosophers must concern themselves with "the human predicament and inner states such as alienation, anxiety, inauthenticity, dread, a sense of nothingness, and anticipation of death." Peter A. Collins, *The Harper-Collins Dictionary of Philosophy,* 2nd ed. (New York: Harper Perennial, 1992), p. 99. If we look at contemporary U.S. society and the schools, we can see that nearly a quarter of the population is plagued by these very same problems and is left with only one option: pharmaceutical remedies, such as Prozac, and drugs for attention deficit disorder, which may be caused by the way our technologies divert our attention from education as it has been traditionally conceived. Clearly, many people are hurting, and the school and society has no answers for them through the security state. Only a reconceptualized school curriculum and school design and integration, backed by a coherent, realistic democratic philosophy and objectives, can restore a common aim and begin to heal these inner states, or at least provide explanations for them.

19. Peter McLaren, *Critical Pedagogy and Predatory Culture* (New York: Verso, 1995).

20. Judith Butler, *Bodies That Matter: On the Discursive Limits of "Sex"* (New York: Routledge, 1993).

21. Copjec, p. 137.

22. John Dewey, *Lectures on the Psychological and Political Ethics, 1898* (New York: Hafner, 1976), p. 160.

23. Donald Woods Winnicott, *Home Is Where We Start From* (New York: W. W. Norton, 1986), p. 93.

24. This was Spinoza's conclusion: Take away final causes (god, judgment, determination, even free will) and you have an open space for living life that is freer than that provided by the structure of metaphysics. Agamben calls for a revision of metaphysics, a matching of the real-world order with the real-world problems. Hardt and Negri call for a Spinoza-like solution, with a smattering of post-structuralism, and Gramsci, to take off the anxiety-producing edge such a metaphysical leap would entail.

Index

About the Editors

DAVID A. GABBARD is Professor, Department of Curriculum and Instruction, East Carolina University, Greenville, North Carolina. He works in solidarity with those who understand that compulsory schooling has failed to serve what is best in the human spirit. Gabbard has edited/coedited two other books: *Knowledge and Power in the Global Economy: Politics & the Rhetoric of School Reform* (2000) and *Education as Enforcement: The Militarization and Corporatization of Schools* (2003).

E. WAYNE ROSS is Professor in the Department of Curriculum Studies at the University of British Columbia in Vancouver, Canada. He is a former secondary social studies and day care teacher in North Carolina and Georgia and has held faculty appointments at the University of Louisville and the State University of New York campuses at Albany and Binghamton. Ross is the author of numerous articles and reviews on issues of curriculum theory and practice, teacher education, and the politics of education. His books include *Image and Education* (with Kevin D. Vinson), *The Social Studies Curriculum,* and *Democratic Social Education* (with David W. Hursh). He is the cofounder of The Rouge Forum, a group of educators, parents, and students working for more democratic schools and society, and the general editor of *Defending Public Schools.*

About the Contributors

TAKIS FOTOPOULOS is a writer and the editor of *Democracy & Nature* since 1992; he is also a columnist for the *Athens Daily Eleftherotypia*. He was previously (1969–1989) Senior Lecturer in Economics at the University of North London. He is the author of *Towards an Inclusive Democracy* (1997), which has been translated into French, German, Spanish, Italian, and Greek. He has also contributed in several other books (*Routledge Encyclopedia of International Political Economy*, 2001; *Education, Culture and Modernization*, 1995). He is also the author of several books in Greek (*Dependent Development; The Gulf War; The Neo-Liberal Consensus; The New World Order; Drugs: Beyond the Demonology of Penalization and the "Progressive" Mythology of Liberalization; The New Order in the Balkans; Religion, Autonomy and Democracy; From the Athenian Democracy to Inclusive Democracy; Globalization, the Left and Inclusive Democracy;* and *The War Against "Terrorism": The Elites' Generalized Attack*). Apart from his numerous writings in D&N and other international journals, he has also made several contributions to French, German, Italian, Dutch, Norwegian, Argentinian, Turkish, Arabic, and Greek publications.

BARRY M. FRANKLIN is Professor and Head of the Department of Secondary Education and an Adjunct Professor of History at Utah State University. His research interests are in the areas of curriculum policy, curriculum history, and urban school reform. His most recent book is a volume edited with Marianne Bloch and Thomas Popkewitz entitled *Educational*

Partnerships and the State: The Paradoxes of Governing Schools, Children, and Families (2003).

DAVE HILL is Professor of Education Policy at University College Northampton, UK. Previously, he taught in schools and colleges in Brixton and in Tower Hamlets in inner city London and in Sussex. He is Founder Director of the Institute for Education Policy Studies, www.ieps.org.uk, founded in 1989. He is also Founding Editor/Chief Editor of *The Journal for Critical Education Policy Studies* (www.jceps.com). He cofounded the Hillcole Group of Radical Left Educators in Britain with Mike Cole in 1989 and cowrote the two Hillcole Group books on education: *Changing the Future: Redprint for Education* (1991), and *Rethinking Education and Democracy: A Socialist Perspective* (1997). With Mike Cole, Dave coedited the trilogy on equality in schooling, *Promoting Equality in Primary Schools* (1997), *Promoting Equality in Secondary Schools* (1999), and *Schooling and Equality: Fact, Concept and Policy* (2001). His two most recent edited collections (with the same cowriters) are *Postmodernism in Educational Theory: Education and the Politics of Human Resistance* and *Marxism against Postmodernism in Educational Theory*. His most recent cowritten book (cowritten with Peter McLaren, Mike Cole and Glenn Rikowski) is *Red Chalk: On Schooling, Capitalism and Politics* (2001). He has forthcoming books on New Labour, education and ideology, and on the restructuring of schooling and teacher education in Britain, 1979–2004.

DAVID W. HURSH is Associate Professor in the Warner Graduate School of Education at the University of Rochester. In the 1970s, he codirected an alternative university, directed two private elementary schools (one of which he founded), and was a consultant on race and gender equity. He is the author of numerous studies on democracy, neoliberalism, and educational reform. He is coeditor of the book *Democratic Social Education: Social Studies for Social Change*.

SANDRA JACKSON is Professor of Women's and Gender Studies at DePaul University in Chicago. Her published works include the following coedited works: *Talking Back and Acting Out: Women Negotiating the Media zcross Cultures; I've Got a Story to Tell: Identity and Place in the Academy;* and *Beyond Comfort Zones: Confronting the Politics of Privilege as Educators*. She is currently working on a book of essays on race and gender as well as an edited book on black women's experiences in the academy.

SHEILA L. MACRINE, Ph.D., is both a Cognitive Psychologist and a Reading Specialist. She is currently working on a large grant to enhance emergent literacy activities for low-income preschool children in urban Philadelphia. Dr. Macrine focuses her research on the intersections of literacy, critical theory, educational psychology, and the nontraditional learner. She has published nationally and internationally. She directs the Reading and Special Education Programs in the Education Department at St. Joseph's University in Philadelphia.

JOHN MARCIANO is Professor Emeritus, Social-Historical Foundations of Education, State University of New York at Cortland. An activist, scholar, and teacher, he is coauthor of *Teaching the Vietnam War* (with William L. Griffen, 1979) and *Civic Illiteracy and Education: The Battle for the Hearts and Minds of American Youth* (1997).

CAMILLE ANNE MARTINA is a doctoral student at the Warner Graduate School of Education and Human Development, University of Rochester, New York. A former high school English teacher in Rochester, she is currently a research assistant on a curriculum development grant from the National Institute of Environmental Health Sciences. Her dissertation focuses on using Bourdieu's concept of social capital to explain why some historically disadvantaged students succeed and others do not. She has presented papers in the U.K., Canada, Mexico, and the United States.

SANDRA MATHISON is Professor and Head, Department of Educational and Counseling Psychology and Special Education, University of British Columbia, Vancouver. Her research is in educational evaluation and her work has focused especially on the potential and limits of evaluation to support democratic ideals and promote justice. She is currently doing research on the effects of state-mandated testing on teaching and learning in elementary and middle schools in upstate New York, research that is funded by a five-year grant from the National Science Foundation.

PETER MCLAREN teaches at the University of California, Los Angeles, where he serves as Professor, Division of Urban Schooling, Graduate School of Education and Information Studies. He is the author and editor of over forty books. His works have been translated into fifteen languages. His forthcoming books include *American Empire: Lessons in Critical Pedagogy* and *Teaching against Globalization*.

THOMAS C. PEDRONI is an Assistant Professor of secondary social studies methods, educational foundations, curriculum theory, and qualitative research methodology at Utah State University. His recent research has centered on issues of identity formation and subaltern agency among urban low-income, predominantly African-American and Latino parents within otherwise largely conservative coalitions for publicly financed private school vouchers. His research interests also include the development of composite critical and poststructural approaches in educational theory and research, the identification of persistent exclusionary power/knowledge regimes in state-level educational reforms, and the analysis of the increasing colonization of the global educational sphere by neoliberal and managerial forms.

KENNETH J. SALTMAN is Assistant Professor of Educational Policy Studies and Research at DePaul University. He is the author of *Collateral Damage: Corporatizing Public Schools—a Threat to Democracy, and Strange Love, or How We Learn to Stop Worrying and Love the Market* (with Robin Truth Goodman) and coeditor of *Education as Enforcement: The Militarization and Corporatization of Schools* (with David Gabbard). His most recent book on The Edison Schools will be published in 2004.

JULIE WEBBER received her Ph.D. from Purdue University in May 2000. She is currently Assistant Professor of Politics and Government at Illinois State University. She is the author of "Why Can't We Be Deweyan Citizens?" an article in the John Dewey Society Publication *Educational Theory*, a chapter in the edited volume *Education as Enforcement* (2003), as well as a recently published book on violence in democratic institutions and societies, *Failure to Hold: The Politics of School Violence* (2003), an edited volume: *Curriculum Dispositions,* with William Reynolds (2004), and *Beyond Global Arrogance* with Janie Leatherman. Dr. Webber's primary research and teaching areas are international political theory, educational theory, and theories of violence and women's studies. She is currently working on her second book, *Virtual Violence and Western Values.*

JOHN F. WELSH is Professor of Higher Education at the University of Louisville where he teaches higher education finance, higher education administration and organization, and college teaching. He has won several institutional and state awards for his teaching. He has published widely in higher education and social science journals on the role of the state in higher education policy formation, the impact of strategic activity in higher education, and critical social theory.